WITHDRAWN 19/06/24.

Microcomputers, Psychology and Medicine

Microcomputers, Psychology and Medicine

Edited by

Robert West
Royal Holloway and Bedford New College, University of London

Margaret Christie
Royal Holloway and Bedford New College, University of London

and

John Weinman
United Medical and Dental Schools of Guy's and St Thomas', University of London

JOHN WILEY & SONS
Chichester · New York · Brisbane · Toronto · Singapore

Other Wiley Editorial Offices

John Wiley & Sons, Inc., 605 Third Avenue,
New York, NY 10158-0012, USA

Jacaranda Wiley Ltd, G.P.O. Box 859, Brisbane,
Queensland 4001, Australia

John Wiley & Sons (Canada) Ltd, 22 Worcester Road,
Rexdale, Ontario M9W ILI, Canada

John Wiley & Sons (SEA) Pte Ltd, 37 Jalan Pemimpin 05-04,
Block B, Union Industrial Building, Singapore 2057

Library of Congress Cataloging-in-Publication Data:
Microcomputers, psychology, and medicine/edited by Robert West,
   Margaret Christie, and John Weinman.
      p.   cm.
   Includes bibliographical references.
   ISBN 0-471-92404-0
   1. Psychiatry—Data processing.   2. Clinical psychology—Data
processing.   3. Microcomputers.   I. West, Robert.   II. Christie,
Margaret J.   III. Weinman, John.
   RC455.2.D38M53   1990
   616.89′00285′416–dc20   89–16732
                                                                 CIP

British Library Cataloguing in Publication Data:
Microcomputers, psychology and medicine.
   1. Medicine. Applications of microcomputers
   I. West. Robert, 1955-   II. Christie, Margaret   III.
   Weinman, John
   610′.28′5416

   ISBN 0-471-92404-0

Typeset by Associated Publishing Services, Petersfield, Hampshire.
Printed and bound in Great Britain by Biddles Ltd, Guildford, Surrey.

Contents

Part 1 Data Processing and Programming

Part II Human Performance Testing: The Effects of External Agents

Part III Human Performance Testing: Client Assessment

List of contributors

Mr Chris Alford — Psychopharmacology Research Unit, University of Leeds, Leeds LS2 9JT, UK

Mr Hassan Alikhan — Biopsychology Group, Psychology Department, University of Leeds, Leeds LS2 9JT, UK

Dr John Blundell — Biopsychology Group, Psychology Department, University of Leeds, Leeds LS2 9JT, UK

Dr Andrew Burton — Department of Psychology, North East London Polytechnic, The Green, Stratford, London E15, UK

Dr Esme Burton — Department of Psychology, North East London Polytechnic, The Green, Stratford, London E15, UK

Dr Margaret Christie — Applied Psychology Research Group, Psychology Department, Royal Holloway and Bedford New College, University of London, Egham, Surrey TW20 OEX, UK

Ms Penelope Earp — Rosemary School, Inner London Education Authority, Islington, London N1, UK

Professor Michael Eysenck — Applied Psychology Research Group, Psychology Department, Royal Holloway and Bedford New College, University of London, Egham, Surrey TW20 OEX, UK

Dr Margo George — Department of Measurement, Evaluation and Computer Applications, Ontario Institute for Studies in Education, University of Toronto, Toronto, Canada

Professor David Hand — Mathematics Department, The Open University, Walton Hall, Milton Keynes MK7 6AA, UK

Dr Colin Hendrie — Pharmacoethology Laboratory, Department of Psychology, University of Leeds, Leeds LS2 9JT, UK

DR IAN HINDMARCH — *Psychopharmacology Research Unit, University of Leeds, Leeds LS2 9JT, UK*

MR RICHARD KEMP — *Psychology Department, Polytechnic of Central London, 77–78 Mortimor Street, London W1, UK*

DR MONICA LAWLOR — *Applied Psychology Research Group, Psychology Department, Royal Holloway and Bedford New College, University of London, Egham, Surrey TW20 OEX, UK*

DR MAURICE LIPSEDGE — *Academic Department of Psychiatry, United Medical and Dental Schools of Guy's and St Thomas', University of London, London SE1 9RT, UK*

MR ALI MEHMET — *Institute of Psychiatry, De Crespigny Park, London, SE5 8AF, UK*

MS KARIN MOGG — *Psychology Department, St George's Hospital Medical School, Tooting, London SW17, UK*

DR MATTHIJS MUIJEN — *Institute of Psychiatry, De Crespigny Park, London SE5 8AF, UK*

DR VEENA PARMAR — *Royal Earleswood Hospital, Redhill, Surrey, RH11 6JL, UK*

PROFESSOR PATRICK RABBITT — *Age and Cognitive Performance Centre, University of Manchester, Precinct Centre, Manchester M13 9PL, UK*

DR JOHN RODGERS — *Pharmacoethology Department, Department of Psychology, University of Leeds, Leeds LS2 9JT, UK*

DR HARVEY SKINNER — *Addiction Research Foundation, 33 Russell Street, Toronto, Ontario, Canada M5S 2S1*

DR BRIAN STOLLERY — *Age and Cognitive Performance Centre, University of Manchester, Precinct Centre, Manchester M13 9PL, UK*

DR ANGELA SUMMERFIELD — *Department of Psychology, Birkbeck College, Malet Street, London WC1E 7HX, UK*

Dr Christine Temple

*Applied Psychology Research Group,
Psychology Department, Royal Holloway and
Bedford New College, University of London,
Egham, Surrey TW20 OEX, UK*

Dr Robert West

*Applied Psychology Research Group,
Psychology Department, Royal Holloway and
Bedford New College, University of London,
Egham, Surrey TW20 OEX, UK*

Dr Sarah Wilson

*Drapers Wing, Royal Hospital and Home,
Putney, West Hill, London SW15 3SW, UK*

Dr John Weinman

*Unit of Psychology, United Medical and
Dentals Schools of Guy's and St Thomas',
University of London, London SE1 9RT, UK*

Preface

Many areas of medical research and clinical practice involve psychology. There are the obvious examples of psychiatric disease and mental handicap. Other applications include the assessment and treatment of patients with brain damage, evaluation of drug side-effects, and assessment of clinical and subclinical effects of environmental pollutants.

The advent of microcomputers has given clinicians and researchers working in these areas a valuable new tool. Microcomputers are now sufficiently powerful to take over from large 'mainframes' in the traditional computer activity of 'data processing'. They are therefore well suited to, for example, statistical analysis and management of large patient databases. Besides this, however, they can be used to control the presentation of stimuli used in psychological assessment and automated recording of responses. They can also be made sufficiently flexible to be used interactively by patients in training and therapy programmes.

Microcomputers are becoming cheaper but increasingly powerful, with larger memories, faster processors and better graphical displays. Thus we are reaching a stage when small groups and even individual clinical practitioners could take advantage of this new technology. Thus there is a growing need for practical information in areas where they may be of use and how one might go about involving them in one's work.

Most of the contributions in this book are based on talks given at a workshop organised by the Applied Psychology Research Group (APRG) based at Royal Holloway and Bedford New College, London University. The aim of the APRG is to facilitate psychological research of relevance to problems outside of the psychological enclave. It has regular working meetings and an annual workshop held at the CIBA Foundation in London with contributions from a small invited group of participants.

Contributors to this volume are using micros on a day-to-day basis in their research or clinical practice. They have been asked to go into the background to their work, the role that micros play and where appropriate some concrete results of their use.

Although the emphasis is on the practical applications of micros, the book is not intended as a manual. This would rapidly become out of date. It is more of a 'guide'. Readers who are thinking about using micros will obtain a good idea of what these have to offer and how they might take their own interest further. Readers already using micros will be able to share the experience of others who may be working in different areas but whose techniques cross the speciality boundaries.

The book is not intended just for computer 'buffs'. It is aimed at psychiatrists and trainee psychiatrists, clinical psychologists and others who use, or are considering using, micros in psychological assessment and therapy. Some of these may wish to get involved in writing or adapting programs. However, most will probably want to use ready-made programs. In some cases, such programs are widely available. In other cases, readers might wish to make contact with the contributors to this volume with a view to setting up their own applications.

We would like to thank Valerie White, who is the secretary of the Applied Psychology Research Group, for her help with large amounts of word processing, distribution of material and liaison between editors and contributors. We are grateful to the CIBA Foundation for their hospitality and Eli Lilly for generously providing funds for the workshop. Finally, we are extremely grateful to Davina French, without whose help this volume would never have met our publisher's deadline.

General introduction: using micros in the collection and analysis of psychological data

ROBERT WEST, JOHN WEINMAN AND MARGARET CHRISTIE

This book is about the use of microcomputers in the collection and analysis of psychological information in clinical research and practice. It is not just about the use of micros in psychiatry and clinical psychology, although these are important areas. It includes topics as diverse as speech therapy and behavioural pharmacology.

Although the areas in which micros can and have been applied are diverse, the methods and techniques have much in common. The commonalities stem from the limited range of fundamental operations which micros perform. The diversity results from the flexible way they can perform these operations.

The microcomputer is essentially a machine which processes information or data. Like its larger cousin, the *mainframe*, it is good at doing arithmetic and storing and retrieving information. These *data-processing* operations are just as useful in medical and psychological endeavour as they are in other fields, from banking to nuclear physics. Part I of this book, on data processing, illustrates diverse aspects of this kind of operation. It considers first of all the mundane, though important area of statistical analysis, and goes on to examine the more esoteric area of artificial intelligence. Part I concludes with a chapter examining tools for developing psychological applications using micros and the considerations to be taken into account when writing programs.

Where the micro diverges most from the mainframe is in its facilities for interaction with the user. These facilities make it a flexible and powerful tool for collection of information from people. Programs can be written which cause information to be displayed on a screen or via a loudspeaker and then responses recorded. This simple format—stimulus presentation and response recording—is a theme which runs through many of the chapters in this book. The nature of the stimulus may vary, as may the kind of response elicited and

Microcomputers, Psychology and Medicine
Edited by R. West, M. Christie and J. Weinman
© 1990 by John Wiley & Sons Ltd

the devices used to control the flow of interaction. but the format remains the same.

Parts II and III are concerned with collection of *performance data* (reaction times, memory, etc.). Part II considers how such data have been used to measure the effects of pharmacological agents and environmental pollutants. The brain is exquisitely sensitive to interference by chemicals which have been ingested—and performance testing can be used to pick up effects which have not yet become manifest in what would conventionally be regarded as clinical symptoms. Part III is directed at assessing the client or patient. Applications range from diagnosis and assessment of brain damage to trying to find out the capabilities of people with severe physical disabilities.

There are occasions in which one is interested in recording behaviour in the field or over a period of time in some particular setting. The computer is not used here to control a sequence of experimental trials each involving presentation of a stimulus and recording of a response. It is used to monitor behaviour as it unfolds over time in the situation of interest. Part IV, on behaviour monitoring, includes two examples of this kind of application, one of which is concerned with drug effects and the other with understanding the mechanisms underlying eating.

One of the first things which psychologists did with micros when these became widely available was to take questionnaires and 'put' them on the computer. This approach continues and many standard personality and mood questionnaires are now computerised. The questions come up on the screen and the respondent presses buttons or types in responses at the keyboard. Some have questioned whether there is anything to be gained by this. The first chapter in Part V, on automated questionnaire administration, illustrates that there are circumstances when this is not only desirable but for practical purposes essential. The second chapter shows how with a little imagination the micro can dramatically extend the power of questionnaire techniques by monitoring indices of reliability or validity as the questionnaire is being completed, and altering the administration of the questionnaire accordingly.

Finally Part VI, appropriately enough, considers how micros have been used in treatment. Applications in this area vary enormously but as with previous parts common themes emerge. Whether it be the provision of aids which speech therapists and others can use in treating aphasics or the development of a suite of programs with which mentally handicapped people can interact, the key to the success of the micro is its flexibility. It can be programmed so that the therapeutic intervention is tailored to the needs of the client.

It seems to some of us that micros have always been with us, and one has to keep reminding oneself that they have impinged on psychology in a major way for less than a decade. We are still very much in the early days of computer applications. As micros become more powerful (and there is no evidence of a slowing in the pace of the technological revolution), their range of application will grow. For example, a major stumbling block at present is the fact that speech synthesis and recognition are currently too crude to allow micros to help a great deal with areas which require these facilities. In the next decade, hopefully, this will change.

The remainder of this introduction will provide for readers unfamiliar with computers an outline of what they are, how they operate, the kinds of microcomputers which are available and what their individual strengths and weaknesses are.

Computer hardware

Computer hardware is the physical circuitry of computer. At the heart of every computer is a *central processing unit* (CPU). This carries out instructions to perform operations on data. In mainframe computers, CPUs consist of a large number of *integrated circuits* (ICs or *chips*), each of which consists of a slice of silicon about the size of a thumbnail onto which a circuit containing the electrical equivalent of thousands of transistors has been imprinted. The CPU of microcomputers is a single IC or chip known as a *microprocessor*. There are many varieties of single-chip CPUs. These are normally classified according to how much data they can manipulate in one go.

The most basic unit of data in the computer is the *bit* or *binary digit*. A binary digit can take only one of two values: 1 or 0. This is represented physically in the computer by a voltage of 5 volts or 0 volts. Binary digits can be grouped into units of 8 bits—these are known as *bytes*. A group of 8 bits can represent 256 different things because there are 256 possible configurations of 1s and 0s:

00000000	0
00000001	1
00000010	2
00000011	3
.	
.	
.	
11111110	254
11111111	255

There are three kinds of things which bytes can be used to represent: numbers, characters and instructions to the CPU. When used to represent numbers a single byte can represent the integers 0 to 255 (see above), or -127 to +127 (with one of the bits being used to represent the minus or plus sign. Usually, however, bytes are themselves grouped into 'words' or two, four, six or eight bytes in length to enable large numbers and numbers with decimal places to

Table I.1

Character	ASCII code	
	Bit pattern	Decimal equivalent
0	00110000	48
1	00110001	49
2	00110010	50
.		
.		
9	00111001	57
A	01000001	65
B	01000010	66
C	01000011 ˙	67
.		
.		
Z	01011010	90
a	01100001	97
b	01100010	98
c	01100011	99
.		
.		
z	01111010	122

be represented. Characters are represented by arbitrarily assigning each character a particular bit configuration. The most widely used assignment is the ASCII code. ASCII stands for the American Standard Code for Information Interchange. Table I.1 shows some ASCII codes and their associated characters. Note that digits are also included as characters. This is important, as will be seen in Chapter 1, because it provides a standard way of representing numerical data for processing by statistical programs.

Finally, instructions to the CPU (known as *op codes*) are a more or less arbitrary assignment of bit configurations to instructions which the CPU can perform. When a string of bytes representing a particular instruction is sent to the CPU it causes it to carry out the instruction concerned. A couple of examples of instructions used by the '68000' microprocessor are shown in Table I.2. Each instruction is contained in two bytes. These would each be followed in actual usage by bytes representing the data with which the instructions were working.

The major division of microprocessors, as stated above, is in terms of how much data they can handle at one go. The early microprocessors were '8-bit', which meant that they could only handle one 8-bit byte at a time. This meant

Table I.2

Instruction	Bit pattern
Move byte from one location to another	01100010 01101110
Compare two 2-byte 'words' with each other	01100100 01010000

that when they needed to perform computations on large numbers they had to perform the task in a sequence of separate operations. This in turn resulted in a considerable slowing of processing speed. Such microprocessors are still in widespread use. The most commonly used microprocessors of this class are:

The Z80 used in Amstrad PCWs, Sinclair Spectrums, and a range of computers known as CPM machines because they used an operating system called CPM (see below).
The 6502 used in Commodore Pets, Commodore 64s and Acorn BBC computers.

The next step up has been the introduction of 16-bit microprocessors. These handle two bytes at a time with a consequent gain in efficiency. Added to this, however, they operate at a faster rate. The speed of a processor depends not only on the amount of information it can handle in one go but also on how many basic instructions it can handle every second. The unit of measurement here is known as the MIP (million instructions per second). There are two factors influencing this: the *clock rate* and the number of clock cycles needed for every instruction. The clock rate is simply the number of operational cycles which the processor can handle per second. Given that it is such an important contributor to overall processing speed, most descriptions of processors or microcomputers give this as the primary index of speed. The number of clock cycles needed to perform a particular instruction depends on the microprocessor and the instruction concerned. It will usually vary between 2 and 16. The 8-bit processors typically work at a clock rate of between 1 and 4 megahertz (MHz)—which meant they could execute 1 to 4 million operational cycles per second. The 16-bit processors typically work at between 5 and 12 MHz. The main 16-bit processors are:

The 8088 family, including the 8086 and the 80186. These form the heart of the ubiquitous IBM PC and its plethora of copies or 'clones' made by hundreds of different manufacturers. The 8086 is exactly the same as the 8088 but, for reasons which we need not go into, operates more efficiently.

The IBM and its clones have become a standard in business and academic use.

The 80286. This is a development of the 8086 and any program which runs on an 8086 will also run on this, its bigger brother. However, it is much faster and more powerful. It is contained within the second generation of IBM PC machines known as the AT of which, as with the PC, there are literally hundreds of lookalikes.

The 68000. This is arguably a more powerful processor than either the 8088/ 8086 or the 80286 but the computers containing this chip have not necessarily reflected this power. It is contained in the Apple Macintosh and Mac Plus computers, the Commodore Amiga and in the Atari ST series of computers.

Finally, there are the 32-bit microprocessors. These are a very recent development. They typically run at between 12 and 20 MHz and can handle 4 bytes at a time. The main ones are:

The 80386. This forms the heart of the latest IBM micros and IBM clones. These micros are compatible with the earlier 8088/8086 and 80286 machines but much faster and potentially more versatile. The 80386 chip has been designed with *multitasking* in mind. That is, it is designed to allow the user to perform several tasks (e.g. word processing, statistical analysis and database management) at the same time.

The 68020 and 68030. These are used in the Apple Macintosh II and III computers. These are developments from the 68000 chips. They are extremely fast and sophisticated but are not particularly well suited to multitasking.

The transputer family of chips (e.g. T800). A lot has been heard about the new super-micros based on these chips with the power of a mainframe. Transputers are extremely fast 32-bit processors with their own memory and, most importantly, the ability to be linked to each other in parallel so that in theory it is possible to double, treble, etc. the speed of the computer by putting these chips together. It is possible to buy transputer add-on boards for IBM machines and ATARI STs. The problem is that at present there are very few commercially written programs which will make use of the power available. Transputer chips have what are known, as 'reduced instruction sets'. This means that instead of having complex circuitry to perform a wide range of operations many of which are only used once in a while, they are built to optimise the speed of the relatively few instructions which they can perform. Note that as far as the user is concerned there is no limitation on the range of instructions that can be performed; when complex instructions have to be performed by the microprocessor, this is done by combining the simpler instructions.

The Acorn RISC (reduced instructions set) chip. This is another very fast chip which has been developed by Acorn for their Archimedes range of micros. The Archimedes has been shown on standard 'benchmarks' (tests of speed) to be by far the fastest micro available at present. It is particularly fast at creating screen graphics.

The second major component of any computer is its electronic memory. The memory stores both data and sequences of instructions (programs) for the CPU. There are two main kinds of memory: random-access memory (RAM) and read-only memory (ROM). RAM can be both read to and written from by a program but its contents are lost when the computer is switched off. Micros typically have between 64 000 and 4 million bytes of RAM. RAM is used to store programs which the user is running at a given time and data which that program is working with (e.g. text if the program is a word processor, or numbers if the program is a statistical package). ROM cannot be altered by the user but it does not lose its contents when the computer is switched off. ROM is used to store special programs which are 'resident' in the computer and are used particularly frequently. Most notably, in the case of some micros, ROMs contain the *operating system* (see below).

In order to be able to keep programs and data when the computer is switched off, or when one wishes to switch between tasks, it is necessary to save these on some permanent memory device. Micros use two main kinds of permanent memory: floppy discs and hard discs. Floppy discs, as the name implies, are thin, flexible discs coated with a magnetic material similar to that on a recording tape. There are three main sizes: 3" used in Amstrad PCWs, 3.5" used in ATARI STs, Macintoshes, some IBMs and clones and Archimedes, and 5.25" used in most Acorn BBC computers and many IBMs and clones. The storage capacity of these discs ranges from 180 000 bytes to 1.4 million bytes. Floppy discs can be removed from the disc drive so that one can have a library of discs, merely inserting the one needed for the task in hand at any one time. Hard discs are not normally removable, but they hold much more information and are much faster. They typically hold from 10 million to 80 million bytes and saving and retrieving programs and data from them is at least 10 times as fast as from floppies.

Both floppy and hard discs store information on *tracks*. These are concentric rings which hold the magnetic patterns which comprise the information. Floppy discs usually have between 40 and 80 tracks. Hard discs have many times as many. The reason that hard discs are much quicker and can store more information is not that they are larger but rather than they spin much faster and the information is much more densely packed. This is only possible because the discs are hermetically sealed inside the drive in a dust-free environment, so that minute dust particules which would otherwise get in the way of the *read–write* heads are excluded. Read–write heads are like the recording and playback heads on a cassette recorder.

Data and programs on discs are stored as *files*. These are similar to files in a filing cabinet. They are discrete entities and can be accessed individually. Each file has a file name which the user gives it when it is created. Typically a hard disc will have hundreds of files, some of which will contain text such as letters, papers or chapters. Others will contain commands to be used by a statistics package for carrying out a particular analysis; others will contain numeric data; and still others will contain programs.

Users interact with computers by means of what are known as *input–output* (IO) devices. The most commonly used input device is the typewriter-style keyboard. This contains many more keys than a typewriter, including special *function keys* which can be programmed to perform specific tasks. The most common output device is the television-like screen (VDU or monitor). There are many different kinds of VDU. Some cheap computers can use an ordinary television screen but the definition is typically too low for any serious applications. Monochrome screens come in a range of colours, from black-on-white, to amber or green on black. Colour screens can be either *composite video* or *RGB*. In the former case, the colour signals are received together down the same wires from the computer. In the case of RGB screens, the red, green and blue signals which make up the colour image are received down separate wires. IBM-type computers have a range of different graphics standards. For example, at the lowest end there is CGA (colour graphics adapter) which has low resolution and relatively few colours; EGA (enhanced graphics adapter) provides for more colours and better resolution; still higher resolution is obtained by VGA systems. These graphics standards do not simply involve the screen. Each has to be 'driven' by a special circuit board inserted into the computer itself.

It is also generally necessary to have a printer. There are three main kinds of printer:

Daisy-wheel printers which operate like typewriters, are slow but produce good quality text. The characters are imprinted on the page by selecting a character on a print wheel and hitting the paper with the character through a ribbon. Daisy-wheel printers generally cannot print out graphics. Different character sets are obtained by changing the print wheel.

Dot-matrix printers which form letters by selecting patterns of pins to hit the paper through an inked ribbon. These are generally faster than daisy-wheel printers and can produce graphics as well as text. Cheap printers of this type usually have 9 pins and their text quality is not very good. Slightly more expensive printers have 24 pins and produce good-quality text and, depending on the program driving them, very good-quality graphics.

Laser printers work rather like photocopiers. A laser is used to imprint a pattern of charge on the paper and *toner* (carbon particles) sticks to that pattern, creating the image. They are quite expensive, fast and quiet and can produce excellent text and graphics (with a resolution of 300 dots per inch). The running costs are much higher than other printers, currently at around 3 pence or 5 cents per page. There are two main kinds of laser printer: bit-mapped and postscript. Bit-mapped laser printers (e.g. Hewlett Packard Laserjet Plus) set up the image pattern by mapping out dot by dot the shapes of characters and graphics. These generally have a relatively limited selection of font (character) styles and sizes. Postscript printers (e.g. Apple Laserwriter plus) use a special language to set up characters and graphics. They are more expensive but have a wider range of font styles and sizes.

Other specialised IO devices for micros include:

Analogue to digital (A to D) converters which can take a continuously variable voltage input and produce a number corresponding to the voltage in a form that the computer can use (i.e. one or more bytes). These are used in some cases to record the position of things such as steering wheels or joysticks when subjects are performing a tracking task of some kind. In other cases they may be used to convert speech sounds into a form which is analysable by the computer. Frequently they are used to enable the computer to record and process electrophysiological data such as electroencephalograms (EEGs), event-related cortical potentials (ERPs), electrocardiograms (ECGs) and electrodermal activity (EDA).

Image scanners which convert a two-dimensional visual image such as a photograph into a form which computers can process. These can be used for inputting images of, for example, faces into the computer for presentation in an experiment.

A crucial piece of hardware for many psychological applications is a timer. All computers have accurate clocks inside them to coordinate the activity of the CPU and memory. However, in many cases, these clocks are not accessible to users in a form which enables accurate timings of responses or stimulus presentation to be made. IBM-type machines are particularly bad in this regard whereas the Atari STs and BBC and Archimedes computers are quite good.

Figure I.1 shows schematically the various parts of microcomputers and how they operate together.

Computer software

Software is the name given to programs which run on computers. Literally everything that a computer does is controlled by some program or other. Programs are sequences of bytes which serve as commands and are stored in the computer memory. A program is run when the memory address of the

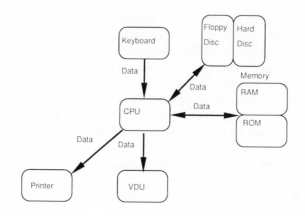

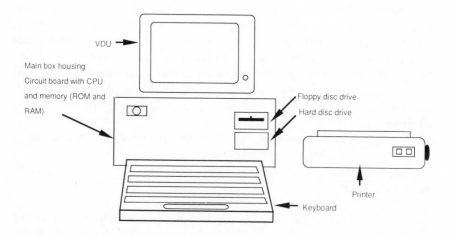

FIGURE I.1   Schematic diagram showing parts of a microcomputer system and how they interact (see text for details).

first byte of the first command is put into a register in the CPU known as the *program counter*. This causes the byte stored at this address to be loaded into the CPU and executed. Unless this byte is the 'stop' command, the program fetches the next command from the next address and continues in this vein, fetching successive commands from addresses in memory until a command is found which says 'stop'.

In the bad old days, in order to program a computer to do something one had to set a bank of switches on a console to a bit pattern of 1s and 0s corresponding to a memory address, press a button to enter that address, then

Table I.3   Examples of operating system commands

Command	Operating system	Meaning
COPY ECG1.DAT+ECG2.DAT ECG.DAT	MSDOS	Copy the contents of files ECG1.DAT and ECG2.DAT to a single file called ECG.DAT
PRINT ECG.DAT	MSDOS	Print out the contents of file ECG.DAT on a printer connected to the micro
TYPE ECG.DAT	MSDOS	Display the contents of file ECG.DAT on the screen
RENAME ECG.DAT=MYDATA.DAT	CPM	Renames a file called MYDATA.DAT to ECG.DAT
DIR	CPM	Displays on the screen a list of files on disc by name

set a bank of switches to the bit pattern corresponding to whatever one wanted to put in that address and then press a button to make that happen. When one wished to run a program, one set a bank of switches to the address of the start of the program and pressed a run button. Happily this is no longer the case.

When a microcomputer is turned on, there is usually present in ROM a program which will do one of two things. It either runs the whole time the computer is switched on, acting as a kind of interpreter between the user and the CPU and memory; or else it enables the user to call up from disc a program which will do this. Programs that act as interpreters between the user and the CPU are known as *operating systems*, and as already mentioned they may be either 'ROM-based' as in the BBC, ATARI, AMIGA and Archimedes, or 'disc-based' as in the IBM types of micro, Amstrad PCWs and Macintoshes. Operating systems control the VDU and interpret keystrokes on the keyboard; they also control the disc drives and, in a limited way, the printer.

There are many different operating systems. Ataris, Amigas, Macintoshes, BBC and Archimedes each have their own. An operating system which became a standard for computers with Z80 processors is known as CPM. It lives on in the Amstrad PCW. IBM-type machines, including PCs, ATs and 80386 machines, use an operating system known as MSDOS (or the near equivalent PCDOS). MSDOS stands for Microsoft (the name of the manufacturer) Disc Operating System. There is also IBM's proprietary OS/2 operating system which allows a degree of multitasking (running several programs at once). Table I.3 gives examples of operating system commands which a user can type in.

Table I.4   Examples of a section of source code in BBC BASIC

Commands	Meaning
DIM RT(10)	Set up space to store 10 reaction times
FOR I = 1 TO 10	Go 10 times through a sequence
CLS	which clears the screen
TIME = 0	creates a delay of 1 second
REPEAT UNTIL TIME > 100	displays a * on the screen
PRINT TAB(20,12);"*"	sets a timer to 0
TIME = 0	waits for a key to be pressed
R = GET	and records the reaction time
RT(I) = TIME	to the appearance of the *
NEXT I	

A new breed of operating systems is gaining in popularity. It uses *mice, windows* and *icons* to control the computer and display computer output. A computer mouse is a small rounded box which sits on the desk top and can be moved by the user around the surface of the desk. This moves a *pointer* around the screen. When the pointer sits on top of a graphical display of, for example, a disc drive, it operates that drive. The user can perform many operations in this way without having to use the keyboard. It is possible in such operating systems to open several 'windows' at once. These are overlaid displays which the user can switch between at will. Macinstosh, Atari ST, Amiga and Archimedes computers have this kind of operating system as standard. IBM-type machines can also run such operatings systems.

Most computer users do not write their own programs. They buy ready-made programs such as word processors, accounting packages, database systems, statistical analysis programs or games programs. However, for psychological applications it is often necessary to write one's own software. Writing programs in *machine code* (using the raw instruction set which the CPU understands) is difficult and error-prone. Therefore most software is written in a *high-level* language which is easier for humans to understand. This is then put through another program which translates the high-level *source code* into machine code. The most commonly used high-level languages are BASIC, FORTRAN, Pascal, Modula 2, C, PROLOG and LISP. Of these, BASIC is used most in psychology. Computer 'buffs' used to be very dismissive about BASIC, saying that it encouraged poor programming style and lacked power. However, modern versions of the language such as BBC BASIC Version V, QUICKBASIC, TRUEBASIC and FASTBASIC are powerful and pleasant to use. Table I.4 shows some lines of BASIC source code.

There are two kinds of program to translate from high-level languages to machine code: *compilers* and *interpreters*. Compilers take the *source code* (the text of the program written in the high-level language) and create a quite separate file containing the machine code. The user then puts the source code to one side and simply runs the machine code program as if he or she had written the program in machine code from the start. Interpreters require the source code to be present at the time the program is run and perform the translation to machine code, line by line, as the program is running. Compilers have the advantage that programs using them run faster because they have already been translated to machine code before the program is run, instead of having to be translated 'on the fly'. The disadvantage of compilers is that during program development the person writing the program has to put the program through the compiler to see whether or not it works as required. This can take several seconds or several minutes depending on the compiler. Given that this has to be done tens or possibly hundreds of times when developing a given program, the time delay can be considerable.

Which computer for which application?

Although it would be desirable in principle to standardise on one kind of micro for all tasks, whether it be word processing and statistical analysis or running an experiment, in practice different micros tend to be useful for different applications.

IBM clones are mainly useful for traditional data-processing activities such as statistical analysis, word processing, database management, etc.

Atari STs, BBCs and Archimedes are best suited for *real-time* applications in which stimuli are presented to subjects and responses recorded and timed.

Apple Macintoshes are particularly good for creating reports with mixed graphics and text.

This concludes the introduction to the world of microcomputers. The main body of rest in this book now considers how micros have been or can be used to help with the work of collecting and analysing psychological data.

Part 1

Data Processing and Programming

Data processing is the traditional use to which computers have been put. Computers excel at 'number crunching', and storing, sorting and retrieving information. Computers are obviously widely used for these purposes in health-care institutions all around the world. This kind of activity can now be carried out on micros. Family practitioners and small teams are putting records and data on computers using either standard 'data-base packages' or special-purpose ones directed at their specialist needs. Part I examines two very different approaches to the use of micros in data processing.

The first chapter examines the process of statistical analysis using ready-made packages available on micros. Statistical analysis is a vital part of most research. It can also play an important role in clinical practice, for example in assessing trends in the kinds of clients who are seeking help with a view to improving delivery of services. Micro-based statistical packages mean that powerful techniques are available to individual practitioners and small teams. These may not have the statistical support of larger organisations and it is important that they understand what can and cannot be done, and how to go about getting the kinds of results they desire.

The second chapter gives us a glimpse into the future. Artificial intelligence has been making the headlines for a few years. One aspect of artificial intelligence which has received a great deal of attention is the development of *expert systems*. These are sophisticated data bases which many believe will either supplement or possibly replace the human expert. This chapter examines principles underlying the development of expert systems in psychiatry, where they offer the possibility of assisting in a range of activities from diagnosis of mental disorders to statistical analysis of data. It is fair to say that none of the psychiatric expert systems developed to date have achieved wide acceptance, but techniques are constantly improving and it should not be long now before psychiatrists and other medical practitioners refer to their micro for a second (or even first) opinion.

The third chapter gives an account of the factors that need to be considered in developing micro-based applications for psychological work; whether it be buying off-the-shelf products or writing programs.

CHAPTER 1

Data analysis using statistical packages on microcomputers

ROBERT WEST

Data collected in medical and psychological investigations will normally need to be subjected to statistical analysis in order to determine what conclusions, if any, can be drawn. Statistical analysis can also be of help in clinical practice, for example in assessing the characteristics of patient populations for the purpose of targeting resources. Powerful programs for carrying out statistical analysis were once only available on large mainframe computers. These have recently been adapted to run on microcomputers. This has meant a huge increase in their accessibility to researchers and clinicians, many of whom are without expert statistical advice. This chapter considers the process of data analysis on micros, giving examples from specific statistical packages where appropriate. It also considers how to make most efficient use of statistical packages.

It was not so many years ago that performing statistical analysis on data collected in medical or psychological research went something like this:

1 Sit at a card-punch machine creating a stack of cards containing numbers and certain magic words and symbols of obscure significance.
2 Place the pack of cards in the computer operator's in-tray and wait for one or more days.
3 Collect a printout indicating that the job had not run because a comma had been left out of one of the statements.
4 Go back to 1 until you obtain a sensible printout or else hand analysis over a statistician (let someone else waste their time on it).
5 When the 'output' finally arrives, try to decipher it.
6 Realise that either there are major errors in the 'punching in' of the data or the wrong analysis has been performed or both.

Microcomputers, Psychology and Medicine
Edited by R. West, M. Christie and J. Weinman
© 1990 by John Wiley & Sons Ltd

And so on . . .

Mainframe computers have become much more powerful and users can now perform a similar exercise in the comfort of their office using a *terminal*. More significantly, microcomputers have become more powerful and so the cycle of frustration is available to all but the most humble organisation at relatively little cost.

This is something of a caricature, but the time wasted in the course of statistical analysis seems little changed in the age of the micro from what it was in the age of the mainframe. This chapter examines statistical analysis using some of the most widely used statistical packages available on microcomputers. The latter part of the chapter will consider how the enormous waste of time involved in using statistical packages can be reduced by adopting particular habits. It concludes by discussing how packages might be designed in the future to make them better suited to the needs of users, many of whom may not be statistically sophisticated.

There are some important points to note before proceeding. First. this chapter is not a statistics guide and it is assumed that the reader knows some statistical terms already. Second, it is not a consumer's guide to all the available statistics packages. This would be impracticable in the space available and in any case would very rapidly become out of date.

There should be something in this chapter for readers with a wide range of statistical expertise. The novice should obtain a flavour of what can be achieved using statistical packages and how one might approach the process of data analysis using these. Other readers may already use one or more of the packages discussed. For them the chapter should indicate alternatives which are available. Readers at all levels of expertise should find something of interest in the discussion of how data analysis may be made more efficient and less wasteful.

The 'hardware' requirements

Computers and the bits and pieces which go with them are known as *hardware*. This is as distinct from *software*, which consists of the programs which run on the computers. This section examines the hardware needed for serious statistical analysis.

Statistical programs are available for a wide range of microcomputers, such as those made by Apple in the US and Acorn in the UK. However, many of these programs are limited in capability and they often contain errors. The major statistical packages are available on only one class of microcomputer— the IBM Personal Computer 'clone' (hereafter referred to simply as the PC). These are computers made by literally hundreds of different manufacturers which are based on an original design by IBM. There are several varieties—

primarily the XT, the AT and the more powerful 80386 machines (see Introduction). The software packages will work on all of these, although they will run faster on ATs and 80386s. The computer will normally need to have at least a 20-megabyte *hard disc*. This is a disc on which information can be stored even when the machine is switched off. The '20 megabytes' means that it can store 20 million characters of information. At least one floppy disc drive will also be needed but these are generally supplied as standard anyway.

Users are advised by the suppliers of statistical packages to buy what is known as a *maths co-processor*. This is simply a chip which plugs into the main circuit board of the computer and speeds up arithmetic operations. In fact this chip does not make a great deal of difference with most of the packages because their speed is influenced much more by the speed of operation of the hard disc. Impatient users would be advised to spend a little more money and buy a faster hard disc. The exception is the package known as BMDP (see below), which will not run unless you have a co-processor.

Overview of the statistical packages

The packages mentioned in the chapter are SPSSPC+, BMDPC, SAS, GLIM, MINITAB, STATGRAPHICS, SYSTAT and EGRET. The first five of these are widely used throughout the world. STATGRAPHICS is mentioned because of its increasing popularity and because it illustrates a different approach from the others. SYSTAT is a newcomer which has had favourable reviews. EGRET performs a very limited range of statistical functions but has a superb user interface which others would do well to emulate. There are other packages but the ones chosen give a good idea of the range which is available.

Almost certainly the best-known statistical package of all is SPSS (Statistical Package for Social Sciences). The micro version is called SPSSPC+ but it will simply be referred to as SPSS in this chapter. Another package which has been around for a long time is BMDP. The micro version is BMDPC but again this chapter will simply use the acronym BMDP. A less well-known package with a rapidly developing following is MINITAB. This was originally developed as an aid to statistics teaching. It is now a major statistical package in its own right.

SAS (Statistical Analysis System) originally ran only on large IBM mainframe computers. It has recently been adapted to run on smaller 'minicomputers' and PCs. The PC version is still in its infancy compared with SPSS and BMDP.

The more statistically sophisticated researcher or clinician will be interested in the GLIM (Gerneralised Linear Modelling) package. This offers a limited range of basic functions from which it is possible to derive more sophisticated ones if one has the statistical expertise to do so. STATGRAPHICS is quite restricted as regards statistical functions. As the name would suggest, the concentration is more on presentation of data in graphical form.

SYSTAT is compact and fairly easy to use, but limited in statistical functions. Its great strength is provision of a flexible programming language with it to perform computations on data prior to use of inbuilt statistical procedures.

EGRET will only perform a statistical function called *logistic regression*, but its user interface is so good that it merits mention for this alone.

Mention should also be made of the fact that business-oriented *spreadsheet* packages designed for financial modelling (e.g. Lotus-1-2-3) can be used for statistical analysis. However, it is unlikely that many medical or psychological researchers will wish to do this, given that ready-made statistical packages are available.

The cost of these packages is of the order of $500 to over $2000 at commercial rates but special deals can reduce the cost dramatically. SPSS, for example, can be obtained for under $200.

Overview of statistical operations on a micro

Statistical packages are designed around the following activities:

Entering data
Editing and selecting data
Recoding and transforming existing variables and computing new ones
Displaying data
Performing statistical analyses
Saving the results of data analysis

Figure 1.1 shows the whole process in outline. Each of these will be considered in turn in the sections which follow.

Entering data

In order for data to be used by a statistical package it has to be entered into a kind of *workspace* (see Figure 1.2). Data can normally be entered either directly from the keyboard or from a *text* file created by a general-purpose editing program or word processor. In most psychological and medical applications entry from data files is by far the most important method. In fact data entry is often farmed out to *coders*, who can use any text editor or word processor to get the numbers into a file on a disc in the form of an ASCII file (see Introduction). This file can then be read by the statistical package. This raises the question of what format the statistical package allows for a data file, and how easy it is to tell the package how your data are organised.

Almost universally, data are organised with one or more rows of numbers representing *cases* (a case usually being a person), with the colomns representing *variables* (e.g. subject number, age, how long they have held a driving

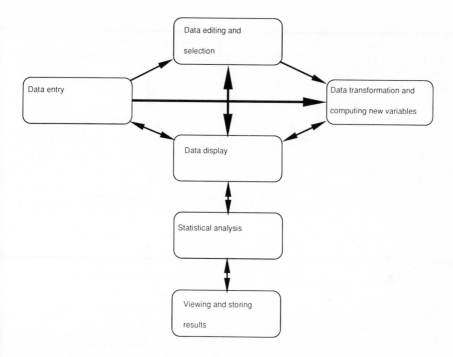

FIGURE 1.1   Activities involved in analysing data on a micro. Arrows represent likely sequencing of activities.

licence, number of road traffic accidents in the past three years, etc.; see Figure 1.3a).

Often the data will be entered in *freefield* format. This involves leaving spaces between the variables. This is the simplest method and has much to recommend it (Figure 1.3b).

Another approach does not require spaces between the observations although the user may include these if desired. The user tells the system where each observation can be located in the data file by providing a kind of 'map' which indicates which variables occupy which columns. No spaces are needed to mark off variables because the system is informed directly where they are by special formulae. Different packages use different kinds of maps.

One kind of map involves indicating the first and last column of each variable. SPSS uses this approach (see Figure 1.3c). The other main approach is to use a kind of formula derived from the programming language FORTRAN. In this formula you work from the beginning of a case through to the end, indicating presence of a variable, example by using *Fa.b*, where *a* is the total number of columns occupied by the variable and *b* is the number of columns after the decimal place (see Figure 1.3d). If you want to skip over one or more

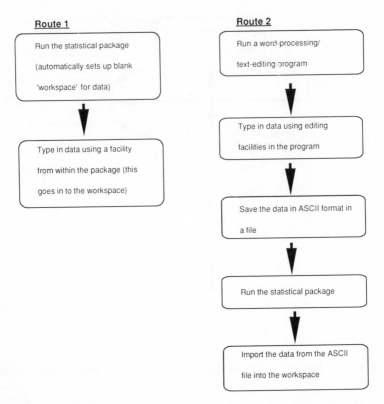

FIGURE 1.2   Two possible routes for entering data into a statistical package. Route 2 is normally to be preferred because it allows use of editing/correction facilities of the word processor.

columns you use X. This system is difficult to learn and likely to lead to mistakes but it does have one major advantage; it allows a very compact statement of where to find the data because of the use of compound expressions contained in parentheses. Thus (3(3F1.0,X),2X,5((2F2.1,X))) will read in 19 variables, nine of which each occupy a single column, while ten occupy two columns with one digit after the decimal place. BMDP, MINITAB and GLIM use this system. EGRET uses this system but has an intelligent interface built in which actually creates the formula for you! The user sees the first case of the data file, and the system provides what it thinks is the most likely format statement. The user then corrects this as necessary in a simple interactive session. It is far and away the best system for reading in data that I have come across.

All the statistical packages under consideration allow you to save time and effort by dumping the contents of the workspace on to a floppy or hard disc. This workspace can be read in directly on another occasion and the user will

DATA FILE CALLED TRRL.DATA   (a)

01 5 10 14 18000 2 1 1 3 1   SUBJECT 1/BASIC INFO

75.09 72.33 68.62 68.44 65.02 68.90   SUBJECT 1/CONDITION 1

000 000 002 002 000 000

71.83 70.54 68.05 68.17 70.35 69.55
                                             SUBJECT 1/CONDITION 2
000 000 002 002 000 000

60.65 67.46 60.71 67.06 66.48 68.10
                                             SUBJECT 1/CONDITION 3
000 000 004 000 000 003

02 5 04 08 19 1 06500 2 1 1 2 1   SUBJECT 2/BASIC INFO

75.31 75.31 74.16 77.26 69.01 74.67
                                             SUBJECT 2/CONDITION 1
000 000 000 000 000 000

....

....

FREEFIELD FORMAT: SPSSPC+
                                                                              (b)
DATA LIST FILE='TRRL.DAT' FREE

/SUBNO AGE LICENCE DRINK MILES GLASSES

BIFOCAL ENDORSE ACCIDENT SEG TRACKA1 TO TRACKA6

ITEMA1 TO ITEMA6 TRACKB1 TO TRACKB6 ITEMB1 TO ITEMB6

TRACKC1 TO TRACKC6 ITEMC1 TO ITEMC6.

FIGURE 1.3   (a) shows the layout of a data file. Only data from subject 1 and part of subject 2 are shown . The data for each subject are organised into seven lines for easier visual inspection. Each subject provides background information and data from three experimental conditions. (b–d) Commands which may be used so that data from this file may be imported into statistics package; (b) shows the commands for a freefield format into SPSS; The words after the / are names which have been given to each variable; (c) shows the same thing using fixed format SPSS style; (d) shows fixed format MINITAB style. Note the greater complexity but also the greater succinctness of the MINITAB command

FIXED FORMAT: SPSSPC+   (c)

```
DATA LIST FILE='TRRL.DAT'

/SUBNO 1-2 AGE 4 LICENCE DRINK 5-10 MILES 11-16

GLASSES BIFOCAL ENDORSE ACCIDENT SEG 17-26

/TRACKA1 TO TRACKA 1-36

/ITEMA1 TO ITEMA6 1-24

/TRACKB1 TO TRACKB 1-36

/ITEMB1 TO ITEMB6 1-24

/TRACKC1 TO TRACKC6 1-36

/ITEMC1 TO ITEMC6 1-24
```

FIXED FORMAT: MINITAB   (d)

```
READ 'TRRL.DAT ' C1-C46;

FORMAT (F2.0, X, F1.0, 2(X,F2.0), X, F5.0, 5(X,F1.0), 3(/,6(F6.2), /, 6(F4.0))).
```

FIGURE 1.3   continued

be in the same position as he or she would have been in at the time the worksheet was saved, with no need to repeat commands to read in data in a particular format or transform data in some way for the purpose of the analyses.

Special mention should be made of a facility in SPSS called the *data entry module*. This is a sophisticated system for entering data which allows error correction and has some nice touches. For example, the user can set it up so that it checks the data as it is being entered to make sure that impossible values for observations are flagged. This reflects the SPSS's philosophy of providing a complete 'environment' for data analysis made up of fully inter-grated modules which satisfy all the user's requirements.

Editing and selecting data

A statistical package is of limited usefulness it allows the user to correct data after it has been entered in. It is also extremely helpful to be able to select parts of a data file for analysis and combine two or more files into a single data file. For example, SPSS allows merging of files in quite sophisticated ways, and selection of cases according to whether they fulfil certain user-definable characteristics. SAS is also particularly well suited to data manipulation and file handling. Most flexible of all is SYSTAT, which allows the user to select, modify or recode variables according to any formula that may be desired.

Recoding of variables is something one frequently has to do. For example, suppose one has collected data on the number of cigarettes smoked per day in a group of patients. One may wish to derive from this a simple categorisation of smokers and non-smokers. Most packages allow one to do this, although some more easily than others. In SPSS the command might be something like:

RECODE CIGSPER (1 THRU HIGHEST = 1).

This assumes that there is a variable called CIGSPER which contains information on cigarette consumption. After the recoding operation, patients with a score of 0 will be non-smokers and those with a score of 1 will be smokers.

MINITAB allows recoding of variables and has a number of editing facilities including copying variables, and choosing or deleting cases whose variables have certain values. A useful facility possessed by some packages (e.g. MINITAB) is the ability to treat a block of data of n cases by m variables as a matrix and perform various matrix operations on it. The usefulness of this is particularly apparent when one wishes to perform correlations, not across subjects but across variables, as in repertory grid analyses. This can easily be achieved by entering the data in the normal way, treating it as a matrix, transposing this matrix and then performing the correlations.

STATGRAPHICS and GLIM have very limited data-editing facilities. STATGRAPHICS is unusual in treating data like a spreadsheet, which comprises a *data dictionary* which may include data from more than one file. In practice, finding and altering data with this system can be very tedious.

Computing new values from existing variables

There are many occasions when one wishes to create a new variable by performing a computation on some combination of existing ones. Most packages allow you to do this. SPSS has the COMPUTE command (e.g. COMPUTE TOTALSCO = SCORE1 + SCORE2, which creates a new variable TOTALSCO equal to the sum of SCORE1 and SCORE2. Just about any kind of arithmetic expression can be used. This makes it relatively easy to generate scores for such things as questionnaire subscales. MINITAB has additional facilities for calculating the sums, means, standard deviations, etc. across a whole set of variables as well as for a given variable. In fact the extensive arithmetic facilities of MINITAB make it possible to construct statistical tests which are not included in the package as standard. These arithmetic operations can be stored in a file and executed at any time. In this way it is theoretically possible

SPSSPC+

```
RECODE MILES (0 THRU 1000=1) (1001 THRU 5000=2) (50001 THRU HI =3).

COMPUTE TRACKA=TRACKA1+TRACKA2+TRACKA3+TRACKA4+ TRACKA5+TRACKA6.

IF (AGE GE 30) EXPER=2.
```

MINITAB

```
RSUM c11-c16 c17

RSTDEV c11-c16 c18

RMEDIAN c11-c16 c19

CODE (999) '"' c17 c17
```

FIGURE 1.4 Examples of commands used to recode existing variables or compute new variables. Note the greater succinctness of the MINITAB commands and the facility (RSTDEV) to calculate standard deviations across variables.

to create statistical tests which are not included as part of the package. However, in practice most users could not, or would not, wish to do this.

STATGRAPHICS is written in a powerful (though rather unfriendly) language called APL. If one purchases APL one can add any range of utilities one wishes to the system (not to be recommended for the non-programmer). SAS has similar facilities for programmers to add their own routines.

SYSTATs main strength is that it includes a programming language very much like BASIC (a simple programming language good for arithmetic operations) which enables users to create their own statistical tests, and also to manipulate data in just about any way imaginable.

Figure 1.4 gives examples of commands used by SPSS and MINITAB to compute new variables and recode existing variables.

Displaying data: descriptive statistics and graphics

All the statistical packages are able to display simple features of data in some form or another. Facilities for bar charts, histograms, pie charts, scattergrams and line charts are widely available. In some cases, one has to purchase additional modules to do this. For example, SPSS has a graphics module which can be added and which together with the third-party programs Microsoft Chart or Chartmaster and a suitable printer or plotter produces bar charts, line charts, etc. which are of a quality suitable for inclusion in scientific papers or books. The graphics produced by BMDP and MINITAB are constructed out of characters such as asterisks and, though useful for visualising the data, are not good enough for publication. STATGRAPHICS offers a superb range of graphics facilities, including the facilities to put in standard errors on regression lines. To take full advantage of this, one should have a special *Enhanced Graphics Adapter* for the PC and a high-resolution colour screen. SYSTAT can provide simple character-based graphics or, with the inclusion of a graphics module, quite good plots including 3-D contour plots.

Basic descriptive statistics such as means, medians, standard deviations, frequency counts, etc. are available on all the packages. MINITAB gives as standard some unusual information, including *truncated means*. These are means produced once the top and bottom 5% of the sample have been excluded. Where frequency counts are available it is usual for the computer to determine for itself the size of the 'bins' to be used.

Statistical testing

Statistical testing is obviously the core of any data analysis package. The facilities offered by the various packages differ considerably.

Regression and correlation are most widely available, together with simple one-sample or two-sample tests such as *t*-tests.

Analysis of variance (ANOVA) is widely available, and in the more sophisticated packages such as SPSS and BMDP unequal cell sizes in multi-way ANOVAs are catered for. MINITAB is very limited in its ANOVAs. The most complex design it can handle is the two-way groups design with equal numbers of observations in each group. This is a major and surprising limitation. Repeated-measures ANOVAs have typically been a major omission in large statistical packages—the notable exception being BMDP, which has a superb suite of modules for ANOVAs. With SPSS one performs a repeated-measures ANOVA by asking for a MANOVA and giving various keywords. The procedure is a big improvement over previous mainframe versions of SPSS in which extraction of a repeated-measures ANOVA was convoluted and difficult to understand. MINITAB has no facility for repeated-measures ANOVAs. GLIM can do any kind of ANOVA, but one has to know the relationship between ANOVA and regression to appreciate how to do the analysis. STATGRAPHICS also does repeated-measures ANOVAs using a regression model. This is not something which a non-statistician would wish to do. SYSTAT is also not recommended for repeated-measures ANOVAs.

One usually wishes to perform a range of planned or post hoc comparisons within ANOVAs. For example, having discovered that there is a significant difference between measures of urinary adrenaline at different times of day one would want to look at where the difference lay. For example, was there a gradual increase, or an increase then a decrease, or was the morning value simply lower than all the others? SPSS allows you to perform planned comparisons relatively easily with independent groups designs, but with repeated measures designs it does horrible things like 'orthonormalising' your specification of what comparisons you want. BMDP is excellent at planned comparisons while at the other extreme MINITAB does not have any specific facilities for these.

The ability to analyse frequency tables using simple chi-squared tests is just about universal. The ability to use log-linear modelling for multi-way tables is available in some packages but not others. For example, SPSS and BMDP allow log-linear modelling of complex frequency tables whereas SAS and MINITAB do not. Log-linear modelling can be obtained in GLIM if you know what you are doing!

Non-parametric tests of various kinds are available in all packages except SAS and GLIM. Most packages have simple one-sample and two-sample tests such as Wilcoxon, Mann–Whitney, and the Sign test. Friedman and Kruskall Wallace tests for repeated measures, and independent groups non-parametric ANOVAs are available. More sophisticated non-parametric tests for multi-way designs are not generally available.

Non-linear regression is extremely well catered for by BMDP. Other packages such as SPSS provide limited means of turning non-linear associations into linear ones, but BMDP allows the selection of a range of non-linear functions to be tested, or the specification of user-defined functions.

A particular form of regression which is widely used in psychological and medical application is *logistic regression*, where one or more variables are used to predict which of two (or more) groups a subject (person, animal or whatever) will fall into. BMDP, SAS and GLIM all have facilities for this. EGRET does only this, but does it very well, giving odds ratios as well as regression coefficients and significance levels.

A wide range of multivariate analyses including cluster analysis, factor analysis and discriminant analysis are available in SAS, BMDP and SPSS. BMDP also allows cluster analysis of variables and clustering of categorical data. STATGRAPHICS and SYSTAT can perform factor analysis, though they offer no choice as to method of factor extraction and what they do would be better considered a principle components analysis, which is slightly different.

An important analysis which is only available on BMDP is *survival analysis*, which as the name implies concerns the inclusion and exclusion of cases progressively over a period of time. This is commonly used for examining death rates for subgroups of patients over time.

Time series analysis of various kinds, including forecasting and spectral analyses, are well provided for. BMDP and MINITAB, for example, both provide 'Box–Jenkins' analyses. BMDP and STATGRAPHICS can perform Fourier analyses—useful for analysing EEG data or other cyclic data, for example.

	BMDP	SPSS	SAS	STATG	MINITAB	GLIM	SYSTAT	EGRET
Descriptive stats	**	**	**	**	**	*	**	-
Simple regression	**	**	**	**	**	**	**	*
Multiple regression	**	**	**	**	**	**	**	*
Logical regression	**	-	**	-	-	*	-	**
Simple correlation	**	**	**	**	*	*	**	-
Partial correlation	**	*	*	**	*	*	*	-
Canonical correlation	**	-	**	-	-	-	-	-
Independent *t*-test	**	**	**	**		*	**	-
Related *t*-test	**	**	**	**	*	*	**	-
One-way ANOVA	**	**	**	*	*	*	**	-
Two-way ANOVA	**	**	**	*	*	*	**	-
Multi-way ANOVA	**	**	**	*	-	*	*	-
Rptd measures ANOVA	**	*	*	*	-	*	*	-
MANOVA	**	**	*	-	-	*	*	-
Non-parametric tests	*	*	-	*	*	-	*	-
Factor analysis	**	**	**	*	-	-	*	-
Discriminant analysis	**	**	**	**	-	-	*	-
Cluster analysis	**	**	**	**	-	-	*	-
Survival analysis	**	-	-	-	-	-	-	-
EDA	*	-	-	**	**	-	-	-
Time series	**	-	-	**	*	-	*	-
Contingency tables	**	**	*	**	*	*	*	-

** comprehensive/easy: * limited/difficult: - not available

STATG = Statgraphics

FIGURE 1.5 Summary of statistical analyses available on eight statistics packages. This is intended only as a rough guide and may change as the packages develop.

MINITAB makes a feature of its *Exploratory Data Analysis* facilities. These are not all that useful when it comes to analysing results of tightly designed studies, but they can be helpful when undertaking 'fishing expeditions' in large and poorly structured data sets.

Figure 1.5 gives a summary of the statistical analyses available on the packages under consideration. The reader should be aware, however, that this information is likely to become out of date as the packages are developed further. It is given merely to show the overall philosophy of each package.

Storing results of analyses

It is important to be able to save the results of analyses in files on the hard disc. In most cases this is simply to avoid having to copy down the results from the screen in long-hand. Stored results can be examined at leisure using a word-processing program or full-screen editor. Another occasion when one wishes to store results is when the statistical analysis has produced data which one then wishes to provide as the input to some further analysis. The most obvious example is *factor scores* which result from factor analysis. SPSS, for example, allows the derived scores for each subject to be saved in the workspace and dumped, if wished, into a data file.

Speed and capacity

There are limits to the amount of data which can be handled by statistical packages running on micros. There limits are very different for different packages. Some packages such as SPSS and SAS can handle very large data sets. In fact there is no theoretical limit on the number of cases. The reason is that the package only reads into the computer's memory small amounts of data at a time from the hard disc. Thus the physical limit on the size of the data set is determined by the size of the hard disc. A 20-megabyte hard disc will typically have some 5 to 10 megabytes available for data after one or two statistical packages and other utility programs have been saved. SPSS is limited to a maximum of 200 variables per case. This may seem like quite a high limit but it is surprisng how often one finds oneself needing more. A single questionnaire, for example, might have 50 questions. If the questionnaire is administered several times in a prospective study, 200 observations can seem very limiting.

Much more restrictive are STATGRAPHICS and MINITAB. The latter, for example, allows fewer than 10 000 numbers in total. It is limited therefore to relatively small-scale studies. STATGRAPHICS allows a maximum of 64 000 bytes of data, which amounts to about 8000 numbers. The reason for these limits is that much greater use is made of the computer's electronic memory. There is far less swapping of data to and from the hard disc. This has one great advantage; typically data analysis is much quicker because access to hard discs is much slower than access to the computer's electronic memory. MINITAB in particular gives the impression of being very fast. SPSS is relatively slow, and SAS is probably the slowest of the packages mentioned. A data set of more than 100 cases will normally require a wait of tens of seconds for a result. This may not seem a great deal but when it is multiplied by the number of analyses one typically performs in a session it can add up to a considerable time spent thumb twiddling.

The user interface

Most users of statistical packages on micros have little time to spend learning the ins and outs of the system. They have a particular requirement and want that requirement met with as little effort as possible. This means that they do not want to have to read a hefty manual; they do not want to have to learn a complex command language; and they want to get their results in a form which they can understand with the minimum of fuss. On top of this, they do not want to spend hours typing (many cannot type anyway).

Different packages have adopted different solutions to this problem—with varying degrees of success. BMDP has without doubt the worst user interface of all. It has developed little from the original 1960s format in which each analysis has to be carried out as essentially a separate operation or 'batch job'. Commands are executed by a cumbersome and unforgiving command language. At the other extreme, in the case of EGRET there is little need even to read the manual. Everything that one has to do so is obvious from prompts on the screen, and one can read in new data or perform new analyses in a given session with the minimum of fuss. The makers of SPSS have paid a great deal of attention to providing a complete user environment, which includes an editor for users to create or modify commands, data or output, and save anything or everything in a disc file. The manual is rarely needed because there are excellent HELP facilities from the program itself. MINITAB is much less sophisticated but has an advantage in the succinctness of the command language. A different approach is adopted by SYSTAT and STATGRAPHICS, which involves the use of *menus*. The user selects items from lists of options displayed on the screen. One problem with this system is that one often needs to go through a convoluted sequences of menus and sub-menus to get what one wants. Figure 1.6 shows the main features of the user interface of the packages mentioned.

Getting the most out of a statistical package

Following this whirlwind tour of the main statistical operations, we turn to how to minimise the wasted time and effort that always seems to accompany data analysis.

The key to this seems to lie in the old maxim 'more haste, less speed'. Because it is relatively easy to obtain statistical output there is a great temptation to dive haphazardly into one's data without system or method. The result in my experience is that one keeps having to go over the same ground, making corrections as one goes along, and one also goes down many blind alleys.

Step 1: plan the method of data entry

The format in which the data are entered can save or waste a great deal of time later on. In general it is better to use freefield format where possible. This saves having to use a map of the data for its entry into the statistical package. However, it is crucial to remember that in freefield format one cannot just

BMDP	Command driven, rather cumbersome, command files available
SPSS	Command driven, rather cumbersome, command files available, excellent command file editor, multiple windows
SAS	Command driven, rather cumbersome, command files available, good command file editor, multiple windows
STATGRAPHICS	Menu driven, cumbersome
MINITAB	Command driven, quick and easy, command files available
GLIM	Command driven, quick but not easy, command files available
EGRET	Menu driven, quick and easy, command files not needed
SYSTAT	Menu driven, cumbersome, possibility to automate user interface

FIGURE 1.6   Summary of the main features of the 'user interface' of eight statistics packages. These provide a rough guide only and may change as the programs develop.

leave a space where there is a missing variable because the computer will just skip over it and go straight to the next proper number—one will then end up with too few variables in the case.

If all the data from a case cannot be fitted on to a single line then one may (depending on the package) have to use fixed format data entry. In that case, it can save a great deal of time and headache later on to standardise as much as possible on the format for each variable. This is worth it even if it means wasting a lot of space. The reason is that the standard fixed format entry systems allow certain short cuts in specifying the map, but these involve treating whole lists of variables in the same way.

This latter point is easily seen in the following example. Suppose we wish to enter the following numbers formatted thus:

2.0 3.45 1 34 60 3.21 2 2 2 3.4 3.5 46.4
3.1 0.21 2 88 59 6.00 1 2 2 3.0 3.5 45.0
etc.

If we were using MINITAB or GLIM we could use the FORMAT statement:

(F3.1,X,F4.2,X,F1.0,2(X,F2.0),X,F4.2,3(X,F1.0),2(X,F3.1),X,F4.1)

This is rather complicated and there is great scope for error in devising the statement. But if the data had been arranged thus:

2.00 3.45 1.00 60.00 3.21 2.00 2.00 2.00 3.42 3.50 46.4
etc.

we could use the statement:

(11(F5.2,X))

which makes the whole thing simpler and less error-prone. The increased simplicity is obvious in this example, but becomes far more important where multi-line cases are involved.

It is a good idea to include subject numbers, and sometimes even names, in the data file. The cases should be ordered in ascending order of subject numbers. At the same time, any written data sheets from which the data file was derived should be kept in the same order so that it is easy to go back and forth from the computer file to the written data sheets to clarify or correct data.

The data from each subject should be structured in a logical fashion, with variables which belong together conceptually being located physically next to each other in the record. Figure 1.3(a) gives an example of such structuring. This enables the user to take advantage of facilities in the statistics package to treat a whole block of variables together.

The 'look' of the data file is also important. It should be clear where one subject's data end and another's begin. It should also be possible just from visual inspection to tell whether variables are missing or misaligned.

Finally, when a data file is being constructed it will typically be added to or modified several times. It is usually a good idea to create a string of files, each one representing a particular stage in development and indicating the version number in the file name (e.g. TRRL1.DAT, TRRL2.DAT, etc.). This allows changes to be undone if necessary.

Step 2: check the data

There are several ways in which data entered into a statistical package can contain errors. First, it can be miscoded. Second, it can be misread into the package (by an incorrect map). Third, values computed from within the statistical package can turn out to be nonsensical because of the numbers used to create them.

Sometimes these errors can be hard to spot but it is essential that every effort is made to check the data *before doing anything else*—it only takes ONE subject's data to be wrong for the whole of the subsequent statistical analysis to have to be redone! Many readers will know that horrible sinking feeling which accompanies the discovery of such an error.

It is advisable, though not often done, to perform some kind of quality control on the coding of the data before putting it into the computer. In an ideal world one would get two coders to enter the same data into separate files, and these could then be matched using the file comparison procedures available in most personal computer operating systems. At the least, it would be worth checking a sample of the coding. If many errors are found then further checks should be made. Most of the cost of a research project is usually in the data collection. It can be a false economy to skimp on the data coding.

Often a simple visual inspection of the data file can reveal coding errors. One of the most common is misalignment of columns. In general, data should be arranged so that each variable occupies a fixed position on the record for each case. This is so that the statistical package knows where to look for it when reading it in. Putting in extra spaces or missing out spaces, or even accidentally adding or omitting numbers, can all cause variable misalignment which will cause problems later on which may or may not be picked up. If the data file is well structured, with spaces between blocks of related variables, it is relatively easy to spot this with a simple visual scan through the data file.

The statistical packages described here have crude error checking at the point where data are read into the workspace ready for use. Sometimes 'warnings' are issued which do no halt execution but merely alert the user to possible mistakes. Never ignore these warnings! One should move heaven and earth to find out what caused them because the chances are there is something seriously wrong with the data file or with the map one is using to tell the package where the variables are.

Coding subject numbers in the data file can greatly ease the task of finding aberrant data values and checking that the data have been read in correctly. For example, a simple listing of the variable containing subject numbers will soon indicate at what point the data file has gone out of step during freefield read-in (for example, because a number has been left out of the data file).

Having read the data in, the error checking continues. It is important to make sure that each variable contains the correct number of cases and that the numbers entered in it are within the expected range. In most packages this can be most easily done by obtaining histograms of the data. This will usually give an overall count of the number of cases and it will be easy to see at a glance whether there are any cases with unwanted values. It would be helpful if packages could point the user to cases with particular values, but unfortunately they do not, so the easiest thing is to go back to a text editor and use the commonly available *search* or *find* command to seek out the unwanted values.

This method should also enable the user to pick out numbers which were used as missing value codes. Commonly, where a particular data value is not available (for example because a respondent has forgotten to fill in the item on a questionnaire) a special number is used to indicate that the value is missing. This should be a number well outside the range of sensible values so that it is easy to pick up. These values are read into the statistical package as ordinary numbers and then the statistical package should be informed that they refer to missing values. It is common for researchers to forget to do this until they perform some statistical analyses and start to obtain surprising results. If the missing value code is set to a number well outside the usual range of values it is possible to spot these using the histogram technique and avoid a considerable waste of time.

A source of error which can cause incorrect results but which is hard to spot arises out of the process of computing new values from old. Often one wishes to transform variable to make them suitable for performing certain statistical tests or for display purposes. The most common are log and square root transformations. Alternatively one might wish to create a new variable by performing some arithmetic operation on two existing ones. For example, one might obtain an adrenaline : creatinine ratio from concentration of the two chemicals in a urine sample. There is always the danger that these transformations will distort the data in unwanted ways. For example, taking logs can create large negative numbers for fractional values but at the same time convert both 0 and 1 to 0. With ratios, it is important to be aware that if the denominator is very small then small differences in it can have a huge effect on the ratio. With weak urine having low creatinines, small differences in creatinine (probably within the measurement error) can have marked effects on the adrenaline : creatinine ratio.

To ensure that data transformations and computations do not have unwanted effects it is always worth performing the histogram procedure on the resulting variables.

Step 3: plan the analyses

It is very tempting to jump in with analyses without any particular method or purpose. Of course in many cases the precise analyses will have been decided upon in the course of designing the study. However, in most large-scale studies in medicine and psychology, data analysis is not simply a question of carrying out preplanned tests. One has (or should have) a good idea of what comparisons and associations one wishes to examine. However, the most appropriate way of doing this is often dependent upon the data itself. Thus data analysis is often a question of trying things out, and seeing where they lead. This process can be haphazard and wasteful, or organised and efficient.

The first step is to determine what, if any, subsamples one wishes to examine and use the data-editing facilities within the package one is using to create a set of subfiles, one for each subsample. Certain packages such as SPSSPC+ allow analyses to be performed on subsets of the data but in practice I have found it generally easier to make these into separate files. One reason for this is that the packages can work much more quickly on the smaller files. Another is that it is easier to keep track of what sample one is looking at.

The second step is to obtain basic statistics on each variable of interest, possibly broken down by subgroups within the sample. These data will form the basis for one or more tables describing subject characteristics or simple aspects of the results. The usual kind of data obtained would be frequency counts, means, standard deviations, etc. It can also be a good idea to obtain information on the nature of the distributions, such as skewness. This can influence decisions about whether to transform variables to normalise them or whether to use parametric versus non-parametric tests.

Having done this one can go through a list of basic analyses which on the face of it should answer the research questions of interest. These may vary from correlations to t-tests and from ANOVAs to factor analysis.

Some of these statistical procedures are essentially descriptive, whereas some are inferential in the sense that they try to assess the statistical significance of difference between conditions or an association or whatever.

From here on there are no simple rules to follow. Obviously there is no substitute for a good understanding of the statistical procedures one is using and the principles of research design. It is a good idea, however, to keep a clear running record of every analysis which one performs and its results and to try to plan analyses as far ahead as possible. Choose one research question which it is hoped the data will answer and plan the strategy for obtaining that answer.

It is generally a good idea, if there are any long commands or sequences of commands required, to put these into a command file (usually a simple ASCII file which can be read by the statistics package as though the user were typing in the commands from the keyboard). If, as is often the case, an error has been made, this can be corrected without having to type in the whole command(s) from scratch. Also, if the command(s) have to be repeated in slightly different form on different variables or data then it is simply a question of making slight alterations to the command file. Equally important, if it turns out that the data had some flaw in it and the analyses need to be re-run, this can be done very easily.

Step 4: plan the presentation

The presumed aim of all this is to produce one or more pieces of written work, often papers in a scientific journal. It is a good idea to draft out the results section of a paper in as much detail as possible as soon as possible. This usually has the result of revealing further analyses that need to be done to clarify the findings.

Some packages, such as SPSSPC+ and SAS, have quite sophisticated report-writing procedures. These are not very useful for writing conventional papers; they are geared much more towards the production of standard reports with similar formats but different data on a regular basis.

If possible, it is desirable to keep the results of the statistical analyses in files so that they can be inspected and returned to at leisure. Given that there will usually be many analyses performed over a number of sessions, a sequence of files should be created.

Sensible use of file names can save a great deal of time latter on. One method which works well is to use the facility in the IBM PC operating system to have a file name consisting of two sections (an eight-letter prefix and a three-letter suffix). Thus one may form a *root* name which applies to all the data, command files and results files for a particular study. This would then be followed by a one- or two-digit version number. The suffix would indicate whether the file was a data file, command file or results file. Thus for the data shown in Figure 1.3 we might have: TRRL1.DAT (the DAT standing for data), TRRL1.RUN (the RUN indicating a command file) and TRRL1.RES (the RES indicating a results file). This practice could be extended to reports or papers arising from the study (e.g. TRRL.DOC).

Table 1.1 summarises the main points made in this section.

Bigger and better packages

Statistical packages are constantly being updated, and new ones are being introduced, and in the main the developments represent genuine advances on what went before. With the advent of more powerful microcomputers with faster processors, larger memories, faster disc drives and better screens and printers, there is no reason why this rapid rate of change should not continue. This final section will consider some of the ways in which these developments could help to make the non-specialist user more productive and more likely to arrive at correct statistical conclusions.

Data entry

Increasingly, data entry will be carried out by people using portable microcom-puters at the site of data collection or in their own homes during free time. The data files thus produced will then be transferred to a larger microcomputer

Table 1.1   Summary of ways of making data analysis more efficient

---

1   Plan data entry
(a) Make all numbers the same length (as far as possible) and/or use freefield format
(b) Use subject numbers
(c) Impose a logical structure on the data for each case with conceptually similar variables being physically proximate in the data file
(d) Block the data for easy visual inspection
(e) Use standard numeric missing value codes
(f) Keep numbered data sheets in the order they were entered in the data file

2   Check the data
(a) Check the data before doing anything else
(b) Do not ignore 'warnings' put out by the stats package when reading in data
(c) Use double coding on at least part of the data
(d) Print out the data file to check visually for misaligned columns or missing variables
(e) When using freefield format, list the variable which contains subject numbers to check that the read-in has progressed satisfactorily and locate the point at which there is an error
(f) Obtain histograms of each variable to check for out-of-range values
(g) Repeat the data checking after every recording or compute operation

3   Plan the analyses
(a) Analyse subsamples using separate data files
(b) Obtain basic statistics first (means, SDs, etc.)
(c) Identify any aberrant distributions
(d) Perform main analyses related to initial research questions and then follow up issues arising from these
(e) Use command files as much as possible

4   Plan the presentation
(a) Draft out the results section of a report as early as possible to identify gaps in the analyses
(b) Keep a record of results in files

---

for data analysis. It would be desirable to have programs which need not be particularly sophisticated but which could be used to perform simple error checking and which could be used on their own, without involving any of the other statistical features provided by conventional packages. Some psychologists already use commercial database packages for this purpose, but I favour something more along the lines of a word processor which instead of having a spelling checker would have a kind of 'numbers checker'. Such a data entry system would output a simple text file such as could be read into ANY statistical package. The data entry program could also keep a record of the number of mistakes which were made and how long it took to code each case. The latter would be extremely useful for purposes of paying coders!

Getting data into the statistical package

There is considerable room for improvement in the way data are read into statistical packages. While every package should have the option of freefield format regardless of how many actual variables there are per subject, there is a need for better built-in safeguards against the errors that can occur with this. The major problem is that if one has one too few or too many numbers in a given case, it throws the whole process out of kilter. It should be possible to specify a given variable as 'subject number' and the read-in process should look at the variable as the data are being read in to check that it is going up one at a time. It should then report immediately if this goes wrong.

There is also a need for an improved freefield format mode of read-in. For example, if one has a data file which includes, say ten items from a questionnaire, where each item is only one digit, one does not want to have to waste space putting spaces between each item as required by freefield format. One should only need to specify that a given block of digits are to be treated singly, in pairs, etc. It should also be possible at this stage to tell the computer about standard missing value codes so that it automatically transforms the numbers to missing values. This saves having to do it later as a separate exercise (an exercise which one sometimes forgets to do).

Editing, recoding and transforming data

The ideal system in this regard would be a cross between SPSS, SYSTAT and MINITAB. The first two offer excellent facilities for controlling which cases one selects, or which cases one performs certain operations on, while the last has powerful commands for performing operations on groups of variables; for example, RSUM C1-C10 C11 will add all the values in variables labelled C1, C2, C3, etc., up to C10, and put the results in a new variable called C11. This is particularly good for deriving subscale scores in questionnaires. There are similar commands for standard deviations and other statistics.

It would be extremely useful to have commands which were more closely related to the actual functions one is trying to perform when transforming data. For example, there could be a command 'NORMALISE' which would try out a range of transformations, testing the results to see to what extent they converted a variable to a normal distribution, and then report which transformation gave the best results.

One often wishes to obtain directories of files, or copy files, or change directories or whatever while running a statistical package. Many word processors allow the user to do this and there is no reason why statistics packages should not follow their example.

It has been mentioned earlier in this chapter that a great advantage of MINITAB is the speed obtained by the fact that the workspace is contained within the computer's electronic memory rather than on disc. The disadvantage is the limited amout of space available. It would be useful to have the option of using a disc-based or memory-based workspace depending on the size of the data set one wishes to work with.

One often deals with frequency data, for example, performing chi-squared analyses to test qualitative associations. There are often occasions when one wishes to enter data for such analyses as frequency counts rather than individually for each case. It would be a simple matter to allow this kind of input.

Statistical analyses

Already some packages have an excellent range of statistical functions. One major area of weakness is in non-parametric statistics. There are techniques available for performing multi-way non-parametric ANOVAs, but these have not yet found their way to the major statistics packages.

Already some packages provide good diagnostic information which helps the user decide whether his or her analyses is invalidated by features of their data. However, this information tends to be presented in rather technical terms that give the user a good excuse for neglecting them. It would be helpful if the statistical analyses could highlight more clearly the nature of problems with the data and suggest ways in which such problems could be ameliorated (for example, by data transformation).

Certain packages such as SPSS produce a great deal of unnecessary detail in their printouts. One should always have the option of a concise versus complete rendering of the results.

Graphical display

Some of the packages already produce excellent graphical output to the screen. Unfortunately this is not always matched by the quality of the printed output. The researcher or clinician needs printed output that can be included directly in reports or sent directly to journals or publishers. Realistically, really good-quality output can only be provided at present with laser printers, but even here current packages do not take full advantage of their capacity for high-resolution output.

User interface

Programs designed for the business community are increasingly moving towards the user of multiple *windows* in which more than one operation can be observed running at one time. The computer keyboard is also being to some extent superseded by *mice*. These are hand-held devices which are used to move a pointer around the computer screen so that the user can select from predefined options. Personally, I find windows and mice a waste of time in most applications but some users, particularly with limited typing skills, might benefit from their introduction to statistical packages. More important is the need (1) to keep the comands brief and stripped of cumbersome subcommands, (2) to have all the commands use a common format, and (3) to make sensible interpretations when errors are made in typing the commands.

As regards the first of the requirements, MINITAB is exemplary. To correlate variables C1, C2, C3 and C4 you simply type:

CORR C1-C4

Similarly, to perform a multiple regression in which variables C1, C2 and C3 are used to predict C4, one types:

REGRESS C4 3 C1 C2 C3

It is hard to see how it could be more simple or concise.

SPSS, for all its strengths, suffers from a weakness as regards the second of the requirements mentioned above. The format varies in unpredictable ways from one command to another, and uses unmnemonic phrases such as OPTIONS = 1 and STATISTICS = 2.

One idea might be to allow the user simply to enter the name of the command, e.g. FACTOR (for factor analysis), and then provide a series of prompts to which the user can either respond or simply accept defaults provided by the program.

As regards the third requirement, for a degree of intelligent interpretation, there is something rather irritating about being told that one's instruction is in error becuse there is a comma missing at a particular place—if the computer can tell that there is a comma missing, why doesn't it put it in itself? There are so many occasions when one types in a long command and finds there is a small typing error which causes the command to abort. It would be a relatively simple matter for a program to match the command with the nearest legal equivalent (e.g. a variable name mistyped), alert the user to the fact that the command is in error and present its interpretation. In 90% of cases all the user need do is acknowledge that this is what was intended and allow the analysis to proceed.

The recommendations for enhancements to statistics packages are summarised in Table 1.2.

Conclusions

This chapter has described the process of data analysis as it may be undertaken using a microcomputer-based statistics package. It has drawn examples from

Table 1.2   Summary of possible enhancements for future statistics packages

---

1   A stand-alone data entry option
2   Improved freefield data entry with missing value recoder
3   Flexible language for performing recoding, transformation and data selction, including statistically oriented commands such as 'normalise'
4   Full access to operating system commands
5   Choice of memory-based or disc-based workspace
6   Facilities to enter matrices, e.g. of frequencies for chi-squared analysis
7   More clearly expressed diagnostic information regarding suitability of statistical test given characteristics of the data
8   More sophisticated non-parametric tests
9   Publication-quality printed graphics output
10   Choice of concise or full rendering of results
11   Concise command lines with option to override defaults, using a standard format
12   Automatic command correction

Note: some of these facilities are already individually available in one form or another in existing packages.

a range of existing packages and drawn broad comparisons between these packages. The second part of the chapter looked at how to make the process of data analysis more efficient and less error-prone, and ways in which packages might be developed in the future to improve efficiency. There will be much in the chapter that those unfamiliar with computers will find difficult to follow. However, hopefully such readers will derive a sense both of the power that statistical packages put at one's finger tips, and the increased opportunities that exist for making a mess of ones analysis. For such readers, it would be fair to point out that most people who have used microcomputers for data analysis find unappealing the idea of going back to hand calculations or even to mainframes, with their slow response times and archaic operating systems. For the initiated reader the chapter should have provided a sense of how their package or packages compare with others which are available, and a few ideas on how the practice of data analysis may be improved.

CHAPTER 2

Artificial intelligence in psychiatric research

DAVID J. HAND

1 Introduction

Artificial intelligence (AI) is usually described as a science, but since the objects of the study are man-made it might be more appropriate to describe it as a technology. It is certainly a technology in the sense that one is trying to create machines using given materials (the materials here being computers), but it is equally a science in that one is exploring the unknown.

Perhaps part of the ambiguity arises from the breadth of the field—researchers working in different areas of AI have different aims and use different theories and methodologies to achieve those aims. One group is concerned with making computers perform tasks which would be regarded as requiring intelligence (such as play chess, diagnose illness, converse rationally, etc). Concern here is with the end result and no constraints are imposed on the software architectures used to achieve it.

Another group is concerned with simulating human cognitive processes using computers. For psychiatrists, undoubtedly the most interesting example of this sort of work is PARRY (Colby, 1981), a simulated psychiatric patient. This has stimulated considerable debate about how such models can be tested.

It might be that the best way to achieve the results that the first group are aiming at is via simulation. Some researchers certainly believe so, dignifying this belief with the name 'The principle of cognitive emulation' (or 'The fourth law of robotics', for science fiction fans). However, it is still an open question.

The division into two groups may be artificial, and certainly others may make different or more detailed partitions. But the point is that, as with any scientific discipline, subdisciplines with different motivations and methodologies exist.

Artificial intelligence overlaps many other areas of scientific research. Obvious ones are computer science and psychology. Less obvious is the overlap with

Microcomputers, Psychology and Medicine
Edited by R. West, M. Christie and J. Weinman
© 1990 by John Wiley & Sons Ltd

linguistics (for example, via natural language understanding systems and machine translation), mathematics (e.g. via formalisation, logic and automatic theorem proving), philosophy (e.g. Sloman, 1978) and other areas.

Although there are overlaps with other scientific disciplines, AI has its own unique flavour. Boden (1977), in a book that is particularly relevant to psychiatry and psychiatrists, and McCorduck (1979), in her excellent history of AI, stress that AI differs from the natural sciences in that it is not reductionist. This point is also discussed in Hand (1985a).

AI is also different from most sciences in that is is not an axiomatic science, attempting to reduce all explanations to the consequences of a few (ideally) fundamental axioms. In contrast, AI is algorithmic—the structures, ideas and methods are written as code to be run on a computer. This leads to the identification of particular structures which have immense power, in that they can be used to describe a range of cognitive activities. Examples of such structures are production systems ('rule-based systems'), frames and scripts, and pattern matchers.

The difference in flavour in the kinds of operations AI programs are expected to perform, compared with computer programs written for other disciplines, has led to the adoption of different computer languages. The two most common are LISP and PROLOG, but many others, often extensions of these or built using these, are in use.

I have remarked above on the fact that there are different subfields within the domain of AI research. Of these, the area which has undoubtedly attracted most general interest is the work on expert systems. This falls squarely within the first of the two categories of research identified above: the aim is to build a system which can perform a task (demonstrate expertise in some area), and the internal way it does this is unimportant. Because of the intense activity in this area, the bulk of this chapter is devoted to them. Section 2 outlines the basic structure of expert systems, and section 3 briefly describes some psychiatric expert systems.

According to Hand (1985b), 80% of the papers in *The British Journal of Psychiatry* and *Psychological Medicine* contain statistical material and concepts. It is thus arguable that statistics is the single scientific discipline of most importance to psychiatric research. For this reason, in section 4, I will briefly examine some of the work on expert systems for assisting in the application of statistical techniques.

Section 5 broadens the discussion to introduce a class of systems with a slightly different objective from conventional expert systems. We call such systems 'knowledge enhancement systems'. They are intended to provide an extremely flexible interface between the user and a chosen knowledge domain.

Finally, section 6 outlines other work involving AI and psychiatric research. Further details of the relationship between AI and psychiatry may be found in Boden (1977) and Hand (1985a).

2 Expert systems in general

Typical expert systems may be described as being composed of two parts: a knowledge base and an inference engine. The knowledge base contains knowledge about the field in which the system is to be an expert, and the inference engine matches information about the current issue with the knowledge base and percolates the deductions and conclusions through the knowledge base to arrive at a final conclusion. Precisely how it does this depends on the way the knowledge base is organised.

The most common basic structure for the knowledge base at present is the production system or *rule-based* system. This has its origins in the early part of this century as a model for the way the brain works, and was developed in detail in this role by Newell and Simon (1972). Such systems are comprised of elements called rules, each of the form:

IF (condition A1 and condition A2 and . . .)
THEN (conclusion or action)

The *conditions* (or antecedents) will be properties of the item under consideration: for example, if the item is a patient who must be diagnosed, the conditions will be of the form 'the patient is disoriented' or 'the patient is overactive'.

The conclusion or action on the right-hand side of the rule could be a diagnosis (the patient has schizophrenia) or could be the identification of a particular syndrome which served as a left-hand side condition for further rules.

Simple systems might have only a handful of such rules, while complicated systems can have thousands. In general, explicit models of cognitive function seem to have only a few while expert systems aimed at performing some practical task have large numbers.

An early attraction of such systems was their modularity. Rules could, at least in principle, be added or removed without requiring the rewriting of the entire system. Simple systems showed a gradual degradation of performance when rules were removed. Contrast this with what happens when one removes lines of code from a FORTRAN or BASIC program. Thus it seemed that one might build very complex systems by a gradual incremental process.

Unfortunately this promise has not altogether materialised. Unforeseen interactions between rules caused unfortunate complications and it was found necessary to impose additional structure on the rule bases—for example, sometimes the rules are grouped into subsets to facilitate the search to identify a matching rule.

Similarly, if the object under consideration (patient in the psychiatric diagnosis case) satisfied the conditions of more than one rule, a way had to be found to choose between them. Several methods of *conflict resolution*, as it is called, have been explored (McDermott and Forgy, 1978), including such things as using the rule with the most conditions (it being the most specific) or random selection from the eligible rules. A very exciting method involves the use of *meta-rules*: rules about rules. Thus, if the left-hand conditions of a meta-rule are satisfied then its right-hand action will be to focus attention on some subset of the rules.

We have described production systems above as working through a series of applications of rules, at each step identifying a rule with left-hand conditions which matched known properties of the object in question, and then carrying out the right-hand action. This approach is known as forward chaining.

Its complement, backward chaining, attempts to reach conclusions by finding rules whose right-hand sides present the conclusions to be demonstrated, and then seeing if the left-hand conditions are true (or can be established as the conclusions of other rules). Studies have shown that humans carry out medical diagnosis in a hypothetico-deductive way which is essentially backward chaining (Elstein *et al.*, 1979). More complex and sophisticated expert systems make use of both approaches.

One vital property of expert systems follows from the rule structure. This is their ability to explain their reasoning. In principle, this follows by immediate translation of the simple structure of the rules into standard English (A was true and B was true, so I know that C was true by rule 123), but in practice more sophistication is usual.

One of the major difficulties in building large rule-based systems has turned out to be formulating the rules—*knowledge elicitation*. It seems that experts, though extremely skilled at applying their knowledge, may not be so good at explaining how they do it. An important topic of research is thus automatic rule induction (e.g. Quinlan, 1982). This is intimately related to statistical techniques for building classification trees (e.g. Breiman *et al.*, 1983).

A second area of contact between expert systems and statistics is in systems which can manipulate uncertain information. In many problem domains, especially in medicine and psychiatry, little of the information can be stated with complete confidence. Many ways of handling uncertainty have been suggested; for a review, see Kanal and Lemmer (1986).

More complex expert systems make use of other knowledge representation schemes, in addition to production systems. Of growing popularity are network-based methods. In medicine, for example, the nodes contain information describing findings and symptoms, and links indicate causal relationships (see, for example, Szolovits, 1982).

3 Some psychiatric expert systems

One of the earliest rule-based medical expert systems, and one which has had a major impact on the field, is MYCIN, a system for diagnosing bacteriological blood infections (Buchanan and Shortliffe, 1984). One reason for its impact is that researchers have stripped out the rules containing the knowledge about blood infections to leave an empty shell (EMYCIN), into which rules containing expertise about other domains can be plugged. The shell is in effect a naked inference engine.

Examples of psychiatric expert systems which use EMYCIN are BLUE-BOX (Mulsant and Servan-Schreiber, 1984), which diagnoses depression and recommends therapy on the basis of symptoms and patient history, and Brooks and Heiser's (1980) system for giving psychopharmacological advice. This latter is not a diagnostic system but chooses a drug therapy. To quote Hand (1985a, p. 184):

> Selection of medication between and within the five major classes of psychopharmacological agent . . . depends on the severity and nature of the symptoms, the history of the patient and his present condition, as well as on diagnosis. As yet there are few theories relating underlying biochemical phenomena to the manifest psychological behaviour patterns. This means that it is not possible to build a theoretical process model, so that an expert system approach, based on the loose modelling of human ways of selecting (treatment) seems eminently reasonable.

Brooks and Heiser have some particularly interesting remarks to make about the application of EMYCIN in this domain.

Sharp (1987) describes a very interesting case study of the use of an expert system for psychiatric assessment. This is not based on EMYCIN, but on the PROPS-2 shell (Fox and Duncan, 1986). He begins by outlining the hypothetico-deductive model for diagnosis common to much of medicine and then points out that in psychiatry there is often a lack of a link between the symptoms and biological model of the disease process. The consequence is that, in psychiatry, 'the diagnosis itself is the ordered pattern of symptoms that are presented, and classification is a shorthand method for summarising this symptom pattern'. This necessitates that the information-gathering process be much more carefully conducted than if one is trying to match symptoms to a model. To formalise the symptom-gathering process psychiatrists have produced structured interviews. One such is the Present State Examination (PSE, Wing et al., 1974), which imposes strict constraints on the conduct of the psychiatric interview, and ends up with ratings on around 500 items. These are then run through a hierarchical grouping process to yield membership of one or more of a set of clinical categories.

The PSE, as described above, has been combined with further diagnostic schedules, containing such things as information about organic brain disease, to produce a broader system known as SCAN.

One criticism of the PSE is its opacity—it cannot explain its inferences, as can an expert system. A second criticism is the difficulty of programming revised versions of the CATEGO program which condenses the PSE symptoms into a diagnosis—again contrast this with the ease of changing rules in a production system.

Based on these observations, Sharp (1987) conducted a study of the feasibility of implementing the SCAN system as an expert system by attempting to translate the CATEGO program into a production system. He makes several points about this exercise, including: (1) that the knowledge elicitation problem has already been solved—it only remains to translate the PSE formatted expertise into production rules; (2) that all of the symptom data are available at the start of applying the system to a case; and (3) that psychiatric diagnosis may be more suited to forward chaining than backward chaining.

The same problem was tackled by Thomas (1987), again rule-based (using a highly structured rule base), but this time using a version of LISP called EXPERLISP. It had three levels of processing. The top level was the seven-step condensation, to a diagnosis, of the original symptoms collected by the PSE. These follow the steps gone through by the CATEGO program to achieve the diagnosis. The second level consisted of meta-rules which controlled the way the diagnostic rules fired in each stage. And the bottom level consisted of the diagnostic rules themselves. Constraints here were that the rule base should be flexible enough to cover all the processing that would be needed for the seven-step condensation, but should not be larger than necessary, could be updated by a person unskilled in LISP, and could be used to formulate explanations.

Each level had associated with it 'objects' which possessed properties which could take various values. For example, there was an object for each stage, which contained three properties: a list of rules governing how the stage was evaluated, a list of items used as antecedents in the rules, and a list of items that occurred as right-hand sides of rules. Both forward and backward chaining was used, initially the former, as the system worked its way down through the stages.

Kolodner (1984) describes a program called SHRINK, which begins with the expertise contained in the DSM-III, a manual for making psychiatric diagnoses (see American Psychiatric Association, 1980), and attempts to improve its diagnosis on the basis of what it learns from the cases it sees. SHRINK is not rule-based, but instead stores records of patients' symptom patterns as deviations from general patterns. The idea is a very interesting one, but may have weaknesses: it may be rather opaque, not permitting ready explanation or justification of its conclusions.

4 Statistical expert systems

A number of papers have recently criticised the quality of statistics demonstrated in medical and psychiatric journals (e.g. White, 1979; Gore et al., 1977). Moreover, we have already remarked that statistics plays a vital role in psychiatric research. Thus if computer programs could be developed which would facilitate the application of statistical techniques by non-statisticians this could have a major impact. This is the aim of statistical expert systems research.

As with all expert systems research, interest in statistical expert systems has grown dramatically over the last few years. Systems have been built or are being built for the entire range of statistical techniques and ideas. For example, for data validation (Dickson and Talbot, 1986), choice of statistical technique (Hand, 1985c), design (Sach, 1986), hypothesis formulation (Salzberg, 1986) and for analysis (Gale, 1986b).

As a consequence of this interest, a number of themes have been recognised and are being explored which have important implications for statistics as a discipline. One such is the notion of a statistical strategy—the steps one should go through to apply a given statistical tool correctly and effectively (e.g. Pregibon, 1986; Hand, 1986).

One of the earliest effective demonstrator statistical expert systems is REX (Regression EXpert) (Gale, 1986b), which guides the user in conducting a simple regression analysis. It is coded in the high-level computer language LISP and uses another language, 'S', for the statistical calculations. REX's strategy was developed by studying how statisticians worked when they analysed several dozen data sets. It includes checks for 14 assumptions and 16 possible remedial actions. An important component of its internal architecture is a hierarchical graph in which the internal nodes represent problems (e.g. non-linearity) and the leaf nodes represent possible solutions (e.g. apply a transformation).

The TESS (Tree-based Expert System for Statistics) (Lubinsky and Pregibon, 1987) adopts a completely different approach to the difficult problem of how the system should make use of external, non-statistical knowledge. This system produces a large number of 'solutions' and lets the user choose. Again trees form a critical component of the representation for strategies.

GLIMPSE (GLIM plus Prolog plus Statistical Expertise) (Nelder, 1987) is an interface to the GLIM statistical package for generalised linear modelling (see Chapter 1 for a brief description of GLIM), a class of techniques which includes such methods as analysis of variance, regression analysis and log-linear modelling. Nelder describes GLIMPSE as a 'libertarian' system, meaning that it offers advice but does not insist the user follows it.

5   Knowledge enhancement systems

Conventional expert systems, as outlined in the preceding three sections, are very efficient for solving certain kinds of problems—the kind they were designed to solve. This is often a classification kind of problem (as in diagnosis). If, however, the user might have any of a very large range of different kinds of problem, perhaps even an unlimited range, then expert systems might be too restrictive to be of great value. This section thus briefly outlines an alternative approach—the *knowledge enhancement system*—which is more flexible and permits the users to interact with the knowledge domain (be it psychiatry, statistics or whatever) in any way they wish.

Part of the motivation for our development of such systems comes from a paper by Coombs and Alty (1984), which describes a study of computer advisory services. Sessions which clients seeking advice found least satisfying were those most closely related to the rule-based approach. The most satisfactory ones were those in which more information was given than was apparently necessary and in which the client gained some understanding of what was going on, rather than a simple instruction to write code in a certain way.

Other motivations come from the inadequacy of books to provide sufficient flexibility and difficulty of updating them. Details are given in Hand (1989) and Hand *et al*, (1989).

At the base of most knowledge enhancement systems lies a graph structure, the nodes of which contain small chunks of knowledge and the edges of which show the relationship between the knowledge chunks. One can steer oneself around this graph, looking at whatever seems relevant in a completely unrestricted manner. Alternatively, one can search the entire graph for specified terms (how this is done depends on the precise system under consideration), yielding a list of nodes referring to the terms in question (or perhaps some Boolean combination of them).

More sophisticated systems also let the system guide a user through a structured discussion of some topic, and this can be done from an arbitrary number of perspectives. Thus a suitably designed system could teach a psychiatrist about non-parametric statistical methods and teach the same material to a psychologist in a slightly different way.

Hand (1987) describes one such system for just this area of knowledge—non-parametric statistics. KENS is a 'Knowledge Enhancement system for Non-parametric Statistics'. At present KENS does not perform any arithmetic calculations but there is in principle no reason why systems such as KENS should not also do this.

6   Other work

This chapter has been almost exclusively devoted to the expert systems kind of AI applications, simply because this is the area which is developing most rapidly and having the greatest impact. Other work is, however, going on. One important such area is computerised interviewing of patients. Early work dispelled fears that no one would wish to 'talk' to a computer and suggested to the contrary that people might be more willing to communicate with a machine about sensitive issues (such as alcohol consumption). A brief summary of work in this area is given in Hand and Glover (1988).

What is quite clear from all of the above is the excitement that researchers working to apply AI technology to psychiatric problems feel. It is also clear that the field is extremely young.

One wishes to avoid predicting great changes just around the corner—such predictions have been made about AI before and have failed to materialise, to the detriment of the discipline. However, some of this research must be regarded as potentially extremely beneficial. We are not merely talking of a minor improvement in treatment or diagnostic accuracy, but the possibility of dramatic changes in the way psychiatry is practised.

References

American Psychiatric Association (1980). *Diagnostic and Statistical Manual of Mental Disorders*. Washington, DC: American Psychiatric Association.

Boden, M. A. (1977). *Artificial Intelligence and Natural Man*. Hassocks: Harvester Press.

Breiman, L., Friedman, J. H., Olshen, R. A. and Stone C. J. (1983). *Classification and Regression Trees*. Belmont, CA: Wadsworth.

Brooks, R. and Heiser, J. (1980). Some experience with transferring the MYCIN system to a new domain, *IEEE Transactions on Pattern Analysis and Machine Intelligence*, **2**, 477–478.

Buchanan, B. G. and Shortliffe, E. H. (eds) (1984). *Rule Based Expert Systems: The MYCIN Experiments of the Stanford Heuristic Programming Project*. Reading, MA: Addison-Wesley.

Colby, K. M. (1981). Modelling a paranoid mind, *Behavioural and Brain Sciences*, **4**, 515–560.

Coombs, M. J. (ed.) (1984). *Developments in Expert Systems*. London: Academic Press.

Coombs, M. J. and Alty, J. (1984). Expert systems: an alternative paradigm. In M. J. Coombs, *Developments in Expert Systems*, pp. 135–157. London: Academic Press.

Dickson, J. M. and Talbot, M. (1986). Statistical data validation and expert systems. In F. de Antoni, N. Lauro and A. Rizzi (eds) *COMPSTAT-86*, pp. 283–288. Heidelberg: Physica-Verlag.

Elstein, A. S., Shulman, L. S. and Sprafka, S. A. (1979). *Medical Problem Solving: An Analysis of Clinical Reasoning*. Cambridge, MA: Harvard University Press.

Fox, J. and Duncan, T. (1986). *The PROPS-2 Primer*, Imperial Cancer Research Fund.

Gale, W. A. (ed.) (1986a). *Artificial Intelligence and Statistics*. Reading, MA: Addison-Wesley.

Gale, W. A. (1986b). REX review. In W. A. Gale (ed.), *Artificial Intelligence and Statistics*, pp. 173–227. Reading, MA: Addison-Wesley.

Gore, S. M., Jones, I. G. and Rytter, E. C. (1977). Misuse of statistical methods: critical assessment of articles in BMJ from January to March 1976, *British Medical Journal*, **i**, 85–87.

Hand, D. J. (1985a). *Artificial Intelligence and Psychiatry*. Cambridge: Cambridge University Press.

Hand, D. J. (1985b). The role of statistics in psychiatry, *Psychological Medicine*, **15**, 471–476.

Hand, D. J. (1985c). Choice of statistical technique, *Bulletin of the International Statistical Institute*, 45th Session, **3**, Amsterdam, August, pp. 21.1-1–21.1-16.

Hand, D. J. (1986) Patterns in statistical strategy. In W. A. Gale (ed.), *Artifical Intelligence and Statistics*, pp. 335–387. Reading, MA: Addison-Wesley.

Hand, D. J. (1989). A statistical knowledge enhancement system, *Journal of the Royal Statistical Society*, Series A, **150**, 334–345.

Hand, D. J. and Glover, E. J. (1988) The impact of information technology. In P. Williams, G. Wilkinson and K. Rawnsley (eds), *Scientific Approaches in Epidemiological and Social psychiatry*. London: Tavistock Publications.

Hand, D. J., Sharp, C. H. and Glover, E. J. (1989) *Knowledge Enhancement Systems* (In preparation).

Haux, R. (ed.) (1986). *Expert systems in statistics*. Stuttgart: Gustav-Fischer.

Kanal, L. N. and Lemmer, J. (eds) (1986). *Uncertainty in Artificial Intelligence*. Amsterdam: North-Holland.

Kolodner, J. L. (1984). Towards an understanding of the role of experience in the evolution from novice to expert. In M. J. Coombs (ed.), *Developments in Expert Systems*, pp. 95–116. London: Academic Press.

Lubinksy, D. and Pregibon, D. (1987). Data analysis as search. In R. Phelps (ed.), *Interactions in Artificial Intelligence and Statistical Methods*, pp. 18–35. Aldershot: Gower Technical Press.

McCorduck, P. (1979). *Machines Who Think*. San Francisco: Freeman.

McDermott, J. and Forgy, C. (1978). Production system conflict resolution strategies. D. A. Waterman and F. Hayes-Roth (eds), *Pattern-directed Inference Systems*, pp. 177–199. New York: Academic Press.

Mulsant, R. and Servan-Schreiber, D. (1984). Knowledge engineering: a daily activity in the hospital ward, *Computers and Biomedical Research*, **17**, 71–91.

Nelder, J. A. (1987). AI and generalised linear modelling. In R. Phelps (ed.), *Interactions in Artificial Intelligence and Statistical Methods*, pp. 36–44. Aldershot: Gower Technical Press.

Newell, A. and Simon, H. A. (1972). *Human Problem Solving*. Englewood Cliffs, NJ: Prentice-Hall.

Phelps, R. (1987). *Interactions in Artificial Intelligence and Statistical Methods*. Aldershot: Gower Technical Press.

Pregibon, D. (1986). A DIY guide to statistical strategy. In W. A. Gale (ed.), *Artificial Intelligence and Statistics*, pp. 389–399. Reading, MA: Addison-Wesley.

Quinlan, J. R. (1982). Semi-autonomous acquisition of pattern-based knowledge. In D. Michie (ed.), *Introductory Readings in Expert Systems*, pp. 192–207 New York: Gorden & Breach.

Sach, S. (1986). Computer support for the design and analysis of survey samples. In R. Haux (ed.), *Expert Systems in Statistics*, pp. 99–110. Stuttgart: Gustav-Fischer.

Salzberg, S. ((1986). Pinpointing good hypotheses with heuristics. In W. A. Gale (ed.), *Artificial Intelligence and Statistics*, pp. 133–158. Reading, MA: Addison-Wesley.

Sharp, C. (1987). Expert systems and structured psychiatric assessment. Unpublished MSc dissertation, Brunel University.

Sloman, A. (1978). *The computer revolution in philosophy*. Hassocks: Harvester Press.

Szolovits, P. (1982). *Artificial Intelligence in Medicine*, Boulder, CO: Westview Press.

Thomas, R. (1987). Expert system for psychiatric diagnosis. Unpublished MSc dissertation, University of Warwick.

White, S. J. (1979). Statistical errors in papers in the British Journal of Psychiatry, *British Journal of Psychiatry*, **135**, 336–342.

Wing, J. K, Cooper, J. E. and Sartorius, N. (1974). *The Measurement and Classification of Psychiatric Syndromes*. Cambridge: Cambridge University Press.

CHAPTER 3

The development of microcomputer-based applications

RICHARD KEMP AND PENELOPE EARP

This chapter is intended as a practical guide for researchers and clinicians who
are thinking of, or are in the process of, developing a microcomputer-based
application of the kind discussed in later chapters in this book. It covers a
range of issues from the purchase of a microcomputer to the evaluation of
software packages and construction of simple hardware 'add-ons' or
'peripherals'.

Choosing a microcomputer

One of the first steps in developing an application is obviously choosing which
micro or micros on which to base it. This section considers some of the factors
which should be taken into account when making the purchase.

1   Aim for compatibility. If colleagues are already using a particular microcomputer one is well advised to choose the same make unless there are strong
reasons to do otherwise. Incompatibility between machines and shared peripherals such as printers probably causes more problems and wastes more time
than any other computing problem. The IBM PC has become very popular in
part because there are a wide range of machines of different capabilities and
price ranges which all share a common standard. This allows easy communication and the development of a large user base; there are many individuals
familiar with the machines and problems associated with them.

2   Avoid the 'leading edge of technology'. Manufacturers love to tell us that
unless we buy their machines we will be left out of the technological advance
in computer hardware. This is not a bad thing. Why should we want to be at
the leading edge of technology and have to risk acquiring an expensive,

Microcomputers, Psychology and Medicine
Edited by R. West, M. Christie and J. Weinman
© 1990 by John Wiley & Sons Ltd

possibly unreliable and unpopular machine when by sitting back and observing the market we can ensure that we obtain the correct machine for our needs and one that is sufficiently popular to be supported by a wide range of manufactured software?

3   Be realistic about the needs of the project. One should make a list of requirements, both current and future, and ensure that the computer meets these. It is always cheaper in the long run to buy a machine that meets all these needs than to struggle with an inadequate machine for which one will have to buy expensive updates. One of the most obvious considerations is disc space; the price of machines including a hard disc is slightly greater than those without, but this expense is almost certainly worthwhile as the risk of losing data is smaller and there is less need to buy hundreds of floppy discs. Many programs such as SPSS, mentioned in Chapter 1, will only run on computers with hard discs. The price difference between a small hard disc (say 20 megabytes) and a large one (say 40 or 80 megabytes) is not great; why not buy the larger-capacity machine? Users are often surprised how much disc space they find they need. Another consideration is that hard discs vary in their access speed. The computer advertisements will quote a disc access speed which is a measure of how quickly information can be read from and written to the disc. The fact that the numbers quoted may be tiny fractions of a second does not mean that it is unimportant; the computer will spend much of its time waiting for the disc drive to respond to its commands and a fast drive can dramatically speed up the rate at which programs will run.

4   Consult with colleagues. Other professionals using computers for a similar purpose will know about the advantages and disadvantages of their machine; it makes sense to tap this pool of knowledge.

5   Try to take advantage of existing peripherals (printers, monitors, etc.). Peripherals are expensive; if one already owns peripherals, it makes sense to buy a machine that is compatible with them.

6   Observe the computer in action. One should never buy a computer until the salesperson has clearly demonstrated that it meets one's requirements and, if appropriate, that it is compatible with existing peripherals.

Software evaluations

Software evaluation is a process of systematically examining a piece of software in order to decide if it meets one's needs and to ensure that it is used in the most appropriate situation. The result of a software evaluation exercise should be a standard checklist which can be used both to decide on the usefulness of the software and to describe its strengths and weaknesses. Much commercially available software, especially that which is designed for use in education, is of extremely poor quality; software evaluation provides a quick means of identifying and avoiding such software.

The process of evaluating software can be divided into four components.

1 Technical Evaluation

This should assess the hardware requirements; one should ask such questions as:

What machine does it run on?
What disc format is it available on?
Does it require a colour monitor?
What extra peripherals does it require?
It it easy to install and run?
Is it dependent upon the machine's precise configuration?

2 Reliability Evaluation

This assesses the robustness of the software. One should ask such questions as:

Will all the options included in the program run correctly without 'crashing'?
What happens if a peripheral required by the program is not attached to the computer or switched on?
What happens if the user gives an unexpected response?
Can the program be stopped by accidentally pressing the wrong key on the keyboard?
If the program does crash does it lose all its data?
What happens if the user removes his or her disc from the floppy disc drive after starting the program?

The fact that the program might fail under some circumstances does not render it useless so long as one is aware that this might happen and that the crash is 'graceful', i.e. data are not lost.

3 Ease of Use Evaluation

This should give some indication of the speed with which a new user can learn to use the program. Of crucial importance here is the extent to which the commands required to interact with the program have a consistent format. One should ask such questions as:

Does the program expect a different form of response to similar questions; for example, does one need to press the <Return> key after all responses or just some?

Is the program 'menu-driven'? That is, does the user select from a set of pre-defined options? If so, does one select options from the menu in the same way throughout the program?

Are 'on-line help facilities' provided? These permit the user to ask for help from the computer as and when needed while it is running.

How good is the manual? Computing manuals are notorious for their obscurity. This is partly a result of wishing to get the product on to the shelves as soon as possible and partly because of the inherent difficulty which computing experts have in putting themselves in the place of the novice user.

Again, failing to pass all these tests is not necessarily fatal. It will help future users greatly though if one takes the trouble to make notes of any idiosyncrasies that one finds.

4   Evaluating the user population

The personal needs of the eventual user should always be borne in mind when evaluating software. In educational and clinical settings one needs to be sure that one has a clear understanding of the objectives; for example, is the program to have some specific therapeutic benefit, to rehabilitate some specific skill, or, just as importantly, is it to provide recreation? One should consider such features as:

Do the users have the physical and mental capabilities required in order to benefit from use of the software—remember that consistent failure benefits nobody.

Is the software appropriate for the users? For example, one should not expect mentally handicapped adults to be motivated by a program written for kindergarten-aged children and involving teddy bears or nursery rhymes. Similarly adult aphasics should not be asked to engage in child-like tasks merely because the only available language development software was written for children.

If the user population is likely to include individuals with some physical handicap then software which requires a complex and lengthy input from the traditional QWERTY keyboard might not be appropriate. Some software allows for the use of special input devices to suit the needs of these individuals.

Would it be more satisfactory for the users not to use the computer to complete the task? Computers are merely one of several means of presenting a task and they do have their limitations. One should always consider whether it would be more appropriate to use a different medium. For example, in teaching money concepts it may be better in some cases to use real coins rather than poor-quality computer representations of the coins.

It is important to be systematic in the way in which one evaluates software and to develop a scheme that suits one's own needs. One should keep a record of the evaluation report and be prepared to modify it as one discovers new aspects of the software. So far it has been assumed that one is evaluating commercially produced software. This need not be the case; it can be a sobering and beneficial experience to expose one's own software to such a critical evaluation.

Using the micro with special populations

As is seen in Chapters 6 and 15 the microcomputer can offer a new range of experiences to disabled populations. Both mentally and physically disabled individuals can benefit greatly from the flexibility and endless patience of the microcomputer. With more severely disabled individuals the computer can offer a real possibility of exercising some control over their environment. The microcomputer is sufficiently flexible to allow us to adapt it to any individual's needs. Unfortunately all too often we expect these individuals to adapt to the computer. Almost every individual is capable of some controlled movement; this might be eye movement, grunting, blowing, head turning or some form of limb movement. Any of these can be used to control the microcomputer. All that is required is a suitable input device, and a wide variety of these are now available. A few examples are listed below:

The *concept keyboard* is a large, flat, pressure-sensitive board which can be configured in a variety of different ways. It is very similar to the till keyboards used in some fast-food restaurants. The concept keyboard can be set up so that the whole area acts as a single key; or this area can be divided into anything up to 128 sections, each acting as separate keys. An overlay can be made to label each of the sections. For example, real objects could be attached to the overlay; pressing one of these would control the computer appropriately.

The *keyguard* is a simple metal shield which fits over the conventional keyboard. Holes cut in the keyguard allow only certain keys to be pressed and help the user to press only one key at a time.

Tilt switches can be attached to the user's limbs so that any movement of their limbs causes the switch to close and hence control the computer.

A variety of devices are available that allow *eye movements* to control the computer. Most of these require electrodes to be attached to the user's face, and unfortunately this can be uncomfortable.

Suck/blow switches are switches which respond to air pressure. Providing the user with one of these attached to a tube through which they can suck or blow can make a wide variety of responses possible.

Voice-activated switches at their simplest respond to the volume of spoken sounds. Others are available which respond to tone and the most sophisticated can recognise complex sound patterns, including individual spoken words.

There is an enormous variety of *pressure switches* which can be adapted to suit an individual's requirements. There are also some more specialised devices designed to train specific fine motor skills; these include door-handle and telephone-dial switches.

Professionals who feel that some of their users may be assisted by these specialist input devices are recommended to contact organisations catering for the disabled, who will be able to provide lists of local manufacturers of such equipment.

Of course input to the microcomputer is only one side of the story. The disabled user can also benefit from specialist output devices such as speech synthesisers and Braille printers. Younger disabled users might also benefit from the use of animated electronic toys as a reward for appropriate behaviour. Cybernetic robots such as the *floor turtle* can be controlled from the microcomputer and can allow severely disabled users to actively explore their environment for the first time.

It should be emphasised that the limiting factor in enabling such special individuals to make use of the computer will most likely be the imagination and determination of the clinician concerned.

Making software accessible

One of the major problems facing someone who wishes to introduce microcomputers into a clinical or educational setting is encouraging colleagues to make regular and efficient use of the resources provided. The first stage must obviously be to introduce the equipment to colleagues, demonstrate its use and discuss its advantages. However, this alone will not guarantee success. If a potential user finds that software is not available or will not run as promised he or she will quickly lose interest. The authors have developed a workable system that both encourages use and monitors success in such settings. It is suggested that a file is made up for each new piece of software which contains the following:

The software itself. Remember to keep a back-up copy elsewhere.
The evaluation of the software (see above).
A description of the user for whom the software is most appropriate.

Instructions outlining how to install and run the software and how to connect
any peripherals.
A comments sheet for the user to complete—this provides useful feedback.

The front of the file should be clearly labelled with the program name and a
description of the machine on which it will run. All these files should be kept
at a central location.

Communication between computers

For a variety of reasons it may be necessary to allow communication between
computers. It may be necessary to send large volumes of data between two or
more microcomputers. Often users wish to use their micros as terminals to a
large computer.

To allow communication we require a physical link between the machines
and a standard *protocol* (set of procedures) for the transmission of the data.
The physical link presents little problem. Almost all microcomputers include a
port designed specifically for this purpose. This port will normally be labelled
'serial port', 'communications', 'RS232' or 'RS423'. RS232 and RS423 are
the code numbers associated with the International Standard for this form of
serial port. The difference between RS232 and RS423 is of no consequence to
us. The serial port will usually use five pins, although sometimes in practice
only three are used. The physical port itself sometimes has 25 pins, of which
most are simply left unconnected. One of the pins is used to transmit data
from the computer, one to the computer, one is the 'ground' or 'earth', and
the remaining two are used to control the flow of information down the cable.

The second requirement is a standard communications protocol which must
be used by both machines to ensure that they transmit and expect to receive
information in the same form. In the academic world a communications
package known as *Kermit* has become a universally accepted standard. Kermit
is available for virtually all computers in use around the world. Kermit was
first written by an American university's computing department and they took
the imaginative decision to make the software freely available to non-profit-
making organisations, together with instructions on how to write versions for
new machines. Kermit is therefore readily and freely available to all schools,
universities and hospitals,

Although other communication programs are available, the authors strongly
recommend the use of Kermit as it is such a widely used standard, is reliable,
and is supported by many other users, providing a ready supply of expert
advice. Kermit also has the advantage of being able to transmit both text and
non-text files equally well and of including comprehensive data-checking
routines that are capable of detecting and rectifying errors that may have been
introduced into the data during the process of transmission. This is especially

important when the transmission route includes a telephone line, as these are notoriously 'noisy'.

Once the micro can communicate with other machines there is the possibility of sharing information. This can be done in two ways:

1   Electronic mail systems allow the user to send and receive messages, text or even programs. Commercial electronic mail systems are readily available and most large computer operating systems include this facility for people working on terminals. A *Local Area Network* allows mail to be exchanged between users on a particular site (say a university campus). These networks usually have *gateways* to national and international networks. In the UK the main university network is known as JANET (Joint Academic Network), and besides allowing near-instantaneous transmission of messages and files between users anywhere in the country, this allows someone sitting at a terminal actually to use mainframes at distant sites (as long as they are registered users). One of the great advantages of electronic mail, apart from its speed, is that in most cases it is free to the user.

2   Bulletin boards are the electronic equivalent of notice boards. Users can pin notices on them and read the notices which others have left. Professionals in a variety of fields are increasingly finding them a useful means of sharing ideas. Specialist, 'single-subject' bulletin boards monitored by an editor are available. For example, researchers in visual perception can contact a bulletin board where they can obtain information about the current research being conducted by colleagues and can ask for assistance with practical problems. Bulletin boards can operate via national or international networks such a JANET (see above), or they can be contacted by connecting the micro to a standard telephone socket via a *modem* and dialling the telephone number of the bulletin board concerned.

Images and the microcompter

New users of the microcomputer are most often disappointed when they discover how difficult it is to present a picture on the computer screen. Advertisements for microcomputers and demonstration packages provided free with them often show elaborate screen displays and users are led to believe that they will easily be able to produce such pictures. The truth of the matter is that the microcomputer is not well suited to the manipulation of complex images. The demonstration packages are nearly always written in machine code by highly skilled programmers. Most microcomputers are designed primarily to present text displays and only images made up of text or text-like characters will be easy to create; this is why the images in early arcade games were so abstract—they were made up of text-like elements.

The problem is that real images are made up of a wide range of luminance values; for example, even a simple black and white photograph looks to be of poor quality unless more than 128 different grey levels are present in the image. Similarly a good-quality image needs to be made up of very large number of small picture elements, the so-called *pixels*. Each of the pixels must be able to display all of the possible grey levels. In practice even a crude image must be at least 200 pixels square, i.e. it will contain over 40 000 pixels. In the computer's memory the image is of course merely a series of numbers required for each pixel, and these numbers must be large enough to be able to represent all possible grey levels. Typically one, two or three bytes are required for each pixel, depending on the number of grey levels required or whether colour is being used. This puts considerable demands on the memory capacity of the computer. The screen used to represent the image must have sufficient resolution to display the pixels. Resolutions of microcomputer screens vary from around 400×200 pixels to 640×480 pixels.

Figure 3.1 shows the same image of a face displayed at a variety of different resolutions—by examining this figure you will be able to see the effect of the pixel size and the number of grey levels present on the image quality. You should also be able to decide what combination of these will produce an image quality high enough for your needs.

Images can be created in several ways. They may be 'drawn' using a programming language such as BASIC (see below), which includes commands to draw lines, circles, rectangles, etc. and colouring or shading these in. More sophisticated images can be drawn using 'graphics' or 'drawing' packages. These provide more poweful line drawing and shading facilities and it is sometimes possible to save the images created on to a disc and import it into a program for purposes of presentation and response timing. More realistic images can be 'captured' using a *scanning device* which scans the grey levels of two-dimensional pictures such as photographs, or an image capture system taking pictures directly from a video camera.

Computer viruses

There has been a great deal of comment in the media concerning so-called 'computer viruses'. Much of this has been hysterical scare-mongering. However, computer viruses do represent a real threat to microcomputer users. Computer viruses come in a variety of forms, but all have the same basic characteristics. The virus is a hidden program that embeds itself into the operating system of the infected machine. The program is written in such a manner that it is extremely difficult to locate and will often remain dormant for many months. When finally it is activated, sometimes by an action of the user and sometimes by time alone, the virus makes its presence felt in one of many ways. Many viruses are fundamentally benign and merely produce some unexpected screen

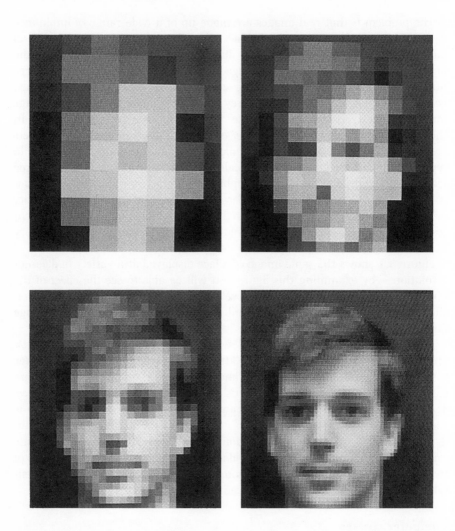

FIGURE 3.1a   A face displayed with varying degrees of spatial resolution.

display. For example, one particularly common virus presents the user with a picture of a Christmas tree during the month of December. However, more worrying are the viruses which destroy data held on disc, or even the disc drive itself.

Viruses are not a new problem; they have been known in academic computing fields for many years. Often they are written by talented but misguided or disgruntled users of a system who derived great pleasure out of leaving these electronic time-bombs. What has changed in recent years is the

FIGURE 3.1a continued.

sophistication of the code and the means of its transmission. One of the first actions of the virus, even when dormant, is to copy itself on to all discs used by the machine. With the advent of mass usage of microcomputers and the legal and illegal sharing of software the spread of a virus can be extremely rapid. If you borrow a disc from a colleague there is an increasingly high probability that it will contain a virus. Even some commercially purchased software is reported to be infected because the machines used to write the software are infected. A recently discovered, and thankfully benign, virus infected thousands of academic users of electronic mail systems across several continents within a few weeks of its release. The virus worked by examining the electronic mail addresses of colleagues which the user kept on disc. It then sent a copy of itself to each of these users, and in the same way that a chain letter can reach thousands of individuals within weeks the virus spread at an exponential rate. Unlike a chain letter though, the virus gave the users no knowledge of their infection or choice as to whether to continue the transmission. If one assumes that on average every user has ten mutually exclusive names and addresses on file then within ten steps of the chain one *billion* users will be infected.

The only certain safeguard against infection is to remain computationally celibate! In other words, not to load any software on to your own machine—clearly not a feasible alternative. Celibacy in humans would result in the extinction of *Homo sapiens*—computational celibacy would render the microcomputer useless. So what can be done to reduce the chances of infection? By far the most likely source of infection is shared software. Unfortunately this covers open-access software as well as pirated software. In the case of open-

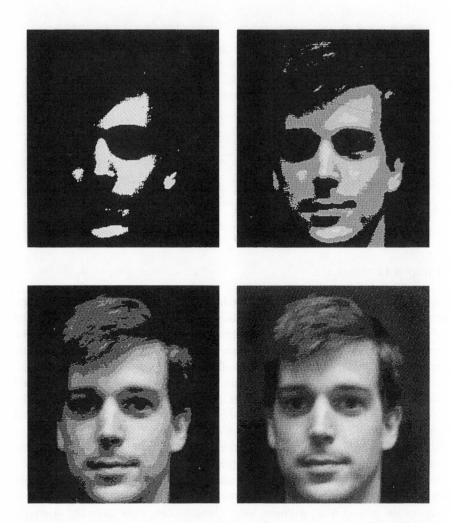

FIGURE 3.1b   A face displayed with varying degrees of grey-scale resolution.

access software, one should try to obtain a version that is as close as possible to the original source. If one pirates software, the price to be paid for this illegality is the ever increasingly high risk of infection. It should be remembered that even if you buy the software but then lend it to someone else for them to pirate they may infect *your* copy. If you share software it is not the number of partners you have but the number they have had that determines your risk factor.

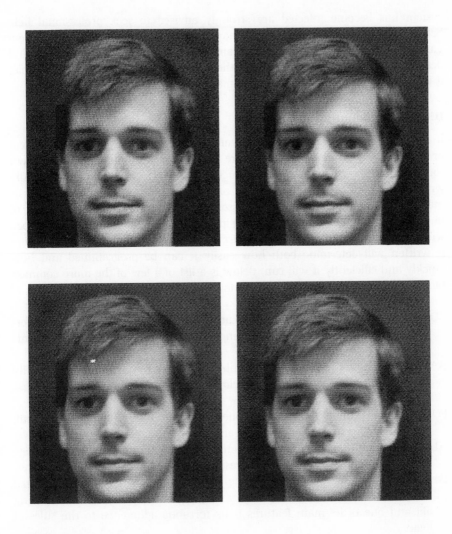

FIGURE 3.1b   continued.

Whether you share your software or not the best precaution that you can take is to take regular back-up copies of the entire contents of your disc(s), including your operating system, and to keep these back-ups indefinitely. Fortunately the analogy with human infection ends here, as in the case of computers it is possible to restore the microcomputer's health to that of the period prior to infection by deleting all current discs and then reloading the healthy back-up copies. Remember one should not inspect back-up copies, as doing so will infect them. Users who are unfortunate enough to find that their system has become infected are strongly advised to seek professional help before attempting anything; years of hard work could be at stake. There are a variety of programs available that claim to be able to seek out viruses and destroy them. Unfortunately most of them appear to be unreliable and some, it is claimed, even contain viruses themselves.

High-level computing languages

It is often the case that existing software packages do not meet one's clinical or research needs. In that case there may be a need to write one's own software. As indicated in the introductory chapter, programs are normally written in *high-level* languages which are much easier to use than binary or machine code which the microprocessor understands. There are a variety of high-level languages available to the programmer and each was developed with a specific task in mind. The nature of the languages in which a program is written will determine both how easily it can be programmed and how quickly and efficiently it will run. Below is a list of a few of the more common high-level languages and the purpose for which they were developed.

COBOL—COmmon Business Oriented Language—designed mainly for commercial business uses such as accountancy and manipulation of large amounts of data.

BASIC—Beginners All-purpose Symbolic Instructional Code—originally developed from FORTRAN (see below) as an accessible and easy-to-use general-purpose language.

FORTRAN—FORmula TRANslator—one of the first high-level languages, still widely used for mathematical programming in scientific settings.

ALGOL—ALGOrithmic Language—another mathematically oriented language in which single statements can represent complex mathematical procedures.

Pascal—named after Blaise Pascal, the French Mathematician who invented one of the first adding machines—the language was developed as a teaching aid and one of its main features is its tortuous adherence to the rules of logic.

C—the third generation of a language of which A and B were pilot versions—this language is becoming increasingly popular with the advent of microcomputers which run the UNIX operating system which is written in C.

Logo—developed by Seymour Papert, a colleague of Piaget, the name was suggested by the child's construction toy 'Lego', which has similar modular properties and, like Logo, was designed for use by children and is now increasingly used by adults—it is used to move images of objects around the screen or cybernetic robots around a flat surface.

LISP—LISt Processing language—this is used primarily for artificial intelligence programs. It has a reputation for being slow and requiring very powerful computers to run anything other than 'toy' applications.

PROLOG—PROgramming LOGic—this is another artificial intelligence language. Its main feature is a built-in system for making deductions from propositions contained in a database.

The fact that two different machines purport to run the same high-level language does not necessarily mean that the same program will run on both. The reason is that different machine *dialects* have developed. An exception to this rule is C and to a lesser extent FORTRAN, for which there are International Standards committees.

As described above, the machine running one of these languages must translate instructions into its own machine language or machine code. This translation can take place in two different ways. In *interpreted* languages, such as most versions of BASIC, each line of the program must be translated immediately before it is executed; this means that even if several identical lines follow each other the machine will translate each independently. Because this translation takes time, interpreted languages tend to be slow in running; however, they are easier to write as, if mistakes are made, an error message is displayed and the program stops at the point of the error.

In *compiled* languages, for example FORTRAN, the entire program is translated before it can be run. This translation process is known as compilation and produces a file known as the *executable image*, which is the machine's translation of the program. Compilation takes time and this delay can be frustrating when developing programs; but the advantage is that the program will actually run faster. Some modern compilers contain optimisation routines which speed up the program still further by modifying it slightly to suit the machine's hardware.

It is occasionally necessary to write programs in which speed of running is critical, for example arcade games or programs to run complex experiments. Compiled, and hence faster, versions of BASIC are available for some machines but when speed is of the essence it is likely that some portions of the program will need to be written directly in the machine's own language—*machine code*. Writing in machine code is not easy as every microprocessor is different and hence a new set of instructions needs to be learnt for each, and these instructions are far from memorable.

The situation is made slightly more manageable by the availability of *assembly languages*, which form a bridge between high-level languages and machine code. An example of a machine code instruction might be to transfer the contents of a memory location to a special store called the accumulator. In the machine code of the 6502 microprocessor (see introductory chapter) this instruction would consist of two 8-bit numbers; in 6502 assembly language the instruction is slightly more comprehensible, taking the mnemonic 'LDA', standing for LoaD memory into Accumulator. Programming in assembly language is not as difficult as is often reported but is a skill that takes some time to acquire, and for most users it would be better to purchase expert assistance.

The newest generation of microcomputers, 'RISC' machines, have somewhat reduced the need to program in machine code. A RISC machine has a different type of microprocessor at its heart. It has long been realised that in a standard microprocessor the vast majority of the time is taken up performing the same few instructions; some of the instructions are only very occasionally used by the program. In a RISC (or Reduced Instruction Set Chip) machine only the most frequently used instructions are made available. As fewer instructions have to be incorporated into the chip when it is made these instructions can be made to run faster. The 'missing' instructions that have not been included can still be carried out by combining several other instructions together. Although it takes longer to perform these tasks, they are so rarely used that the overall effect is to speed up massively the rate at which programs run. One of the first RISC microcomputers to be widely available is the Archimedes, made by Acorn Computers in the UK. It is claimed that this is by far the fastest micro in the world; in fact it is said to be so fast that programs previously written in machine code for speed will run when written in standard BASIC on this machine. If this type of machine proves to be as fast as is claimed and becomes popular, the need to write in machine code will be considerably reduced.

Writing a program

Clearly, in the space available here we can only offer the briefest advice to those readers considering writing their own software. However, we hope that the suggestions listed below will be useful and will ease the process of programming.

The first question which needs to addressed is: why is one writing one's own software? Writing software always takes many times longer than was imagined. One should only embark on this process if it is certain that there is no alternative. It is always worthwhile, for example, checking that there is no commercially available software suitable for the job in hand. One should also consult with colleagues; there is nothing more frustrating than, after weeks of stressful programming, discovering from colleagues that one has 'reinvented the wheel'.

It is important to decide exactly what the program needs to do and to write a program specification. This should include a list of the component tasks that will make up the program. One should not to be too ambitious at this stage; it is better to get one element of the program working at a time than to be faced with a huge and incomprehensible program which does not work.

The specification can be expressed as a *flowchart* or possibly a *structure diagram*. Flowcharts and structure diagrams are diagrammatic representations of the specification and include such features as *loops*, where several instructions are carried out many times, and *branches*, where the sequence of instructions is dependent upon a decision; the result of this decision will determine which path through the program will be taken. The need to write flowcharts is always stressed by programming tutorials, and in practice is almost always ignored by programmers. This is a mistake; although it takes time to write a flowchart, one nearly always benefits from this initial outlay. The elements of the final flowchart should be translatable into one or two lines of a program.

The choice of a high-level programming language to use is critical. Some programs are easier to write in one language than another. If it seems that there is a need to use machine code, one should stop and think again. Realistically, most researchers and clinicians are unlikely to develop expertise in more than one or two languages. One of these will be BASIC and another may be a more specialised language such as PROLOG. Happily modern BASICs are sufficiently powerful and easy to use for most purposes.

It is important to make sure that one uses the chosen high-level language to the full. For example, if the language includes *procedures* (small blocks of program which are give a name and can be referred to at any point in the program), one should use them. A well-written program using procedures will be easy to read, especially if these are given names which reflect what they do. If, for example, a procedure in a program measures a subject's reaction time then it should be called something like 'REACTIONTIME' rather than, say, 'X'.

All languages allow the programmer to include comments written in English, which are ignored by the computer when running. These comments are an enormous help when modifying the program. At the time of writing the program one feels that one understands it perfectly and believes it to be self-explanatory; within a week, without comments written into the program, one may not even recognise it, let alone remember what it does.

As the program develops one should keep a paper record, including the flowchart, and a listing of the program and any modifications made to it. Whenever a change is made to the program this should always be noted in the documentation; not doing so will only result in chaos and potential disaster at a later date.

Using micros to control experiments

As will be discussed in Chapter 9, without the availability of the microcomputer much modern research would not be possible. The microcomputer is undoubtably an invaluable tool to the researcher. However, it is dangerous to use the

microcomputer to control experiments without at first having some understanding of its workings. In this section it is our aim to draw the reader's
attention to some of the pitfalls that can face the researcher and to offer
possible solutions.

The microcomputer is most often used to present a stimulus to subjects or
patients in a controlled manner and monitor their responses to it. If the precise
timing of these two types of events, presentation of stimuli and collection of
response, is not critical then there is no problem in writing the software in a
high-level language such as BASIC. However, when the timing is critical, as is
often the case in psychological experimentation then two types of problem
arise: namely, the measurement of time by the computer and the delays
involved in the computer controlling and monitoring peripherals such as the
keyboard and screen.

Most versions of BASIC include a timer. For example, in BBC BASIC there is
a clock which measures time in centiseconds (100ths of a second); some
versions of BASIC written for IBM and its compatibles purport to measure time
accurately to a tenth of a second. For many experimentation purposes these
levels of accuracy are often not sufficient. Ideally reaction times should be
measured to an accuracy of one millisecond. This limitation of the language
can be overcome in a number of ways; machine code routines are available to
speed up the clock on many machines, but some care should be taken in using
them as there is usually some cost to be paid for this added speed. The
manufacturers would have implemented faster clocks if it had been easy to do
so. The machine's operating system has access to the very high-speed clock
that controls all the machine code operations in the computer. The clock
available to the programmer is incremented about every 20 000 cycles of this
high-speed clock. To make the high-level language timer run faster the
operating system is altered so that it increments this clock after fewer cycles of
the machine's clock. Clearly doing this disrupts the smooth running of the
operating system. Timing is critical to the operating system as the machine's
memory and peripherals need to be serviced at specified intervals. The cost
then associated with speeding up the clock is a loss of reliability; disc drives
are likely to be especially vulnerable to these changes. The alternative is to use
an add-on board in the computer which contains a separate but machine-
readable clock running at the desired speed. Some modern microcomputers
already contain such a clock which can be read and controlled safely from
machine code.

Even after the desired level of timing accuracy is achieved it cannot be
assumed that events on the screen or keyboard can be measured to this degree.
The problem can best be illustrated by a brief anecdote. When one of the
authors first started using microcomputers in experimentation he was interested in measuring finger-tapping performance. The subjects were required to
tap as fast as they could on the keyboard of the computer. To the author's

amazement he discovered that all human tapping performance seemed to have a fundamental frequency of 60 Hz—clearly an important discovery. Fortunately, before seeking publication the computer manual was examined and it was discovered the computer keyboard was 'read' by the operating system 60 times a second! Early microcomputers were difficult to use because a skilled typist could type faster than the operating system could cope with; in all modern machines this problem is overcome by all key presses being automatically stored in a buffer—the operating system reads the contents of this buffer when it has time do so, in the case of the example above once every 60th of a second. This means that no matter how fast the high-level language clock might be running one cannot detect key presses faster than the rate at which the buffer is emptied.

A similar problem applies to screen output. Servicing a monitor is a slow process for the operating system. Exactly when a character appears on the screen is extremely difficult to determine. Using the screen to output stimuli in an experiment also generates another problem. The chemicals used to coat the screen are designed to glow for some time after they have been activated. If this were not the case the screen would flicker. A consequence of this is that for some time after the moment when a stimulus is removed from the screen an image of it remains slowly decaying. This might seem of trivial importance; however, in some experimental paradigms this can be critical. For example, in a divided visual field presentation, stimuli must not be visible for more than 200 milliseconds. The only way to ensure that the stimulus is no longer visible is to cover it with a *mask* (a second, visually dense stimulus) that obscures it at the appropriate time.

The ultimate solution to these problems is to use non-buffered inputs and outputs. This may involve using the computer to control peripherals such as an optical shutter on a slide projector via a port on the computer (see Chapter 7). Similarly the subjects' responses may need to be measured via special buttons connected to this port. A fuller description of how to achieve this is given in the following section.

Controlling external devices

As explained earlier it is often necessary to use the microcomputer to control or monitor external devices which in turn present stimuli to, or collect response from, a subject. These devices are connected to the micro via special *ports* or sockets. The easiest port to control is one that is *memory-mapped*; the pins on such a port directly reflect the value contained in a section of the computer's memory. It is as if a section of the computer's memory is exposed to the outside world; changing the value of the memory location on to which the port is mapped changes the voltages presented on the pins of the port. The simplest memory-mapped ports to control are parallel ports which are mapped on to a single byte of the computer's memory. These ports are described as parallel because they transmit all the elements of the information in this byte of memory simultaneously. By comparison a serial port transmits the elements of information sequentially—one bit at a time. A special kind of parallel port is generally used to control a printer. Serial ports can be used for this purpose but are also often used to connect microcomputers together for purposes of communication. On some computers there is a parallel port provided to allow the user to control external devices; it is often referred to as the *user port*. The BBC microcomputer, despite its age and now outdated technology, is still very widely used in UK universities, schools and hospitals, in part at least because of the provision of a versatile user port. This port provides the user with eight pins, the voltages on which can be controlled or monitored simply by either changing or reading the value of the memory location on to which the port is mapped.

In a digital computer a value is represented by the presence or absence of 5 volts on a wire. If the wire is carrying 5 volts then the value represented is 1; if it carries 0 volts then the value represented within the computer is 0. In the microcomputer, eight of these wires make up a single byte of memory, allowing us to represent any number between 0 and 255. This means that eight independent devices can be turned on or off simply by making them respond to the presence or absence of 5 volts on the wire to which they are connected. So, for example, we could switch on or off a tape recorder simply by changing the value of the memory-mapped byte. Similarly we can monitor subject's responses simply by connecting a button which they press between one of the pins of the user port and a zero voltage ground wire also present on the user port. Pressing the button will now change the value of the memory-mapped byte in a predictable way. Figure 3.2 shows a simple circuit diagram showing how an external device can be controlled or a button press monitored.

A problem with the IBM PC and many other modern microcomputers is that user ports of this type are not normally provided. Almost all computers have a serial port which can also be used to control external devices. However, it is in the nature of a serial port that the external device must be able to decode the signal that is sent to it down the cable. This coding and decoding might introduce time delays into the system and will certainly complicate the circuitry required to connect even the simplest of switches to the microcomputer. However, the IBM PC and most of its compatibles are provided with a number of *expansion slots* into which special circuit boards can be plugged. Several manufacturers produce boards which either mimic the action of the user port or are specifically designed to control individual pieces of equipment. The disadvantages of such a system are increased cost and reduced flexibility.

An alternative means of monitoring the action of a subject is via the 'analogue to digital' or 'A to D' input port on a microcomputer. As explained above, modern computers are digital devices in which values are represented

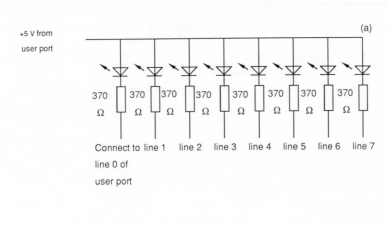

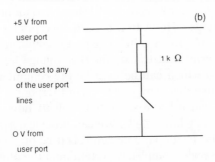

FIGURE 3.2 Simple wiring diagrams for using a parallel 'user' port as provided on the BBC computer to control peripherals. (a) This shows how a set of light-emitting diodes (LEDs) connected between the 5-volt pin and each of the eight remaining data pins can be used to indicate when these pins are set at 0 or 5 volts, thus monitoring the state of the user port. When the pin is set to 5 volts the associated LED will go out. (b) This shows how to make the user port monitor a subject's response. The switch shown could be a simple button press. When it is closed, the pin on the user port will go from 5 volts to 0 volts (1 to 0 in digital terms) and this can be detected by reading the byte at the appropriate memory address. The resistor is not essential but will help the line to the user port reach the appropriate voltage quickly. The circuit can be repeated eight times, each switch being connected to one of the eight user port lines. (c) This shows how to make the user port switch on or off an external device. The device is connected between A and B. When the line connected to the user port pin at C is at 0 volts, then the relay will be activated and the device will be turned on. When C goes to 5 volts the device will be turned off. The circuit can be repeated eight times, with one such circuit for each user port line. The diode between C and the 5-volt pin of the user port is necessary to avoid a current surge in the reverse direction damaging the computer circuitry when the reed relay switches.

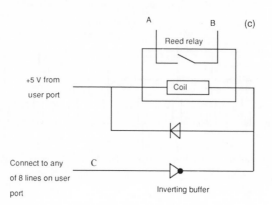

FIGURE 3.2   continued.

by combinations of 1s and 0s. It is often useful though to monitor continuously varying ('analogue') voltages. The A to D port can accept any voltage between two values (usually + 5 volts to –5 volts). The port is connected to an analogue to digital (A to D) converter that transforms this voltage into a digital value (either one or two bytes) which can be used by the computer. With a simple additional piece of circuitry this allows us to record responses on a continuous scale. For example, we can ask the subjects to tell us how certain they are about a judgement that they have made. We can provide a slide potentiometer (a variable resistor similar to the volume controls used on some hi-fi systems) and label one end of the scale 'completely certain' and the other end 'complete guess'. The subject can then indicate their level of certainty by placing the slide anywhere in this range. The analogue port will include a reference voltage line which is equal to the highest voltage the port can accept; we can connect the potentiometer between this reference voltage and the analogue ground also provided at the port. The voltage on the wire connected to the slide will now be dependent on the position of the slide and will automatically vary between 0 and the maximum value that the port can represent, allowing us to detect the exact position that the subject has left the slide at on the scale. Some modern microcomputers (such as the BBC series) come with an 8-bit analogue port, and those that do not will often accept add-on boards.

Figure 3.3 shows the simple circuit needed to use the analogue port in this way. A high-resistance (e.g. 10-kilohm) potentiometer should be used to ensure that little current is drawn. It is important to choose one with a linear rather than a logrithmic scale. The capacitor shown in the circuit helps reduce 'noise' in the circuit and its exact value is not important.

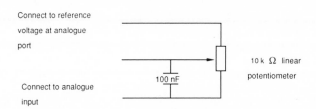

Connect to reference
voltage at analogue
port

100 nF

Connect to analogue
input

10 k Ω linear
potentiometer

FIGURE 3.3   This shows how to use the analogue port of a micro such as the BBC to allow subjects to make continuously variable responses. The position of the slider on the potentiometer will determine the voltage at the connection to the analogue port.

Conclusions

This chapter has considered some of the major aspects of developing a micro-based application for psychological research or clinical practice. There are numerous introductory books on the more common operating systems and programming languages. Many of these are readily comprehended by researchers or clinicians who are considering developing expertise in this area. However, the greatest benefit can be obtained by subscribing to one or more of the more 'serious' computing magazines. The two most suitable are *Byte*, published in the US, and *Personal Computer World*, published in the UK. Just reading through the advertisements of the magazines is a lesson in itself.

FIGURE 3.? ... shows how to use the ... set of traits such as the five-factor model to allow subjects to rate continuously which is happiness. The position of the slider on the continuum will determine the values of the continuum to the application, etc.

Conclusion

This chapter has considered some of the major aspects of developing a user-based application for psychological research or clinical practice. The sections introduce the basics on the more common operating systems and programming languages. Many of these are widely comprehensible to researchers or clinicians who are themselves developing something in this area. However, the greatest benefit can be obtained by subscribing to one or more of the many serious computing magazines, the very most substantive now published in the USA and elsewhere. Contact by the publisher can be aided by reading through the advertisements of the magazines, or found in itself.

Part II

Human Performance Testing: The Effects of External Agents

Micros are ideally suited to assessing human cognitive and psychomotor performance. In former times, reaction time testing, visuo-spatial tracking ability, memory tests and so on required purpose-built equipment, which was expensive, cumbersome, tricky to use and above all inflexible. All these activities can now be undertaken by micros. Information can be displayed on the screen and all manner of responses recorded and timed. Sometimes it is necessary to attach special-purpose apparatus to the computer to present stimuli which cannot be shown on a screen, or record responses when the conventional computer keyboard is inappropriate. However, these *peripherals* can usually be bought 'off the shelf' or cheaply constructed.

Part II examines the use of micros for assessing the effects of external agents operating on people. In the case of the first chapter this means the side-effects of drugs. The chapter focuses on antidepressants but it could equally be tranquillisers, pain-killers, antibiotics or antihistamines. The second chapter focuses on environmental pollutants in the workplace. The two chapters have in common the principle that there is little point in performing just one or two performance tests—one needs a wide battery of such tests to obtain a 'profile' of the action of the external agents. Micros permit this wide range of tests to be performed by the same apparatus, and indeed the tests to be readily adapted so as to achieve the greatest possible sensitivity. These tests can be used by anyone with a suitable micro. Their ease of application and low cost of setting up could mean a widening of the research base, with interested practitioners getting involved in the data collection process.

CHAPTER 4

Measuring the effects of psychoactive drugs, with particular reference to antidepressants

CHRIS ALFORD AND IAN HINDMARCH

The use of microcomputers in psychology and medicine is rapidly increasing. This volume bears testimony to the ever-increasing range of applications to which microcomputers can successfully be put for the control, collection and analysis of data. Microcomputers are used widely in psychopharmacology, ranging from management and coordination of clinical trials (Severe, 1987; Smith and Glaudin, 1987) via data handling and collection (Greenhill et al., 1987; Rhoades et al., 1987); to specific tests for the assessment of behavioural and cognitive deficits (Corwin and Snodgrass, 1987; Ismond et al., 1987; Maulucci et al., 1987; Solanto and Lewitter, 1987).

Work in the Human Psychopharmacology Research Unit has centred on the evaluation of psychoactive drugs by profiling their effects on a battery of tests of psychomotor and cognitive function (Hindmarch, 1975, 1980, 1986). The reliable evaluation of psychoactive compounds has only been possible through the use of microcomputers and microprocessors. As well as being used for controlling stimulus presentations and recording responses, microprocessors have enabled accurate data collection from large numbers of subjects using simultaneous testing in tightly controlled laboratory environments, through to the study of hospitalised patients recovering from anaesthesia and the testing of individuals whilst driving motor vehicles.

Advantages of microcomputer- and microprocessor-controlled test systems for psychopharmacological evaluation

The main advantages of using microprocessor- and microcomputer-based systems for psychopharmacological test batteries may be summarised as follows:

Microcomputers, Psychology and Medicine
Edited by R. West, M. Christie and J. Weinman
© 1990 by John Wiley & Sons Ltd

1   The use of microcomputers enables testing to be carried out in a tightly controlled environment where standardised programs enable precision control of test variables.

2   Parallel testing with multiple test stations using identical microcomputers and computer programs enables relatively large numbers of subjects to be dealt with simultaneously without recourse to using different experimenters. Extraneous variables, including circadian/ultradian rhythms and experimenter effects, are thereby limited.

3   Results obtained from sensitive and reliable tests improve confidence for comparative drug evaluations. For example, critical flicker fusion threshold (CFF) has been found to exhibit both an ultradian and circadian rhythm (Frewer, 1986), as well as good test–retest reliability with the same drug (Hindmarch, 1982).

4   Simultaneous testing of subjects using standardised computer test systems provides a cost-effective means of evaluating psychotropic compounds. Similarly, inexpensive alterations to control programs can be made as required from the results of further research and experience. An updated program suite can easily and cheaply be installed in all microcomputer test units.

5   Each test within a battery may have a wide variety of pre-programmed variables which may be selected to provide appropriate task demands for the specific psychopharmacological evaluation required, e.g. the need to reduce memory load when testing the elderly in comparison to young adults. Programmed flexibility of test variables optimises test battery sensitivity and validity for a given experimental group or situation.

6   The results obtained with microcomputer-based testing are highly reliable, being free from human recording errors and related experimental variables. The recording format (e.g. floppy discs) is compatible with economic back-up procedures to prevent data loss, and reliable data transcription for further analysis. This includes file transfer to more powerful mainframe computers for statistical evaluation, or the use of modems or other electronic transmission systems for centralising data collection and evaluation. The increased capacity of available software for modern microcomputers often enables complete data processing to be carried out in situ. Modern file-coding techniques, which automatically encode such information as the date and time for each response file, improve reliability and cross-checking of data. Data for registration with drug regulatory authorities has to guarantee that there are no false file identifications and related subject/user errors.

7   Microcomputers enable the rapid generation of a standardised database which may be constantly added to and updated. It is only through the existence of such a base that both valid and reliable comparative psychopharmacological evaluations of different compounds may be made.

8   The operational flexibility of modern microcomputer-based test systems enables comparative evaluations to be undertaken in a variety of situations. These may vary from the controlled laboratory situation to hospitalised patients recovering from anaesthesia (Moss *et al.*, 1987), and the assessment of 'on-the-road' driving performance (Hindmarch, 1986).

9   Inter-test validity and compatibility may be determined by different centres exchanging programs. In this respect there is a need for various research groups to adopt a common computer system to facilitate the interchange of test programs.

10 The use of microcomputers enables the integration of a variety of peripheral assessment devices into a single stimulus presentation and data-recording device; for example, a simple driving simulator can comprise a steering wheel and a brake and an accelerator pedal connected to the I/O (input–output) port of the computer.

In summary, the use of a microprocessor- and microcomputer-based test battery for the psychopharmacological investigation of different compounds has provided a sensitive, reliable and valid means of evaluating different psychoactive drugs.

Baldessarini (1985) observed that there had been few systematic comparisons of large numbers of agents under identical conditions. However, standardised test batteries and common methodologies now enable such comparisons to be made. A review of the effects of antidepressants analysed with the microcomputer-based test battery provides a suitable vehicle for illustrating how a systematic comparison of a group of psychoactive drugs can be made.

General methodology

The results described were typically obtained from volunteer subjects. Following morning drug administration the test battery would be used to assess acute and subacute effects with an initial test after 1–2 hours and repeated test sessions up to 4–5 hours to plot the pharmacodynamic course of events. Patient studies show that results obtained with volunteers generalise to the recipient patient population (Hanks, 1984; Khan *et al.*, 1984; Hindmarch 1987a,b), adding a certain 'ecological validity' to the findings from volunteers.

Results are obtained with respect to placebo and/or a verum (usually amitriptyline) with subjects acting as their own controls in cross-over design studies, with drug administration schedules balanced and randomised according to Latin squares. In all repeated measures designs a drug-free washout period separates each test drug treatment.

Test measures and assesments

The Leeds Psychomotor Tester

The Leeds Psychomotor Tester is a microprocessor-controlled test apparatus which measures both Critical Flicker Fusion (CFF) and choice reaction time (CRT) (Hindmarch, 1975, 1980).

Critical Flicker Fusion Threshold (CFF)

The test device (Hindmarch, 1975; Hindmarch and Parrot, 1978; Hindmarch, 1982) is comprised of four light-emitting diodes which the subject holds in foveal fixation by sitting at a distance of 1 m from the test apparatus. It is a means of measuring discrete sensory data and is taken as an index of overall CNS activity and information-processing capacity. The lights flicker on and off at a constantly increasing or decreasing rate of 1 Hz per second over a range of 12–50 Hz under microprocessor control. An increasing or decreasing rate of change is selected, first increasing from 12 Hz then decreasing from 50 Hz, so that individual thresholds are determined by the psychophysical method of limits (Woodworth and Schlosberg, 1958). Three ascending and three descending scales are administered in alternate order, with the flicker fusion threshold being automatically registered and displayed by the microprocessor.

The validity of CFF as a measure of information processing may be seen from its correlation with other accepted measures of CNS function, notably the EEG (Bobon et al., 1982) and other measures of information processing and subjective alertness (Parrott, 1982). The reliability of the measure has been shown in test–retest situations with the same drug (Hindmarch, 1981).

From Figure 4.1 it may be seen that three categories of results have been obtained with CFF from a comparative evaluation of antidepressants. Interestingly, amitriptyline (a first-generation tricyclic), mianserin (a tetracylic) and trazodone (a triazolopyridine derivative) all share common sedative effects when assessed using CFF. These results clearly indicate that biochemical properties alone cannot be used to provide an index of drug effects.

Similarly, those drugs which do not differ significantly from placebo include the tricyclics lofepramine and desipramine, as well as members of the new generation of specific 5-HT reuptake inhibitors, zimeldine and fluoxetine. The final group comprises compounds which significantly improve information-processing ability, having an opposite effect to the sedative antidepressants and yet again including 5-HT reuptake inhibitors (paroxetine). Serotonin enhancement is common to trazodone, zimeldine and paroxetine, and yet these three compounds have sedative, neutral and performance-enhancing effects, respectively.

Acute/sub-acute	effects		(a)
	mg	CFF	CRT
Amitriptyline	50	-	-
Mianserin	10	-	-
Trazodone	50	-	-
Dothiepin	50	O	O
Desipramine	50	O	O
Lofepramine	140	O	O
Zimeldine	200	O	O
Midalcipran	100	O	O
Buproprion	100	O	O
Fluoxetine	40	O	O
Sertraline	100	+	O
Paroxetine	30	+	O
Nomifensine	100	+	O

Acute/sub-acute	effects		(b)
	mg	STM IPR	SUB SED
Amitriptyline	50	-	-
Mianserin	10	-	-
Trazodone	50	-	-
Dothiepin	50		-
Desipramine	50	O	O
Lofepramine	140	O	O
Zimeldine	200		O
Midalcipran	100	O	O
Buproprion	100	O	O
Fluoxetine	40		O
Sertraline	100	O	O
Paroxetine	30		O
Nomifensine	100	+	+

FIGURE 4.1   Drug effect and side-effect profile of a range of antidepressant drugs on a variety of measures. Minus sign means significant impairment when compared with a placebo; a zero means no effect compared with placebo; a plus sign means significant improvement compared with placebo. CFF = critical flicker fusion threshold, CRT = choice reaction time, STM IPR = short-term memory and information processing, SUB SED = subjective ratings of sedation, SIM CAR = simulated car driving, OTR CAR = on-the-road car driving.

Acute/sub-acute effects	mg	SIM CAR	(c) OTR CAR
Amitriptyline	50	-	-
Mianserin	10	-	-
Trazodone	50	-	-
Dothiepin	50	O	
Desipramine	50	O	
Lofepramine	140	O	
Zimeldine	200	O	O
Midalcipran	100	O	
Buproprion	100	O	O
Fluoxetine	40	O	
Sertraline	100	O	
Paroxetine	30	O	
Nomifensine	100	+	O

FIGURE 4.1   continued

These results demonstrate yet another aspect of CFF threshold; that they are sensitive to both decrements and improvements produced by psychoactive compounds. This bimodal sensitivity is an important aspect for appropriate classification of drug effects.

Choice Reaction Time (CRT)

The subject response part of the CRT apparatus comprises a central touch-sensitive pad, surrounded in an arc of a circle by six similar pads each having a red light next to them. The microprocessor illuminates each of these lights in a random order using a variable foreperiod of 1–3 seconds. The subject is required to extinguish the illuminated light by pressing the appropriate response pad as quickly as possible. The microprocessor records three reaction time components: recognition reaction time (RRT)—between stimulus light and lift-off from central pad; motor reaction time (MRT)—between central and appropriate peripheral pad; and total reaction time (TRT)—between stimulus light and contact with the appropriate peripheral pad.

Results for the comparative evaluation of antidepressants share similarities with those for CFF. Amitriptyline, mianserin and trazodone show significant sedative effects registered as increases in reaction time. However, whilst the results for setraline, paroxetine and nomifensine significantly increased with CFF, the effects on total reaction time failed to achieve significance. These results may reflect the superior sensitivity of CFF as a measure of psychoactive response, or the specificity of CFF response does not extend to the psychomotor activity measured by CRT.

Microcomputer-Based Tests

A wide variety of microcomputer-based tests have been developed for inclusion in the psychopharmacological test battery. These include Sternberg-type memory tests for digits, a word recognition task, the Stroop test of hemispheric discongruity, adaptive tracking tasks with or without a divided-attention reaction time component, a car-driving simulator test involving tracking and reaction time, and subjective assessments of sedation using visual analogue scales. The Sternberg-type memory task and the subjective sedation scale are selected as examples.

Sternberg Memory Scanning Task (STM)

This test assesses high-speed scanning ability and retrieval from short-term memory, being based on the reaction time method in memory research (Sternberg, 1969, 1975). 'Sets' containing different length sequences of words or letters or digits are presented to the subject to be memorised. The subject is then required to indicate whether a subsequent test stimulus was one of those previously presented in the 'set' sequence using a yes/no response button. Response latency and correct or incorrect responses are recorded by the computer. The set size for memorisation may be varied to adjust for age or other performance deficits. Typically 20 test probes for each of three different set sizes would be presented during each test session.

The results for the Sternberg-type memory task indicate a good correlation with the microprocessor-controlled CFF and CRT measures. Amitriptyline, mianserin and trazodone all produce a significant decrement in information processing. Interestingly, nomifensine revealed significantly improved results for the memory task, reflecting the results for CFF and suggesting that the information-processing aspect of this test is sensitive to drug effects rather than reaction time *per se*.

Line Analogue Rating Scale (LARS)

This subjective measure of sedation employs a set of 10-cm line analogue rating scales separating verbal descriptors such as 'more tired'and 'less tired' (Hindmarch and Gudgeon, 1980).

The test is available both as a printed sheet and as a microcomputer program. The latter version requires the subject to use left and right keys to position a cursor on a 10-cm line, displayed on the VDU, in order to indicate their subjective state. Whilst the printed paper version is useful outside the laboratory, along with other similar questionnaires and checklists, the computer version shares the advantages for the microcomputer-based tests. The mean score of ratings, including 'tiredness', 'drowsiness' and 'alertness', which are included amongst several distractor scales, are taken as measures of subjective sedation.

The subjective response to different antidepressant compounds indicates a good correlation with other objective measures of cognitive state. With this measure dothiepin, amitriptyline, mianserin and trazodone showed significant sedation. Again, nomifensine was found to have a significant stimulating effect in concordance with the results for memory and CFF.

Such a high correlation is perhaps surprising when differences between objective and subjective measures of drowsiness and alertness are often found (Herscovitch and Broughton, 1981; Thayer, 1978). This can have serious repercussions when patients receiving a sedative pharmacotherapy may not realise the degree of impairment. Equally important are the subjective effects of a drug and compliance. Drugs which are poorly tolerated may lead to a lack of compliance with clinical dose regimens.

Analogues and tests of car-driving skills

Tests of car driving and related psychomotor ability are an important adjunct to a psychopharmacological test battery as driving is a commonplace activity.

Driving simulator (SIM CAR)

The driving simulator comprises a steering wheel and a brake and accelerator pedal connected to the microcomputer. The program provides a steering/ tracking task where performance accuracy is measured as subjects follow a computer-generated 'course' which varies in position on a simulated road. Brake pedal reaction time to red traffic light symbols is also measured.

'On-the-road' tests of driving performance (OTR CAR)

A variety of tests of on-the-road driving skills have been employed (Hindmarch, 1976, 1986, 1987b; Hindmarch and Gudgeon, 1980). These include parking, braking, three-point turn, slalom and width estimation. Brake reaction time is measured on a microcomputer mounted in the boot of the test vehicle which controls a rear-facing brake light mounted on the bonnet of the car. The stimulus light appears as the rear brake light of an imaginary lead vehicle. Approximately 20 stimulus presentations of the brake light are used during a driving task (e.g. slalom), with the computer recording the reaction time to activation of the brake pedal via a micro-switch.

The results for both simulated and 'on-the-road' tests of car driving indicate a good correlation with the other microcomputer-controlled tests. Amitriptyline, mianserin and trazodone again produced significant decrements in performance, indicating the possibility of increased risk of accidents in road traffic situations for car-driving patients treated with these compounds. Nomifensine produced a perforance-enhancing effect registered as an improvement in simulated driving performance. In general, actual tests of driving can fail to pick up drug effects, perhaps due to reduced control of extraneous variables in a 'field' test situation, or the limitation of the tests themselves. In a recent review (Alford and Hindmarch, 1987) of benzodiazepine hypnotics, 'on-the-road' tests of driving performance failed to produce significant effects whilst microcomputer-controlled analogues of driving, particularly the lateral tracking task, revealed significant decrements with several compounds. These results emphasise the high degree of experimental control available with microcomputer-based laboratory tests. This review of results of experiments using microprocessor- and microcomputer-based psychopharmacological tests demonstrates the sensitivity of these measures in discriminating between different antidepressant compounds. Through the use of microcomputers it is possible to control the test procedures from stimulus presentation to data and response recording. This has enabled the development of sensitive test procedures having a high test–retest reliability, and a valid correlation with related measures of psychomotor performance and information processing. Sensitivity of the test system enables screening of new therapeutic compounds.

Conclusions

The results indicate that although a given class of therapeutic compounds, e.g. antidepressants, may be equipotent and yield clinically similar results, they may be differentiated using psychopharmacological tests. Measures of psychomotor performance and information processing reveal the behavioural toxicity of a drug. Such profiles provide information of substantial value to the prescribing physician dealing with ambulant patients where the integrity of psychomotor and cognitive function is important.

The use of microcomputers enables testing in different environments, but maintains tightly controlled test presentation standards so that confidence may be gained from the results recorded. The program options available enable the standard test battery to be tailored towards specific test situations and subject groups as exemplified by older subjects. In this way test sensitivity can be maintained over a variety of test situations.

The data storage medium provided by microcomputer-based systems enables the rapid and accurate generation of a database which can be constantly updated. This again is important for the comparative evaluation of psychoactive drugs. Equally, the database can provide information to other research teams working at other locations but using the standard test battery. Because the test battery is based on software using minimal and inexpensive peripheral accessories, a cost-effective system is produced. Relatively cheap and accurate test systems are the cornerstone of modern psychopharmacological test batteries where relatively large numbers of subjects undergo parallel testing within a tightly controlled test environment.

References

Alford, C. and Hindmarch, I. (1987). The residual effects of benzodiazepine hypnotics on cognitive function, psychomotor ability and car driving performance. *Second International Symposium on Medicinal Drugs and Driving Performance*, July, 1987. Maastricht, Holland.

Baldessarini, R. J. (1985). Drugs and the treatment of psychiatric disorders. In A. Goodman Gilman, L. S. Goodman, T. W. Rall and F. Murad (eds), *The Pharmacological Basis of Therapeutics*, 7th edition. New York: Macmillan.

Bobon, D. P., Lecoq, A., von Frenkell, R., Mormont, I., Laverque, G. and Lottin, T. (1982). La frequence critique de fusion visuelle en psychophathologie et en psychopharmacologie, *Acta Medica Belgica, Brussels*, **82**, 112.

Corwin, J. and Snodgrass, J. G. (1987). The picture memory and fragmented pictures test: use with cognitively impaired populations, *Psychopharmacology Bulletin*, **23**, 286–290.

Frewer, L. J. (1986). Some psychopharmacological variables affecting the critical flicker fusion threshold. PhD Thesis, University of Leeds.

Greenhill, L. L., Solomon, M., Cornblatt, B. and Martin, J. (1987). Multiple microcomputers for data entry and analysis, *Psychopharmacology Bulletin*, **23**, 264–268.

Hanks, G. W. (1984). The effects of amitriptyline and nomifensine on critical flicker fusion threshold in an elderly patient population. In W. Linford-Rees and R. G. Priest (eds), *Nomifensine: A Pharmacological and Clinical Profile*, Royal Society of Medicine International Congress and Symposium Series No. 70, pp. 47–52. Oxford: Oxford University Press.

Herscovitch, J. and Broughton, R. (1981). Sensitivity of the Stanford Sleepiness Scale to the effects of cumulative partial sleep deprivation and recovery oversleeping, *Sleep*, **4**, 83–91.

Hindmarch, I. (1975). A 1,4-benzodiazepine, temazepam: its effects on some psychological aspects of sleep and behaviour, *Arzneimittel-Forschung (Drug Research)*, **25**, 1836–1839.

Hindmarch, I. (1976). The effects of a sub-chronic administration of an anti-histamine, clemastine, on tests of car driving ability and psychomotor performance, *Current Medical Research and Opinion*, **4**, 197–206.

Hindmarch, I. (1980). Psychomotor function and psychoactive drugs, *British Journal of Clinical Pharmacology*, **10**, 189–209.

Hindmarch, I. (1981). Measuring the effects of psychoactive drugs on higher brain function. In G. Burrows and J. S. Werry (eds), *Advances in Psychopharmacology*, **II**, 79–106.

Hindmarch, I. (1982). Critical flicker fusion frequency (CFF): The effects of psychotropic compounds, *Pharmacopsychiatria*, **15**, (Suppl. 1), 44–48.

Hindmarch, I. (1986). The effects of psychoactive drugs on car handling and related psychomotor ability: a review. In J. F. O'Hanlon and J. J. de Gier (eds), *Drugs and Driving*, pp. 71–82. London: Taylor & Francis.

Hindmarch, I. (1987a). Antidepressant drugs and cognitive function. Diagnosis and treatment of depression. In K. Biziere, S. Garanttini and P. Simon (eds), *Quo Vadis: Diagnosis and Treatment of Depression*, pp. 356–363. Paris: Medsi/McGraw Hill.

Hindmarch, I, (1987b). The effects of antidepressants on information processing and analogues of car driving skills. *Second International Symposium on Medicinal Drugs and Driving Performance*, July, 1987. Maastricht, Holland.

Hindmarch, I. and Gudgeon, A. C. (1980). The effects of clobazam and lorazepam on aspects of psychomotor performance and car handling ability, *British Journal of Clinical Pharmacology*, **10**, 145–150

Hindmarch, I. and Parrot, A. C. (1978). A repeated dose comparison of the side effects of five antihistamines on objective assessments of psychomotor performance, central nervous system arousal and subject's appraisals of sleep and early morning behaviour, *Arzneimittel-Forschung (Drug Research)*, **28**, 483–486.

Ismond, D. R., Rasband, W., Smith, B. M. and Rapoport, J. L. (1987). Patient activity monitor (PAM) software for the Macintosh: A system for collecting activity data, *Psychopharmacology Bulletin*, **23**, 298–299.

Khan, M. C., Mahapatra, S. N., Stonier, P. D. and Thomas, E. M. (1984). Nomifensine and mianserin: non-tricyclic with distinct clinical profiles: a randomised double-blind study. In W. Linford-Rees and R. G. Priest (eds), *Nomifensine: A Pharmacological and Clinical Profile*, Royal Society of Medicine International Congress and Symposium Series No. 70, pp. 71–76. Oxford: Oxford University Press.

Maulucci, R. A., Eckhouse, R. H., Jr and Herman, R. M. (1987). A microcomputer work station for assessing function, *Psychopharmacology Bulletin*, **23**, 294–297.

Moss, E., Hindmarch I., Pain, A. J. and Edmondson, R. S. (1987). Comparison of recovery after halothane or alfentanil anaesthesia for minor surgery, *British Journal of Anaesthesia*, **59**, 970–977.

Parrott, A. C. (1982). Critical Flicker Fusion Thresholds and their relationship to other measures of alertness, *Pharmacopsychiatria*, **15**, 39–43.

Rhoades, H. M., Overall, J. E., Cecil, S. and Faillace, L. A. (1987). A clinical assessment and documentation template for psychopharmacology research, *Psychopharmacology Bulletin*, **23**, 272–278.

Severe, J. B. (1987). Computers in coordination of a multicenter clinical trial, *Psychopharmacology Bulletin*, **23**, 261–263.

Smith, W. T. and Glaudin, V. (1987). Microcomputers in managing psychopharmacology clinical trials, *Psychopharmacology Bulletin*, **23**, 269–271.

Solanto, M. V. and Lewitter, M. (1987). The delayed response task for ADD children, *Psychopharmacology Bulletin*, **23**, 283–285.

Sternberg, S. (1969). Memory Scanning: Mental processes revealed by reaction time experiments, *American Scientist*, **57**, 421–457.

Sternberg, S. (1975). Memory Scanning: New findings and current controversies, *Quarterly Journal of Experimental Psychology*, **27**, 1–32.

Thayer, R. E. (1978). Towards a psychological theory of multidimensional activation (arousal), *Motivation and Emotion*, **2**, 1–34.

Woodworth, R. S. and Schlosberg, H. (1958). *Experimental Psychology*. London: Methuen.

CHAPTER 5

Measuring marginal toxicity in work environments

Brian Stollery

Introduction

In the sixteenth century the physician Paracelsus described chronic lung inflammation in miners and heavy metal poisoning in smelters, drawing attention to the possibility that a person's work may be a source of disease. The first systematic study of occupational diseases was begun by Ramazzini in the eighteenth century, leading to advocacy of basic hygiene measures for their prevention. That work added a new diagnostic question to the physician's arsenal: what is your job?

The Industrial Revolution brought about a wide range of new working conditions and new diseases, and the ensuing series of Factory Acts were the first attempts to protect the health of people at work. Modern health and safety legislation has continued that trend by requiring employers to maintain a safe and healthy work environment for their employees. The rationale behind this approach to health and safety is the prevention of disease through the identification, control and removal of harmful substances before irreversible damage can occur.

Occupational Medicine

The guidelines specified in health and safety legislation govern the permissible workplace levels of toxins when no personal protection equipment is used. All organisations, no matter how small, must comply with this legislation and many organisations now provide full-time health services for their workers. In the UK for example it has been estimated that over 700 full-time and 2000 part-time physicians are currently working in occupational medicine (Lee,

Microcomputers, Psychology and Medicine
Edited by R. West, M. Christie and J. Weinman
© 1990 by John Wiley & Sons Ltd

1981). Supporting the occupational physician is a wide spectrum of health-care professionals who are actively involved in the day to day provision of an occupational health service. Because the prevention of occupational ill-health requires that formal workplace health surveillance is carried out, there are likely to be increased demands for these specialised health-care professionals in the future.

With the increasing sophistication and complexity of modern industrial processes, the workplace became a unique source of exposure to a wide range of potentially hazardous agents (e.g. radiation, metals, solvents and pesticides). The range of industrial diseases is correspondingly wide and includes cancers, skin and respiratory disorders, diseases of the blood and body organs, and disorders of the cardiovascular, peripheral and central nervous systems (see Raffle et al., 1987, for reviews).

Exposure standards and marginal toxicity

Guidelines with respect to 'allowable' exposure are established through wide-ranging discussions between management, trade unions and government regulatory agencies. The final standard adopted takes into account knowledge of toxic properties, the socio-economic costs of introducing the legislation and the likelihood of compliance. Compliance is achieved by monitoring and maintaining the agents's airborne concentration below a statutory 'threshold limit value' or TLV. This TLV specifies the average level of the agent that nearly all workers can be exposed to, on a long-term basis, without any adverse health effects being apparent. For certain agents periodic biological monitoring is required, but this is seen as complementing rather than replacing environmental monitoring. In the case of inorganic lead, for example, workers whose level of lead in blood exceeds 70 µg/dl must be excluded from the source of exposure until levels return to normal (Waldron, 1987).

As epidemiological and clinical methods improve, and toxicologists provide more detailed descriptions of a toxin's properties (e.g. the kinetics of absorption, distribution, metabolism and excretion), data emerge which serve to reduce TLVs. Although clinical toxicity remains a problem of serious concern in industrially poorly developed countries (Misra et al., 1985), in developed countries the preventive approach has been so successful that workers now rarely present with clinical signs of toxicity. As the more debilitating disorders came under control, research shifted to the early detection of disease (Grand-jean and Tarkowski, 1985).

Psychological Toxicology

One rapidly growing area of occupational medicine concerned with marginal toxicity is behavioural or psychological toxicology. The central aim of this work is the detection and description of central nervous system (CNS) disorders due to toxic insult (see Feldman *et al.*, 1980, for a recent review). This interest in CNS dysfunction took root in the 1960s and can be traced to three main trends. First, it was becoming quite clear that the brain, with its rich vascular supply, was a particularly sensitive target for toxins and their metabolites. Second, a worker's early complaints often took the form of symptoms indicative of CNS dysfunction (e.g. changes in affect, poor memory) and appeared to herald the more severe symptoms associated with over-exposure and toxic brain dysfunction. Third, psychological techniques were gaining acceptance by the medical community, perhaps through the successes of neuropsychology, and to many investigators seemed an ideal way in which to quantify CNS disorders in a functional non-invasive way (Hanninen, 1971, 1985; Seppalainen *et al.*, 1980; Weiss, 1983; Xintaras *et al.*, 1974).

The psychological techniques introduced quickly found a unique niche in the study of toxic reactions, and because it has long been suspected that chronic low-level exposure may have effects which go unrecognised by the affected workers (e.g. Hanninen, 1971), current research efforts are concerned with characterising the states of marginal CNS toxicity.

A review of assessment methods of CNS function reveals that the tests have predominantly been imported from clinical psychology. The preponderance of clinical tests is mainly due to their historically important role in the classification of patients with organic brain damage (Lezak, 1973) and it was assumed that such tests might help detect early toxicity. Initially the test batteries adopted were wide-ranging, drawing upon a multitude of clinical tests (e.g. Baker *et al.*, 1983; Cherry *et al.*, 1981; Grandjean *et al.*, 1978; Hanninen and Lindstrom, 1976; Hogstedt *et al.*, 1980; MacKay *et al.*, 1987; Valciukas and Lillis, 1980), although the nucleus of most test batteries has been drawn from the subtests of the ubiquitous Wechsler Adult Intelligence Scale and Wechsler Memory Scale. The dominance of clinically based tests continues and has found its most recent expression in the standard 'core' battery advocated by the World Health Organization (WHO), in conjunction with the National Institute of Occupational Safety and Health (NIOSH), in their attempt to standardise assessment of psychological toxicity (Johnson *et al.*, 1985).

Whilst test batteries have been constructed essentially to provide a basic level of screening for neurotoxicological effects, the long-term aims are to provide a means for the prospective monitoring of workers and evaluating the effectiveness of exposure reduction programs. In constructing their test batteries, investigators have been motivated to produce a short series of tests (normally lasting less than 60 minutes) because asymptomatic workers must be released from their normal production duties for testing. Although this time pressure obviously compromises the provision of a comprehensive assessment, it gives a strong impetus for developing short sensitive tests in which the microcomputer will play a substantial role.

Computerised neurotoxicological assessment

As with many areas of applied psychology, the widespread availability of cheap microcomputer systems has facilitated the development of computerised tests of psychological assessment. Many authors now use some microcomputer assessment in their studies of neurotoxic agents (Baker *et al.*, 1985; Cherry *et al.*, 1981; Iregren *et al.*, 1985), but with few exceptions (e.g. Stollery, 1986, 1987; Williamson and Teo, 1986; Williamson *et al.*, 1982) the tests are simple adaptations of the earlier clinical tests. For example, pencil-and-paper versions have simply been administered by a microcomputer which acts as an 'electronic scoreboard'. Baker and Letz (1986) have recently tabulated the main test batteries used in workplace neurotoxicological assessments, with particular emphasis on those which have been adapted for computerised administration. Although tests adapted from the clinical literature still feature predominantly, this form of automated testing offers several advantages over the traditional methods, especially when population samples are large. It has eliminated some of the more time-consuming aspects of test administration which, in turn, facilitates widespread testing of asymptomatic workers with suspected workplace toxicity. It has reduced the necessity of employing specially trained testing personnel in the data collection phase and has helped to create a standardised testing situation. Finally, it offers the hope of increasing comparability between different studies—one of the central aims of the WHO initiative (Johnson *et al.*, 1985).

From a theoretical point of view, however, there is little advantage merely in automating established clinical tests. First, the effectiveness of these tests for detecting states of marginal toxicity remains uncertain. Computerised tasks need to be developed which are more sensitive than clinically oriented tasks in detecting marginal CNS toxicity. Second, clinical tests are limited in terms of their capacity to characterise a deficit in functional terms. Frequently, they attempt to provide a global measure of functioning, and since the tasks are multi-faceted, making demands on many cognitive functions, it is not possible to identify specific underlying disorders of functioning. A priori, it is unlikely that neurotoxins give rise to global impairment of functioning and it becomes important to be able to specify a 'profile' of functional impairment for various toxins with some precision. The increased power offered by microcomputer-based assessment offers the prospect of developing the necessary tasks.

Our approach to the study of marginal toxicity has been from the perspective of 'normal' cognitive psychology rather than 'abnormal' clinical psychology (Stollery, 1985) and task construction draws on current theorising with its emphasis on multiple measures of performance and appropriate attention to the micro-structure of task performance. The tasks described below are an attempt to apply such techniques. However, much work remains to be done. What is required ultimately is a series of tasks, each of which allows a number

Table 5.1 Computerised tasks used in various studies

Electromagnetic fields—solvents	Lead—anaesthetic agents
Number search with STM load (10 min)	Syntactic reasoning (6 min)
Syntactic reasoning (10 min)	Delayed 5-choice RT (9 min)
Continuous 5-choice RT (20 min)	Category Search (2 min)
Semantic reasoning (5 min)	Visual spacial memory (5 min)
Mood checklist	Free recall (2 min)
	Mood checklist
50–60 min	20–30 min

of functionally independent but interacting cognitive systems to be examined in some detail. Test batteries for industrial use can then be formed by selecting from the overall series, selection being guided by suspected areas of functional difficulty or the need to explore possible reasons for impairment in further detail. The more precise 'targeting' of impairment achieved by this process can then be used to guide further study of marginal toxicity.

Microcomputer assessment of cognitive function

In our studies of suspected neurotoxic agents, we have used a Research Machine's Limited (RML, Oxford) 380Z microcomputer equipped with twin double-density disc drives, 56K memory and with a CP/M operating system. The tests have been programmed in the popular BASIC language to facilitate transportation to other computer systems, but limitations are inherent in the machine code routines used to provide millisecond timing. One disc drive contains the task materials and the programs for the psychological tasks, and the other drive is used to save raw data. A separate series of analysis programs process the raw data to provide multiple measures of performance as a function of various task parameters.

At present, stimulus presentation is limited to the visual modality: the task materials are presented on a 17-inch black-and-white video monitor and responses made by pressing keys on a standard keyboard. A large stimulus–response panel, placed adjacent to the monitor, is used in tests of serial reaction time and is currently the only peripheral device controlled by microcomputer. We have developed a wide range of tasks to assess the major cognitive functions of memory, attention, verbal and spatial skills. The tests have been designed primarily for use in field studies of asymptomatic workers, but have also proved useful in laboratory and clinical work.

Table 5.1 outlines the computerised tasks we have used in assessments of marginal toxicity. The construction and usefulness of these tasks is illustrated with reference to our research into the effects of exposure to inorganic lead,

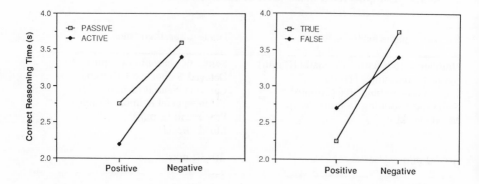

FIGURE 5.1   The general pattern of effects due to problem complexity on reasoning speed in the syntactic reasoning task.

(e.g. Stollery and Banks, 1985; Stollery *et al.*, in press), organic solvents (unpublished), the presence of anaesthetic agents in scavenged operating theatres (Stollery and Keen, 1987; Stollery *et al.*, 1988) and a laboratory-based study of power–frequency electromagnetic fields (Stollery, 1986, 1987). Not all the tests developed will be described and the following discussion deals with the 30-minute sequence we have used in industrial studies.

Syntactic reasoning. This task is a version of one used by Baddeley and Hitch (1978) to explore the role of working memory in a verbal reasoning task. In this task, subjects decide whether a sentence correctly describes the order of a pair of letters (e.g. A is followed by B: AB). The sentences are phrased in a positive or negative form, with the verb in either the active or passive voice, and can either correctly or incorrectly describe the order of the letters (see Stollery, 1986, for further details).

Current task analysis involves assessment of the following performance measures at 2-minute intervals during a 6-minute task: trials attempted (including errors), number of errors, correct reaction time and the variability of correct reaction times. The linguistic aspects of the task permit more detailed study and have proved particularly useful: speed and accuracy are assessed as a function of the truth, voice and negation conditions. In normal populations, distinctive patterns of results are found: strong reliable main effects are seen for the voice and negation factors, and the truth of a statement interacts with the presence of negatives. Figure 5.1 shows the effects of these factors on correct reaction times in the absence of toxic agents (Stollery *et al.*, 1988). This robust pattern of effects (see also Baddeley and Hitch, 1978; Stollery, 1986) forms the basis for exploring possible effects of toxic agents.

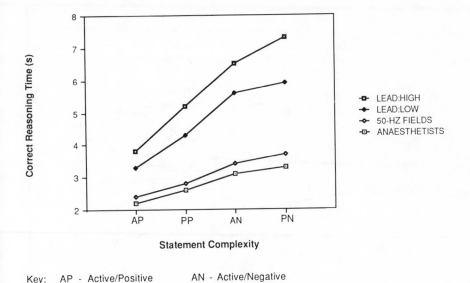

Key: AP - Active/Positive   AN - Active/Negative
       PP - Passive/Positive   PN - Passive/Negative

FIGURE 5.2   Variations in reasoning speed as a function of problem complexity in three studies.

Figure 5.2 shows correct reasoning times as a function of the voice and negation conditions from three seperate studies. In our field studies of occupational exposure to inorganic lead, the more exposed workers showed a slight slowing in speed but, more critically, this slowing tended to become progressively greater as difficulty of the reasoning problems increased; particularly for 'false' statements (e.g. A does not follow B: BA). This result helped to localise the functional impairment to the central processing requirements of the task, rather than the stimulus encoding, working memory and response components. Both our laboratory study of power–frequency electric currents (Stollery, 1986) and our field studies of anaesthetists occupationally exposed to trace concentrations of anaesthetic agents (Stollery et al., 1988) conformed to a cross-over design and only overall levels of performance are shown in Figure 5.2. In both of these studies, correct reaction times were considerably faster than in our study of inorganic lead, but nevertheless the main effects of voice and negation are clearly evident. While we did not observe poorer reasoning following anaesthetic exposure, exposure to power–frequency electric currents showed independent exposure effects for the voice and negation factors. Interestingly, these effects were only observed on the second day of the two-day experiment, possibly reflecting a state-dependent transfer of learning. Finally, in our study

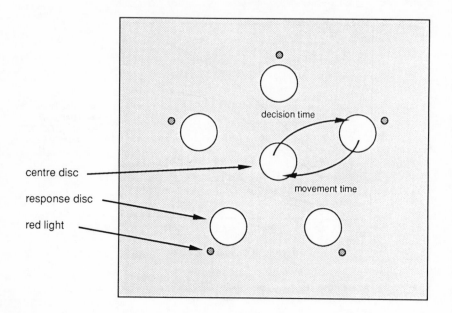

FIGURE 5.3   The five-choice serial reaction time board.

of the long-term sequelae of an accidental workplace solvent intoxication, we observed an overall slowing of reasoning speed, but more importantly the critical finding was a difficulty with the conceptually more complex negative problems.

Delayed serial reaction time. In this version of the classic five-choice serial reaction time task (Figure 5.3), subjects extinguish a light by touching its adjacent response disc (decision and movement time) and return to a centre disc to initiate a new trial (movement time). In laboratory studies we have used a 20-minute task in which the next light is triggered immediately the centre disc is touched (Stollery, 1987). For industrial studies we have developed a 9-minute task which incorporates a randomly varying delay of up to 4 seconds between the touching of the central disc and the presentation of the next light (Stollery *et al.*, 1988).

Task analysis currently involves the examination of some 12 performance measures (e.g. correct decision times, variability, gap rates) as a function of time on the task and duration of waiting for light illimination, although analysis of performance is undergoing further development. Once again, distinctive patterns of results are observed. With respect to the duration of waiting, for example, decision times are longer when the light is illuminated

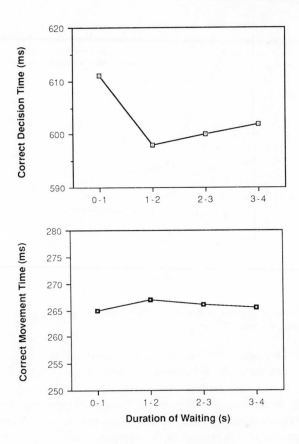

FIGURE 5.4 General pattern of decision and movement times in the serial reaction time task as a function of the duration of waiting for light illumination: anaesthetic study.

within 1 second of completing the movement response, but movement times are not affected (Figure 5.4). Similarly, decision gaps (extra-long decision times) are also more frequent after short periods of waiting, but movement gaps are not (Figure 5.5). These typical patterns of performance have proved particularly useful in specifying impairment due to lead exposure. Workers with blood lead levels in excess of 40 µg/dl (the High group) were 'impaired' on most aspects of performance, except errors and movement gaps, but the performance patterns indicated that this impairment related mainly to the sensorimotor aspects of performance. For example, decision times did not slow down disproportionately as a function of task duration, and the slowing observed on the decision and movement phases of the task was not adversely affected by the duration of waiting for light presentation (Figure 5.6).

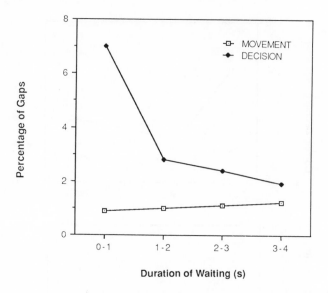

FIGURE 5.5   General pattern of decision and movement gap rates as a function of duration of waiting: anaesthetic study.

Category search. This task, which examines the speed and accuracy of semantic classifications, was specially developed for field studies. Subjects classify a sequence of 80 nouns with respect to membership of a semantic category (e.g. Birds), normally in 2 minutes. The category nouns comprise equal numbers of typical and atypical instances which are classified in two discrete lists of distractor nouns: (a) nouns related to the category through a near superordinate (e.g. other animal nouns); and (b) nouns unrelated to the category (e.g. century).

Task analysis consists of analysing speed, accuaracy and variability as a function of the 'truth × distractor type' and the 'category typicality × distractor type' factorial designs. In general, category exemplars are classified faster than unrelated distractors, which in turn are classified faster than related distractors (Figure 5.7). For category exemplars, typical members are classified faster than atypical members, and both types of category member are slowed by the presence of related distractors, particularly atypical members (Figure 5.8). Again, these distinctive patterns of performance are used in the specification of the nature of functional impairments.

While occupational exposure to anaesthetic agents did not impair category-search performance, performance was clearly impaired by lead exposure, and examination of performance patterns was again crucial in establishing that impairment related mainly to the sensorimotor aspects of performance rather than semantic processing per se. For example, the classification of atypical

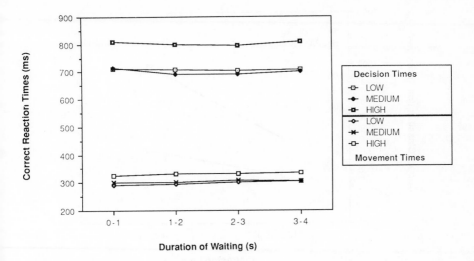

FIGURE 5.6 Decision and movement times in the serial reaction time task as a function of duration of waiting and level of lead exposure.

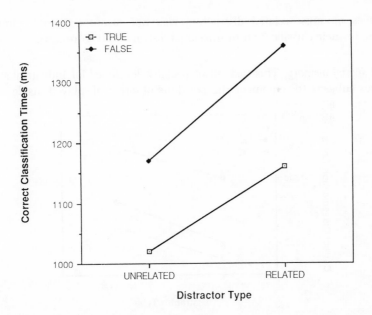

FIGURE 5.7 Classification of category nouns (TRUE) and distractor nouns (FALSE) in the category search task: lead study.

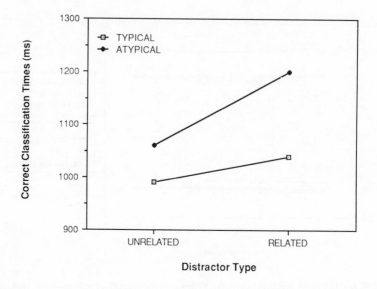

FIGURE 5.8   Classification of typical and atypical instances as a function of distractor relatedness: lead study.

instances amongst related distractors was not disproportionately impaired relative to their classification in unrelated distractors (Figure 5.9).

Visual spatial memory. This task, also specially developed for industrial studies, requires subjects to remember the positions of circles displayed inside a large

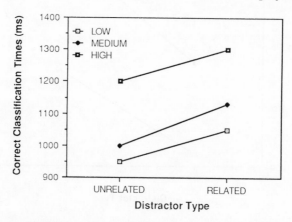

FIGURE 5.9   Classification speed of atypical instances as a function of distractor relatedness and level of lead exposure.

square on the video monitor. Shortly after the circles (memory-set) have been erased, a question mark probe is presented and subjects decide whether the probe marks the location of an item in the memory-set, i.e. true–false recognition memory. Five replications of the factorial combination of probe truth (true/false) and memory-set size (2, 4 or 6 circles), with a constant 1-second delay between memory-set and probe, are normally completed in about 5 minutes. The delay between erasure of the memory-set and presentation of the probe can be factorially combined with the other conditions, but this feature has yet to be used in industrial studies because of time limitations.

Task analysis consists of examining speed, accuracy and variability as a function of the truth × memory-set factorial design. The typical finding is that speed and accuracy decline as the size of the memory-set increases: Figure 5.10 shows these patterns based on our study of anaesthetic exposure. Once again, lead workers tended to respond more slowly, but because the magnitude of this slowing did not vary as a function of memory-set size the findings provided further evidence of a simple slowing of sensorimotor reaction time.

Category search recall. This task requires subjects to write down as many nouns as possible, in 2 minutes, from the category-search task described earlier. It is a delayed recall task since the visual spatial memory task is interposed between the category-search and free-recall components. Correct recall protocols follow a clear pattern since recall levels decline progressively in the order: typical instances, atypical instances, related distractors and unrelated distractors (Figure 5.11). Once again, while anaesthetic exposure did not impair recall, the critical effect for workers with high blood lead levels was the poorer recall of distractors; recall levels for the category nouns did not differ significantly. Thus, the difficulty in remembering information was specific to nouns which were not of central importance to the classification task and a general impairment in recall was not indicated.

To summarise, distinctive patterns of performance are observed in each of the tasks described above; the patterns serving as frameworks for understanding why performance is impaired following neurotoxic exposure. It has been proposed that in order to characterise deficits in functional terms, it is essential to examine qualitative and quantitative changes in performance. The former changes are particularly important since they play a central role in characterising the deficit in functional terms. Not only do they provide insight into why performance was impaired, but they also give us valuable information about the vulnerability of certain functions to toxic insult. Of course, our theoretical understanding of any particular pattern of task impairment may well permit several hypotheses for the locus of 'functional' impairment to be specified. In these cases, more 'precise' targeting of the tasks may help to resolve difficulties

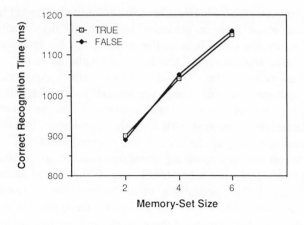

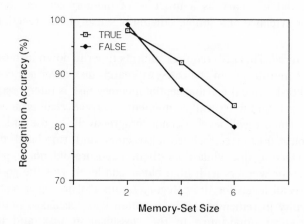

FIGURE 5.10   Overall recognition speed and accuracy in the visual–spatial memory task: anaesthetic study.

of interpretation, although the cooperative and multi-functional nature of cognition implies that functions may never be fully isolated from each other.

The description of neurotoxic impairment necessarily involves some consensus on what constitutes exposure and, given the complex nature of biological systems, several 'exposure monitoring' strategies naturally coexist. Thus, environmental monitoring provides measures of day-to-day exposure, whereas biological monitoring provides details about the biotransformation and excretion of the toxin over periods of days to months. Techniques for estimating cumulative exposure over several years have only recently been proposed (Fidler *et al.*, 1987; Scott and Chettle, 1986) and as yet there appears to be no simple solution to the problem of assessing the relative contributions of acute,

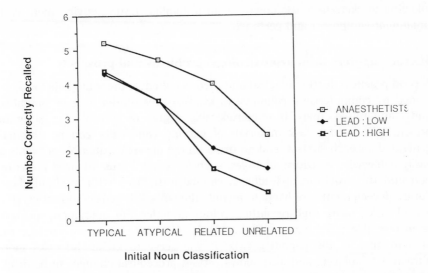

FIGURE 5.11   The influence of initial noun classification on delayed free-recall scores in two studies.

recent and chronic exposure to the development of neurotoxic reactions. However, it is suggested that closer attention to the micro-structure of task performance may improve these chances. In this context, the microcomputer provides a convenient, adaptable and portable 'laboratory' in which the necessary psychological experiments for addressing these issues can be performed.

Microphobia

We have found the provision of a familiarisation session to be an extremely important prelude to the formal testing session. Many people are initially wary of 'computers' and may not perform optimally without familiarisation. In the session, subjects acquaint themselves with the keyboard and task procedures by completing a shortened test battery. Speed and accuracy information is provided in the syntactic reasoning and visual spatial memory tasks to encourage fast accurate responding, and subjects are encouraged to press 'wrong' keys in order to acquaint themselves with the instructions shown when wrong key presses occur during formal testing. The purpose of this practice is not to eliminate task learning, but to provide a firm basis on which future learning can take place. We have also found the session to be an ideal one in which to develop a rapport with subjects and to collect basic personal details. This prelude to the formal testing session helps reduce test anxiety by allowing workers to 'settle down' in an unfamiliar testing environment with unfamiliar equipment and personel.

Microcomputers in neurotoxicology: problems and prospects

Several practical, methodological and theoretical advantages may obviously be gained by computerising cognitive tasks. Test presentation can be optimised and standardised, there is a considerable degree of control over stimulus presentation factors, task materials of varying complexity can be uniquely generated for each subject, and accurate timing of rapid sequences of events is easily achieved. Procedural changes, such as paced versus unpaced presentation and the provision of feedback, can be introduced with minimal effort. Future developments are likely to include the embellishment of formal psychological tasks, using high-resolution colour graphics and animation, to make them resemble video games. While this development should not sacrifice the original aims of the cognitive task, it will serve to make the tasks more attractive to subjects and also allows certain procedural changes to be incorporated more naturally. In certain cases the provision of immediate feedback can serve to increase task interest, and performance may become optimal through self-competition, but task difficulty may need to be interactively adjusted to avoid the negative effects on performance of excessive failures. As this game approach to task development continues, assessment of metacognitive skills is likely to gain increased attention.

The ability of the microcomputer to rapidly store large quantities of information allows raw data to be stored on a trial-by-trial basis. The saving of raw data implies that appropriate task analysis programs be developed and it is essential these are developed in parallel with the tasks themselves. The analysis programs can then be used to derive the multiple measures of performance used in the micro-analysis of task performance. Another obvious advantage of storing raw data is that it permits future advances in theory and data analysis techniques to be fully exploited.

The machine interface is at present poor and the keyboard represents a major barrier to widespread applications. Additional response devices such as touch-sensitive screens, joysticks, graphics tablets and specialised response panels need to be developed further. Sensory systems other than vision (e.g. touch, sound) are currently difficult to assess, and the expressive elements of responding are also difficult to capture with current response formats. Improvements in the quality of current voice synthesisers would allow sophisticated auditory material (e.g. text) to be presented and would increase the range of cognitive tasks which could be adapted for the microcomputer. If successful, the development of automatic speech recognition systems would have wide-ranging repercussions. The availability of standardised programming languages, incorporating machine code routines for millisecond timing, a variety of experimental designs, randomisation, stimulus construction and presentation, would also greatly facilitate the application of microcomputer-based cognitive assessment.

As methodologies become more sophisticated and theoretical perspectives evolve, it is natural to expect that the tools of the psychotoxicologist will undergo revision. Notwithstanding the problems of existing data interpretation, research findings in neurotoxicology are accumulating at such a rapidly accelerating rate that unless theoretical perspectives are evolved to organise these findings they will become impossible to assimilate (Stollery, 1988). The use of microcomputers will facilitate this process and promises to revolutionise workplace assessment over the next decade. It also seems clear that the ever-decreasing costs of microcomputer systems will play a not insubstantial role in developing methods for the detection of marginal toxicity in work environments.

References

Baddeley, A. and Hitch, G. J. (1978). Working memory. In G. Bower (ed.), *The psychology of Learning and Motivation: Advances in Research and Theory*, Vol 3. New York: Academic Press.

Baker, E. L. and Letz, R. (1986). Neurobehavioural testing in monitoring hazardous workplace exposures, *Journal of Occupational Medicine*, **28**, 987–990.

Baker, E. L., Feldman, R. G., White, R. F. *et al.* (1983). Monitoring neurotoxins in industry: Development of a neuro-behavioural test battery, *Journal of Occupational Medicine*, **25**, 125–130.

Baker, E. L., Letz, R. A. and Fidler, A. T. (1985). A computer-administered neurobehavioural evaluation system for occupational and environmental epidemology, *Journal of Occupational Medicine*, **27**, 206–212.

Cherry, N., Venables, H. and Waldron, H. A. (1981). *A Test Battery to Measure the Behavioural Effects of Neurotoxic Substances*. TUC Centenary Institute of Occupational Health, London.

Feldman, R. G., Ricks, N. L. and Baker, E. L. (1980). Neuropsychological effects of industrial toxins: a review, *American Journal of Industrial Medicine*, **1**, 211–227.

Fidler, A. T., Baker, E. L. and Letz, R. E. (1987). Estimation of long term exposure to mixed solvents from questionnaire data: a tool for epidemiological investigations, *British Journal of Industrial Medicine*, **44**, 133–141.

Grandjean, P., Arnvig, E. and Beckmann, J. (1978). Psychological dysfunctions in lead-exposed workers, *Scandinavian Journal of Work Environment and Health*, **4**, 295–303.

Grandjean, P. and Tarkowski, S. (1985). Preventative aspects of neurobehavioural research. In *Environmental Health 3: Neurobehavioural Methods in Occupational and Environmental Health*, pp. 1–3. Copenhagen: World Health Organisation.

Hanninen, H. (1971). Psychological picture of manifest and latent carbon disulphide poisoning, *British Journal of Industrial Medicine*, **28**, 374–381.

Hanninen, H. (1985). Twenty-five years of behavioural toxicology within occupational medicine: A personal account, *American Journal of Industrial Medicine*, **7**, 19–30.

Hanninen, H. and Lindstrom, K. (1976). *Behavioural Test Battery for Toxicopsychological Studies*. Helsinki: Institute of Occupational Health.

Hogstedt, C., Hane, M. and Axelson, O. (1980). Diagnostic and health care aspects of workers exposed to solvents. In C. Zenz, (ed.), *Developments in Occupational Medicine*.

London: Year Book Medical Publishers.

Iregren, A., Gamberale, F. and Kjellberg, A. (1985). A Microcomputer-based behavioural testing system. In *Environmental Health 3: Neurobehavioural Methods in Occupational and Environmental Health*, pp. 75–79. Copenhagen: World Health Organization.

Johnson, B. L., Anger, W. K. and Xintaras, C. (1985). Progress report on the WHO/ NIOSH neurotoxicology programme. In *Environmetal Health 6: Neurobehavioural Methods in Occupational and Environmental Health: Symposium Report.*, pp. 6–10. World Health Organiztation/Commission of the European Communities.

Lee, W. R. (1981). Developments in education in occupational medicine, *American Journal of Industrial Medicine*, **2**, 203–208.

Lezak, M. (1973). *Neuropsychological Assessment*, 2nd edn. New York: Oxford University Press.

MacKay, C. J., Campbell, L., Samuel, A. M., Alderman, K. J., Idzikowski, C., Wilson, H. K. and Gompertz, D. (1987). Behavioural changes during exposure to 1,1,1-trichlorethane: time-course and relationship to blood solvent levels. *American Journal of Industrial Medicine*, **11**, 223–239.

Misra, U. K., Nag, D., Khan, W. A. and Ray, P. K. (1985). Clinical neurotoxicology in Indian context. In *Environmental Health 3: Neurobehavioural Methods in Occupational and Environmental Health*, pp. 4–8. Copenhagen: World Health Organization.

Raffle, P. A. B., Lee, W. R., MaCallum, R. I. and Murray, R. (1987). *Hunter's Diseases of Occupations*, London: Hodder & Stoughton.

Scott, M. C. and Chettle, D. R. (1986). In vivo elemental analysis in occupational medicine. *Scandinavian Journal of Work Environment and Health*, **12**, 81–96.

Seppalainen, A. M., Lindstrom, K. and Martelin, T. (1980). Neurological and psychological picture of solvent poisoning. *American Journal of Industrial Medicine*, **1**, 31–42.

Stollery, B. T. (1985). Psychological toxicology: New methods for detecting subclinical effects. In *Environmental Health 3: Neurobehavioural Methods in Occupational and Environmental Health*, pp. 80–85. Copenhagen: World Health Organization.

Stollery, B. T. (1986). Effects of 50-Hz electric currents on mood and verbal reasoning skills. *British Journal of Industrial Medicine*, **43**, 339–349.

Stollery, B. T. (1987). Effects of 50-Hz electric currents on vigilance and concentration. *British Journal of Industrial Medicine*, **44**, 111–118.

Stollery, B. T. (1988). Neurotoxic exposure and memory function. In M. M. Gruneberg, P. Morris and R. N. Sykes (eds), *Practical Aspects of Memory: Current Research and Issues*, Vol 2, pp. 242–247. Chichester: Wiley.

Stollery, B. T. and Banks, H. A. (1985). Cognitive functioning in lead workers: preliminary report on a longitudinal study. In *Heavy Metals in the Environment*. Edinburgh: C.E.C. Consultants Ltd.

Stollery, B. T. and Keen, R. I. (1987). Cognitive functioning in anaesthetists. *British Journal of Anaesthesia*, **59**, 655p.

Stollery, B. T., Broadbent, D. E., Lee, W. R., Healy, T. E. J., Keen, R. I. and Beatty, P. (1988). Mood and cognitive functioning in anaesthetists working in actively scavenged operating theatres. *British Journal of Anaesthesia*, **61**, 446–455.

Stollery, B. T., Banks, H. A., Broadbent, D. E. and Lee W. R. (in press). Cognitive functioning in lead workers. *British Journal of Industrial Medicine*.

Valciukas, J. A. and Lillis, R. (1980). Psychometric techniques in environmental research. *Environmental Research*, **21**, 257–297.

Waldron, H. A. (1987). Metals. In P. A. B. Raffle, W. R. Lee, R. I. McCallum and R. Murray (eds), *Hunter's Diseases of Occupations*, pp. 239–296. London: Hodder & Stoughton.

Weiss, B. (1983). Behavioural toxicology and environmental health science. *American Psychologist*, 1174–1187.

Williamson, A. M. and Teo, R. K. C. (1986). Neurobehavioural effects of occupational exposure to lead. *British Journal of Industrial Medicine*, **43**, 374–380.

Williamson, A. M., Teo, R. K. C. and Sanderson, J. (1982). Occupational mercury exposure and its consequences for behaviour. *International Archives of Occupational and Environmental Health*, **50**, 273–286.

Xintaras, C., Johnson, B. L. and de Groot, I. (1974). *Behavioural Toxicology: Early Detection of Occupational Hazards*. Washington, D.C: USDHEW (NIOSH) Publication No. 74–126.

Part III

Human Performance Testing: Client Assessment

Part III develops the theme of performance testing, this time with regard to examining the capabilities and processing strategies of individuals or groups. The concept is the same as before—present tasks to individuals using the computer and record their responses. There is even some overlap in the actual tasks used. However, as will be seen, the design of the tasks and their use in particular contexts stem from a different philosophy.

In some cases, as in Chapter 6, the aim is to discover the capabilities of people with severe physical disability. In such cases the micro can provide a window between these people and the outside world which allows them to look out and take advantage of what it has to offer, and others look in and observe the intellectual capacities which may be difficult to appreciate under normal circumstances.

The chapter on micros in neuropsychology shows how micros are changing the face of assessment of deficits resulting from brain lesions. This kind of work is important for individual patients because only after their cognitive deficits have been assessed can retraining be appropriately targeted. There is also a major research component to this work because mapping brain lesions to performance deficits can provide important clues to the organisation of cognitive functions in the brain. Often the extent and location of the lesion cannot be precisely specified; even in these cases, obtaining a profile of performance deficits can illuminate the modularity of cognitive functioning.

In some cases, as illustrated by the chapter on anxiety and cognition, the purpose is to try to understand the nature of some psychological disorder. Groups of anxious patients can be compared across a range of tests with relevant controls to help determine how far their cognitive style predisposes them to anxiety or follows as a consequence of it.

This part concludes with a chapter containing some general observations on the role of micros in performance testing and an examination of the directions which this kind of work seems to be taking. In particular, the value of micros is seen to lie in their ability to obtain data from sequences of trials which would not be possible with conventional apparatus. It is also noted that micros have an important role to play not merely in acquiring performance data but also in running simulations of processes which are presumed to underlie these.

CHAPTER 6

Psychologial assessment and severe physical disability

SARAH WILSON

Background to the project

One of the principles of psychometric assessment is that those carrying out the assessment should have established a reliable method of communication with the client so that they may be unequivocally certain of the responses they collect. Conventional tests can require the client to speak, write, draw or manoeuvre objects and sometimes may require such responses at speed. According to the pattern of impairments suffered, the physically disabled individual may find such methods of communication difficult, if not impossible. For the psychologist there is the problem in interpreting test performance of deciding to what extent cognitive abilities are confounded by physical disabilities.

The answer to this problem is to develop alternative forms of communication. In some cases this is quite simple, the obvious one being that when a client cannot write they could perhaps dictate their answers; however, if timing is an element of the test, then the interpretation of results will be affected. Pointing can be used in multiple-choice tests or a letter board can be used to spell out answers if speech is impaired. Reynell (1970) and Shakespeare (1975) both suggest that in the most disabled cases head nodding or shaking or eye pointing can be used. These methods are dependent on the client having reliable control over head or eye movements. Since both Reynell and Shakespeare gave this advice, there has been a proliferation of aids to communication for disabled people spurred on by developments in microtechnology and these are undoubtedly proving useful as an aid to assessment. Most tests are standardised for one method of presentation and one method of response, and changing one or both of these may make the validity of the use of the normative data questionable. In order to make assessments quantitatively as

Microcomputers, Psychology and Medicine
Edited by R. West, M. Christie and J. Weinman
© 1990 by John Wiley & Sons Ltd

well as qualitatively interpretable then the development of a system where presentation and response collection can be standardised, or as near standardised as possible, for use with severe physical disability seems desirable.

People with severe physical disabilities, particularly when normal methods of communication are not feasible, can be very easily labelled, both by lay people and professional staff, as mentally handicapped. In some cases this may be accurate, in others not. There have been several celebrated cases of people with severe physical disability being wrongfully assumed to be mentally handicapped until an effective method of communication was found with them. One case is that of Anne McDonald (Crossley and McDonald, 1982), who was found to be of at least normal intelligence.

The Royal Hospital and Home, Putney (formerly the Royal Hospital and Home for Incurables) cares for some 300 adults who, on admission, suffer severe physical disability. It was an awareness of the difficulties using conventional techniques of identifying cognitive abilities and deficits in members of the hospital population that prompted the initiation of the project to develop a computer-based psychological assessment system.

Why computer-based assessment?

There have been a number of reviews published on the advantages and disadvantages of the use of computers in psychological assessment in general (Thompson and Wilson, 1982; Sampson, 1983; Bartram and Bayliss, 1984; French, 1986). This section will, however, concentrate on the advantages and problems for this specialist application.

One of the primary reasons for use of computer-based assessment with a physically disabled population is the ease with which communication can be enabled between the disabled individual and the microcomputer. There are a range of devices available commercially, although within the UK the majority of these have been developed for use with the Acorn BBC microcomputer. If help and advice are available from somebody with skills in electronics then the construction of response media for specific requirements can be accomplished and not necessarily at great cost. When using conventional tests with severely disabled adults the client may find the act of responding very effortful and this will add to the stress of the test. The use of computer-based tests allows the development and application of response media that utilise the actions that clients can perform most easily; the objective being to make it as easy for the disabled client to respond as it is for the able-bodied.

Testing people with severe physical disabilities can be very time-consuming; due to various factors associated with their disability or illness, they can take far longer than an able-bodied person to complete a test. Test protocol permitting, the computer can 'wait' for as long as is necessary for the client to complete the test, which can be far less stressful for the human examiner. Also the clients can become anxious if they feel they are keeping the examiner waiting and may subsequently not perform as well as they might.

Computers have no body language. This may seem an obvious statement, but it is a very important consideration. It is very easy to subconsciously cue somebody, particularly if they take a long time to answer, by changes in posture, gesture or tone of voice. The use of the micro ensures a standardised presentation of the test material every time it is used.

Another problem which the use of the microcomputer can overcome is difficulty in interpreting clients' responses. For example, in testing somebody with severely dysarthric speech, the examiner's interpretation of the client's speech sounds could be biased by beliefs about the client's capabilities. Similar problems can occur with the use of other methods of response, such as eye-pointing. The application of a response device with the computer that the client can use without difficulty avoids such problems.

If the clients' abilities to operate response media are extremely limited and they are able to operate one or two switches at most, then again the microcomputer comes into its own. The number of choices the individual can select from can be increased by using a feature such as a moving cursor on the computer screen. The clients respond by operating their response device when the cursor reaches the answer of choice.

Microcomputer-based techniques can also be used in the assessment of individuals who need material to be presented aurally. This can be done through the use of computer-controlled audio tape systems or through the use of synthetic speech. The latter varies greatly in quality but fortunately good synthetic speech is becoming relatively cheaper as time goes on. The advantage of using either method is to give an entirely standardised presentation of the material every time as well as being a source of relief to the examiner's vocal cords! The administration of the aural presentation can be controlled through the software and can permit as many repeats of the material as necessary.

Another advantage is that questions can be presented one at a time, precluding the possibility that answers may be recorded in the wrong place. It also prevents the client misreading material from one question into another. Tests presented on the computer screen are usually easier to read as the print is larger than in standard forms of tests.

There are also limitations to the use of computers for psychological assessment. One is that the complexity of graphics used is dependent on the resolution of the visual display unit in the computer system. Bartram et al. (1987) recommended a minimum resolution of 512×512 for using well-defined oblique lines, and for complex graphics involving fine detail and curved lines a minimum resolution of 1024×1024. The automation of tests in which the standard form tests behaviour in three dimensions in space is problematic as a computer test can only be in two dimensions (although depth can be represented by the use of perspective).

Another disadvantage, particulary when developing new tests, is the necessity for collecting normative data on the test. However, this may be circumvented if the requirement is for comparison of a particular client's performance on subsequent occasions rather then making comparison with the norm.

The advent of substitutes for the 'qwerty' keyboard designed for use by people with physical disabilities can make possible the application of test material which uses open-ended questions. Depending on severity of disability, however, typing in answers can be a very laborious process. Furthermore if the test being used involves memory, then there is evidence that the act of key pressing may interfere with recall (Wilson, 1987). In order to make the test battery as widely applicable as possible, the best strategy is to use tests which can be presented in either a multiple-choice format or with precisely defined answers such as a number string. The employment of this strategy also means that the test can be scored by the computer. In the case of open answers, scoring these demands an expert systems approach, and this is limited by the state of the art in the use of natural languages.

Overall, there are many more advantages to use of the microcomputer in the psychological assessment of people with severe physical disabilities than there are disadvantages. One factor that has not been mentioned so far is that, unlike many devices used as aids for the disabled, microcomputers are not exclusively used by this group; they are widely used in society and their use bears prestige rather than stigma. The acceptability of the microcomputer to this client group is not a problem.

The chief reason for the use of the microcomputer is that is enables in some instances an objective psychological assessment of indviduals to take place that was not hitherto possible.

The project at the Royal Hospital and Home, Putney

The work on this project may be divided broadly into three areas; developments in hardware, developments in software and evaluation.

Hardware

Initially the system was based on a Apple II microcomputer, but three years ago we changed to using Acorn BBC machines because of the greater ease with which colour, graphics and sound can be used. The basic system consists of the microcomputer, medium-resolution colour monitor, dual disc drive (although for most functions a single drive will suffice) and printer. The system also includes a range of special response media to enable communication between people with severe physical disabilities and the machine, which have been developed as part of the project.

It was mentioned earlier that a number of special devices are now available commercially to help physically disabled people to use computers. We have not made use of these (as yet) for several reasons. First, they were not available in the early stages of the project. Second, there is the problem that different devices interface with the microcomputer through different inputs, and modifications have to be made to software to cope with this; no single device, as yet, can cope with all disabilities. Third, the commercially available devices, particulary those which are intended as substitute qwerty keyboards, tend to have rather more switches/keys than are needed for testing and the redundant keys could prove a source of distraction. Lastly of course there is cost; having had to develop the expertise for response media design and production, it is cheaper for us to produce our own devices.

Our response media all interface with the microcomputer via an analogue-to-digital converter built in to the computer. This means that whatever device the client uses, if it has the requisite number of switches for the test, all that has to be done is to plug it in. Most of the clients can use keyboard-type devices. The largest one consists of a row of ten pressure pads, 3.5 cm wide × 10.5 cm long; the pads are separated by 1.5-mm-wide baffles which extend 1.0 cm above the height of the pads and prevent accidental lateral movement from one key to another, essential when assessing people with problems such as tremor.

Experience has taught us that when multiple switches are used they have to be arranged in a row rather than in a matrix as, for a variety of reasons, the switches in the bottom row tend to be operated by the client when aiming for a switch on the top row. We have other keyboards with rows of three or four pressure pads and several single switches developed for coping with different sorts of disabilities; for example, one that can be operated by a slight movement of a finger, and another for clients who have no reliable control over individual digits but who can bring the whole hand down on the switch. For those who have no reliable use of their limbs but who have control of their tongue a buccal switch could be used (Parker, 1981). The general principle is to identify a movement over which the client has reliable control, or at least for which reliable control can be established, and make use of it.

The system described so far can be used for the presentation of visual and auditory stimuli. The aural presentation of speech sounds can also be required as some tests use spoken words or there is the problem of testing people with deficits in visual acuity. In order to assist with such problems, two forms of computer-controlled aural presentation have been developed.

The first of these is a computer-controlled tape deck for presenting multiple-choice tests (Wylie et al., 1984). The tape is controlled through software. Each question and its multiple-choice answers are played through. If the client does not respond by operating his or her switch when the answer of choice is heard, then at the end of the answers the tape is automatically wound back to the beginning of the question and it is repeated. The system will repeat individual questions as many times as necessary for the client to respond. If the client does not know the answer, he or she is given the opportunity to pass. The same principle applies to the instructions at the beginning of the test. As each section is read aloud the client signifies comprehension by operating a switch at the end of the section; to hear the instructions repeated the client does nothing. No matter how many times individual questions are repeated the presentation is always standard. The problem with this system is that the test material has to be recorded and perfect renditions of questions may not always be achieved first time.

The voice-over system described above was developed at a time when good-quality synthetic speech was beyond our budget; it is now more affordable. We have made use of a cheap (£14) off-the-shelf ROM, which includes numbers in its 'vocabulary', to produce an aurally presented digit span test. Again the presentation is completely standardised, if lacking in prosodic qualities. The use of synthetic speech can now be superseded by digitised speech.

Software

The software for the project has all been written in the high-level computing language BASIC. The test software developed can be divided into two categories: direct transcriptions of 'pen and paper' tests and tests developed specially for computer-based presentation. The test battery is primarily aimed at providing a neuropsychological assessment although a personality measure has also been included. The initial strategy in the development of the battery was to produce automated equivalents of existing tests. The rationale for this was that once the comparability of the two forms of the test were established use could be made of existing normative data. This strategy, however, has its limitations since many tests are either not amenable to automation, or may be amenable to automation but not suitable for use with this particular population. Memory tests, for example, are particularly problematic since most use free recall. The answer to this problem is the development of new tests.

Our experience has shown that computer-based tests for use with severely physically disabled adults should conform, whenever possible, to a number of criteria:

1   They should be operable from a single switch whenever possible, although the option of using a bank of switches (if appropriate) should be available since this may be preferable for more able clients.
2   To avoid confounding motor and cognitive disabilities, time should not be a factor in the test. We are, however, experimenting in one test with pacing presentation according to the individual client's reaction time.
3   The fewer instructions to the client that are needed, the better.
4   Presentation of material should be clear, bold and attractive.

5   In the design of a test, it is important to ensure as far as possible that performance on a measure of one particular aspect of behaviour is not being confounded by deficits in another aspect of behaviour. For example, when the answers to a multiple-choice test presented in two columns side-by-side, some individuals were observed as having the tendency to visually neglect one column of answers which depressed their score.

The test battery developed to date includes: vocabulary scales, a vigilance task, a card sorting test, a line bisection task, tests of visuospatial orientation and organisation and a personality test. There is also a program to help train the most severely disabled individuals to use their response medium reliably. The test battery is still in the process of development; we are particularly concerned with the problems of assessing individuals who suffer combined severe physical and cognitive disabilities as can be found, for example, following severe brain injury.

Evaluation

Having well-designed hardware and test software is of no consequence unless they actually work together to produce the desired result. As well as design and development of hardware and software it is axiomatic that evaluation of the sytem should also be considered. The members of the population on which the system is being evaluated are all severely physically disabled adults and include diagnostic groups such as multiple sclerosis, head injury, stroke, Parkinson's disease, spinal injury, cerebral palsy and rheumatoid conditions.

First of all the evaluation of software: a number of authors have published studies where comparison has been made of automated against standard versions of tests (e.g. Calvert and Waterfall, 1982; Wilson *et al.*, 1982; Watts *et al.*, 1982; Beaumont and French, 1987). On the whole correlations between automated and standard forms of tests are high and comparable with the test–retest reliability for the standard forms of the test. For example, Beaumont and French (1987) found a correlation of 0.90 between automated and standard forms of the Mill Hill Vocabulary Scale synonyms in a study using psychiatric patients. Wilson *et al.* (1982), in an early study from this project using an Apple II-based system, found a correlation of 0.87 for the same test; Watts *et al.* (1982), using a system incorporating a slide projector, found correlations of between 0.82 and 0.87 when testing an elderly group. Beaumont and French (1987) also compared automated and standard presentations of the Standard Progressive Matrices; they found an overall correlation of 0.84. Watts *et al* (1982) found correlations of between 0.83 and 0.87, and Calvert and Waterfall (1982), who were also using a system incorporating a slide projector to test student nurses, found correlations of between 0.82 and 0.96. Similar findings have been reported for personality tests (Ridgway *et al.*, 1982; Beaumont and French, 1987).

From these findings, it is reasonable to assume that similarly good results will be achieved with the current system. A recent study carried out with the BBC-based version of the Mill Hill Vocabulary Scale synonyms gave an overall correlation between automated and standard forms of 0.87 (as in the earlier study). In this version the multiple-choice answers were in one column, as opposed to the two columns in the earlier version. Also in this study alternative versions of the test were used; when the results from automated and standard forms of each version were correlated, the coefficients were between 0.91 and 0.93. This finding vindicates the strategy mentioned earlier for helping to cope with problems of visual inattention, i.e. arranging multiple-choice information in a column rather than a matrix. We are also using a personality test— Cattell's 16PF—as part of a study of the role of psychological factors in rehabilitation. The automated form of this test has also been evaluated against the standard. Although the correlations between automated and standard versions of each of the 16 scores were positive and highly significant (ranging from 0.47 to 0.79), they are not as good as the retest reliabilities published in the manual (which range from 0.68 to 0.86). A study is at present in progress to evaluate the retest reliability for the standard form of the test in our patient population.

Not all forms of tests have such a high degree of comparability between automated and standard forms. One of the tests in the battery is a line bisection task for the assessment of unilateral neglect. This test operates from a single switch and both horizontal and vertical lines are presented. The horizontal lines are presented centred either on the left side of screen, middle of screen or right side of screen, and the vertical lines centred in the top half of the screen, middle or bottom half of screen. During the test a moving cursor, which could start from either end of the line, would scan along each line. The test subject had to operate a switch to stop the cursor when they perceived it was at the middle of the line. When the line was bisected a reward was given regardless of accuracy. The lines were scored by measuring the percentage deviation from the centre of the line. Performance on this test was compared with performance on a pen and paper version of the test as described by Schenkenberg *et al.* (1980). The sizes of the percentage deviations from the centre were on the whole smaller for the pen and paper version of the test than for the automated version, and mostly significantly so. For the horizontal lines the correlation between the two forms were all positive and significant but also small (left centred 0.38, middle centred 0.41, right centred 0.51). For the vertical lines the correlations were smaller and non-significant. The first hypothesis to account for the differences in the results was that when the vertical lines were considered those on the computer screen were presented in a different plane from those on paper. The pen and paper test with the vertical lines was repeated with the paper pinned to a drawing board positioned so that the vertical lines on the paper were in the same plane as those on the screen. This, however, produced no change in the results. We were therefore left with two further hypotheses: one is that culturally we are more practised at dealing with horizontal rather than vertical lines and therefore proprioceptive feedback may have an important role in dealing with vertical lines and proprioceptive feedback was not possible for the automated version of the test; second, the variability in results could have reflected the pathology of the subject population.

As has been mentioned earlier in the chapter, we use a range of response media. The objective is to make it as easy as possible for the client to respond. Whenever it is feasible, we design the test to be operable from a single switch. A small study has been carried out to see whether use of a single switch with a multiple-choice test produces different results from when a bank of switches was used for response. This study used the Mill Hill Vocabulary Scale synonyms and was carried out as part of the earlier-mentioned study evaluating the automated against the standard form of the test. It was found that no significant difference was produced in the score sizes, and the correlation between the tests for the two different forms of response media was 0.86. Using a single switch, at least with this test, produced comparable results with those from a bank of switches and of course the standard form of the test.

Concluding remarks

The rapidity of development of modern technology produces the effect that no sooner have you started to develop a computer-based system then you find the hardware has been superseded. There is also a proliferation of development of computer-based communication aids for disabled people. The art is in achieving compromise between taking advantage of new developments in technology and achieving the objectives for which the system was acquired in the first place. Tests developed for one computer system, for example, can look quite different when converted for use on another.

The use of an entirely automated battery with a population of severely physically disabled adults is not necessarily always advocated, since some standard tests are amenable to use with this population. However, computer-based assessment is very acceptable to the client population at this hospital and has shown itself to be an effective means of eliciting objective information about the cognitive state of adults with severe physical disabilities. In some instances it has proved the only way of yielding such information.

Acknowledgements

The author wishes to thank Geoffrey A. Wylie for development of the special hardware required by the project and for writing software; Sarah Abbess for carrying out studies to evaluate the BBC-based test software; and residents of The Royal Hospital and Home, Putney, for taking part in the evaluation studies, also the Development Trust for the Young Disabled, The Frances and Augustus Moody Newman Foundation and The Wolfson Foundation for supporting this research.

References

Bartram, D. and Bayliss, R. (1984). Automated testing: past, present and future, *Journal of Occupational Psychology*, **57**, 221–237.

Bartram, D., Beaumont, J. G., Cornford, T., Dann, P. L. and Wilson, S. L. (1987). Recommendations for the design of software for computer based assessment (CBA), *Bulletin of the British Psychological Society*, **40**, 86–87.

Beaumont, J. G. and French, C. C. (1987). A clinical field study of eight automated psychometric procedures: the Leicester/DHSS project, *International Journal Man-Machine Studies*, **26**, 661–682.

Calvert, E. J. and Waterfall, R. C. (1982). A comparison of automated and standard administration of Raven's Standard Progressive Matrices, *International Journal of Man-Machine Studies*, **17**, 305–310.

Crossley, R. and McDonald, A. (1982), *Annie's Coming Out*. Harmondsworth: Pelican.

French, C. C. (1986). Microcomputers and psychometric assessment, *British Journal of Guidance and Counselling*, **14**, 33–45.

Parker, C.B. (1981). A linguo-buccal aid to control an electric wheelchair, *British Dental Journal*, **151**, 263.

Reynell, J. (1970). Children with physical handicaps. In P. Mittler (ed.), *The Psychological Assessment of Mental and Physical Handicap*, pp. 443–469. London: Tavistock Publications.

Ridgway, J., MacCulloch, M. J. and Mills, H. E. (1982). Some experiences in administering a psychometric test with a light pen and a microcomputer, *International Journal of Man-Machine Studies*, **17**, 265–278.

Sampson, J. P. (1983). Computer-assisted testing and treatment: current status and implications for the future, *Measurement and Evaluation in Guidance*, **15**, 293–299.

Schenkenberg, T., Bradford, D. C. and Ajax, E. T. (1980). Line bisection and unilateral visual neglect in patients with neurologic impairment, *Neurology*, **30**, 509–517.

Shakespeare, R. (1975). *The Psychology of Handicap*. London: Methuen.

Thompson, J. A. and Wilson, S. L. (1982). Automated psychological testing, *International Journal of Man-Machine Studies*. **17**, 279–290.

Watts, K., Baddeley, A. and Williams, M. (1982). Automated tailored testing using Raven's Matrices and the Mill Hill Vocabulary tests: a comparison with manual administration, *International Journal of Man-Machine Studies*, **17**, 331–344.

Wilson, S. L. (1987). The development of an automated test of immediate memory and its evaluation on severely physically disabled adults, *Applied Psychology: An International Review*, **36**, 311–327.

Wilson, S. L., Thompson, J. A. and Wylie, G. A. (1982). Automated psychological testing for the severely physically handicapped, *International Journal of Man-Machine Studies*, **17**, 291–296.

Wylie, G. A., Wilson, S. L. and Wedgwood, J. (1984). The use of microcomputers for the psychological assessment of physically disabled adults, *Journal of Medical Engineering and Technology*, **8**, 224–229.

CHAPTER 7

Neuropsychological assesssment of congenital and acquired disorders

CHRISTINE TEMPLE

Historical background

At the turn of the nineteenth century Gall advocated cranioscopy and phrenology to enhance understanding of people's behaviour. He discovered 26 locations which he called faculties on the surface of the head corresponding to particular characteristics of an individual's personality. His student, Spurzheim, was responsible for the widespread communication of these ideas and in 1814 he lectured and gave demonstrations on phrenology in England. It was the Victorians who developed some of the first machines which were claimed to measure the psychological functions of the brain. These were phrenometers, 'sophisticated' measuring devices which charted the relative dimensions of the bumps and indentations on the exterior of the skull. These measurements were considered to reflect the relative strengths of the phrenological faculties which combine together to produce character. Imbalance of individual faculties leads to particular behaviours. For example, excess of vivativeness produces a hyperactive, overtense disposition, incapable of relaxation, whereas deficiency causes a soulless attitude or hollow feeling. Phrenological surgeries appeared during the nineteenth century and phrenological schools, foods, doctors and instruments became widespread. Queen Victoria had her children's heads read and George Elliot had her head shaved twice by phrenologists to facilitate the measurement process (Cooper and Cooper, 1983).

Subsequently phrenology fell into disrepute, though recently some of its ideas have re-emerged in modified form. Some researchers now argue that the strength of particular cognitive abilities may be reflected in the volume of cortical tissue devoted to their function. Significance has been attached to the finding that the planum temporale is larger on the left side in 65% of adult brains and on the right side in only 10%; the majority of adults also having

Microcomputers, Psychology and Medicine
Edited by R. West, M. Christie and J. Weinman
© 1990 by John Wiley & Sons Ltd

left hemisphere dominance for language. In contrast, symmetry of the planum temporale has been observed in developmental dyslexia (Geschwind and Galaburda, 1985).

Traditional neuropsychology developed and rapidly expanded in the first seventy years of the century. During this period, localisationists had been concerned with mapping the location of specific lesions with respect to particular functional deficits. Such work accelerated following the world wars, when large numbers of patients with focal wounds to the brain were studied (e.g. Newcombe, 1969). Such patients often showed dissociation in performance with defective performance on one type of task but not in another. Just as patients with left hemisphere injury often showed language impairment, patients with right hemisphere lesions performed more poorly on visual tasks such as mazes and tests of 'closure'. Moreover, there were dissociations within the visual tasks. For example, patients with adequate maze performance but poor closure had posterior temporal lobe lesions, whereas patients with poor maze performance and adequate closure had high posterior parietal lesions (Newcombe and Russell, 1969). Numerous tachistoscopic studies of normal subjects have provided complementary information regarding hemispheric asymmetries.

However, the simple dichotomy of left hemisphere with language and right hemisphere with non-linguistic functions has proved to be a simplification. Studies of commissurotomy patients (whose corpus callosum has been cut) indicate that the right hemisphere may also be involved in some language functions (Zaidel, 1978), though the extent and precise nature of this involvement is debated. Recently, Mehta et al. (1987) retested some of the men with chronic focal unilateral bullet injuries to the brain on four tasks: two visuoperceptual and two visuospatial. As expected there was a predominantly right hemisphere deficit on the visuoperceptive tasks but a relatively greater left than right hemisphere deficit on the spatial ones. Such findings indicate a left hemisphere contribution to visuospatial processing.

As sophisticated brain imagery has increased, the clinical importance of lesion localisation per se for neuropsychological data has reduced. However, there has been increased interest in the mechanisms involved in brain organisation, and increased computer technology has led to information-processing approaches to neuropsychological disorders. Following the papers of Marshall and Newcombe (1966, 1973), cognitive neuropsychology emerged. Cognitive neuropsychology has been concerned with developing models of underlying systems on the basis of the selective fractionation of functional performance observed after brain injury or disease. Cognitive neuropsychology has expanded the models which cognitive psychologists have developed of normal psychological processing and has also led to increased understanding by neuropsychologists of their patients' impairments and potential for remediation. Several recent volumes speak of the growing interest in this field (Patterson et al.,

1985; Coltheart *et al.*, 1987; Ellis and Young, 1988).

As the models of cognitive function have improved, so the brain-imaging technology has also developed. Nuclear magnetic resonance (NMR), though not yet widely used in the clinical health service because of its prohibitive cost, has been employed in a number of research studies. Evidence of brain damage following stroke can be seen with NMR at an earlier time than with computerised tomography (CT) scan. Structures which are not clearly visualised on CT scan can be pictured with clarity using NMR. Thus, for example, the structure of the corpus callosum can be seen clearly and it is possible to determine in cases of callosal agenesis whether the fibre tract is absent or partially formed.

Functional activation can be investigated by studying regional cerebral blood flow or positron emission tomography. It is now known that local blood flow varies with the functional and metabolic level of neuronal tissue (Raichle *et al.*, 1976). Studies of regional cerebral blood flow employ a radioactive isotope (^{133}Xe) which is injected into the carotid artery or inhaled in a non-invasive technique. Although the effects may be highly localised, possibly relating to columnar organisation (Sokoloff, 1975), the spatial resolution of most commercially available systems has been 3–5 cm (Risberg, 1986) though this is currently improving. Five minutes of activation is required per task. Most neuropsychological studies have employed two-dimensional recording systems, though three-dimensional systems are now being introduced (e.g. single photon emission computed tomography SPECT). New tracers are also being investigated which will provide better spatial and temporal resolution.

Positron emission tomography (PET) measures local cerebral metabolic rate of glucose with [^{18}F]2-fluoro-2-deoxy-D-glucose (FDG) using a technique (Reivich *et al.*, 1979) derived from [^{14}C]deoxyglucose autoradiography (Sokoloff *et al.*, 1977). FDG is transported into cells by the same carrier system as glucose and phosphorylated to [^{18}F]deoxyglucose-6-phosphate, which can be metabolised and accumulates in brain cells. Its concentration in small volumes of tissue is measured and reconstruction algorithms then compute the topographical images of spatial tracer distribution (Heiss *et al.*, 1986). Using PET, metabolic disturbances have been shown to extend far beyond the site of primary focal lesions, thus explaining impairments which cannot be ascribed to the focal lesion itself. In Alzheimer's disease, abnormalities on PET are visible before atrophy can be viewed on CT scanning (Heiss and Phelps, 1983).

Microcomputers in neuropsychology

Lateralised studies

When microcomputers first began to appear in human neuropsychology laboratories they were rapidly adopted for visual field studies and supplemented many box tachistoscopes for studies of visual field asymmetries. One of their major advantages was in time-saving. Stimuli could be constructed by the computer and did not have to be individually written, drawn or traced on tachistoscopic cards. Further, reaction times could be recorded automatically, without the necessity for individual manual records as testing proceeded. Thus testing time itself was shortened and the experimenter was able to concentrate on checking the subject or patient rather than the dials and meters. For experiments involving large numbers of reaction times, data analysis could be pre-programmed, thus considerably shortening access to experimental results. Microcomputers continue to be used in such investigations.

Reading and dyslexia

Microcomputers have also been widely employed in other research on memory or language which does not require lateralised stimulus presentation but for which reaction time measures provide useful data. A recent example is the work of Seymour (Seymour and MacGregor, 1984; Seymour, 1986, 1987), which presents a systematic analysis of development dyslexia and normal reading variation.

Seymour used a set of measurement procedures, adapted from standard experimental paradigms and automated on a microcomputer, in which error and reaction time data were used to probe the various components of an information-processing model of reading. Most reading models now incorporate two 'routes' by which a word may be read aloud correctly: a phonological route, which 'sounds out' words to attain their pronunciation; and a semantic reading route, in which the pronunciation of words is attained via the activation of an abstract representation of the concept represented by the word, i.e. via a semantic system. In cases of acquired dyslexia, one or other of these routes may be selectively impaired following brain damage with relative preservation of the alternative route. In surface dyslexia (Marshall and Newcombe, 1973) there is a regularity effect, with words with regular spelling-to-sound patterns read aloud more easily than words whose pattern is not regular. Errors to the latter tend to be in the form of regularisations, e.g. yacht→'yatched', in which a systematic set of rules appears to have been over-applied. Reading of unfamiliar but regular words and ability to pronounce non-words is preserved. There are a number of other features but those outlined illustrate why the disorder is interpreted as reflecting impairment of the semantic reading route but with relative preservation of phonological reading skills. There is a double dissociation between surface dyslexia and phonological dyslexia. In phonological dyslexia (Beauvois and Derouesne, 1979) there is no regularity effect. However, there is a lexicality effect with impaired ability to read aloud pronouncable non-words. Other features also contrast with surface dyslexia. This disorder is interpreted as reflecting impaired reading by the phonological route with relative preservation of semantic-route reading. The two disorders have both been described in analogous developmental form: developmental surface dyslexia (Holmes, 1973; Coltheart *et al.*, 1983; Temple, 1984a, 1985), in which there is impaired *establishment* of the semantic reading route; and developmental phonological dyslexia (Temple and Marshall, 1983; Temple, 1984b,c; Seymour and MacGregor, 1984; Campbell and Butterworth, 1985; Snowling *et al.* 1986), in which there is impaired *establishment* of the phonological reading route. In his analyses of developmental dyslexia Seymour was therefore interested in investigating both phonological access and semantic access. Further, he describes in detail a visual processor which precedes both phonological and semantic access and whose functions he also tested.

Visual processor functions were tested by means of identity and array-matching tasks and assessment of the capacity to read words written in distorted format, e.g.

```
TABLE   v.   T  B  E   v.   T
             A  L            A
                             B
                             L
                             E
```

Phonological access was assessed using word and non-word vocalisation tasks, with the former varied for frequency, regularity, concreteness and syntactic function, and the latter varied for homophoneity (boan v. poan). Semantic access was examined in lexical decision and semantic decision. Latterly even wider ranges of tasks have been employed.

Seymour's experimental work was automated on an Apple II microprocessor. Word and letter stimuli were presented in standard Apple upper case characters at the centre of a green screen monitor, viewed at an approximate distance of 75 cm. In experiments requiring a vocal response, reaction times were detected by a microphone and voice switch which were linked to the computer through the games 'port' (normally used for a joystick). Two micro-switches, designated 'yes' and 'no', were used in the decision experiments. Displays were presented by switching out of a blank 'graphics screen' to a 'text screen' on which the stimulus had already been printed. An assembly language routine, based on interrupts generated at 1 ms intervals by the Apple Mountain Hardware clock, was used to control interstimulus intervals, to measure reaction times (RTs), and to detect closure of a switch on the games port.

In general a trial involved presentation of a warning signal—an array of five asterisks for 500 ms—followed, after blank interval of 1500 ms, by the stimulus, which remained on the screen until the response occurred. Reaction times were recorded in milliseconds from the onset of the stimulus to the onset of the response. The experimenter indicated on the computer keyboard the correctness of the response and whether there had been equipment failure. Trials designated as failures were replaced. In vocalisation experiments, the program asked the experimenter to type a representation of the incorrect response following the signal of an error. Order of presentation of stimuli were randomised prior to testing.

Using such an experimental design, Seymour conducts case studies of dyslexics and controls. Dyslexics are compared to the range of normal performance and are found to lie outside it (Seymour 1986). Developmental phonological dyslexics are poorer at reading non-words than at reading words. Seymour and MacGregor (1984) show that there is also a sharp difference in RT between the two types of material. Similarly, just as a homophony effect has been reported for accuracy in reading non-words in developmental phonological dyslexia (Temple and Marshall 1983), so Seymour and MacGregor (1984) show a significant effect of homophony on vocal RTs. Difficulty in reading function words is a feature of acquired phonological dyslexia but has only been reported in developmental phonological dyslexia when text reading is involved. However, by using vocal RT measures, Seymour shows that there are significantly slower vocal RTs to function words as compared to other words even if final responses are accurate.

Such dissociations are not observed in developmental surface dyslexia (called developmental morphemic dyslexia by Seymour). Seymour also describes visual analytic dyslexia in which vocal RT measures reveal dissociations within the matching and format distortion tasks. Results from these experiments suggest an impairment affecting the speed at which the visual processor can operate in analytical or serial mode.

Seymour suggests that even within the categories of phonological, surface and visual analytic dyslexia there are variations in performance so that description merely in relation to such a group may lead to 'over-simplification'. He concludes in a recent paper:

> These observations have important implications for the manner in which reading disability might most usefully be described and investigated. The main contention is that studies should be conducted within an information processing framework, exploiting the full potential of factorial experiments and latency measurements, with the aim of accepting a minimally complete description of each individual case. The results so far obtained indicate a radical degree of heterogeneity in the dyslexic population.

Face recognition

One disadvantage of microcomputer use for RT studies is that the graphic limitations of the machines restrict potential stimulus sets. Thus although studies employing verbal stimuli are straightforward and schematic pictorial representations can be produced, most microcomputers are not able to present realistic photographs of objects for studies of naming, nor present photographs of faces for face recognitition.

In recent years there has been increased interest in the mechanisms involved in face processing. A range of studies of normal subjects have led to the development of a theory of face recognition which incorporates several abstracted processing codes (Bruce and Young, 1986). Face recognition units are comparable to the input logogens (Morton, 1979) of reading and language comprehension. They are internalised stores of structural codes describing the appearance of familiar faces. Output from the accessed face recognition unit activates a 'person identity node' which is connected with identity-specific semantic codes. Subsequently, name codes are retrieved. Parallel studies have been employed with prosopagnosics, who have lost the ability to recognise faces following brain damage. One recent such study has shown that in prosopagnosia much of the processing of familiar faces can remain intact despite absence of awareness that recognition has occurred. The patient (P.H.) of de Haan (de Haan et al., 1987) showed the normal advantage in making same/different identity judgements for familiar over unfamiliar face photographs. As normal, faster matching of familiar faces was found only for identity matches involving the face's 'internal features'. Yet P.H. is quite unaware of any ability to recognise familiar faces although he can recognise familiar people from their names.

In conducting recent studies of prosopagnosia and many of the studies which led to the current theories of face processing, slide stimuli have been employed. These have been used in back-projection tachistoscopes linked to response keys and reaction time monitors. However, it is notable in reading the description of these studies that recording of reaction times has been done manually. In principle a back-projection tachistoscope can be linked to a microcomputer for data recording. Automation of these procedures would facilitate these studies and speed up the process of data analysis. Such developments are now beginning.

EEG topographical mapping

Many of the sophisticated brain-imaging techniques are prohibitively expensive. However, some of the new EEG topographical mappers are substantially more affordable. Data collection, storage and analysis is controlled by microcomputer, which also displays the topographical map.

Topographical mapping involves recording EEG or ERPs from multiple electrodes attached to different locations on the scalp from which reconstruction algorithms interpolate a map of regional activation in the brain. Systems vary in the number of electrodes which are employed, but tend to be in the range 16–28. A large number of electrodes provides more data upon which to employ the mathematical transformation to produce the topography. However, there is argument regarding the number of electrodes which should be seen as minimal.

The electrodes are mounted on caps of various sizes. The obvious advantage of the cap is that it substantially reduces the time required for electrode attachment. The obvious disadvantage is that the precise placement of the electrodes is constrained. Although they remain constant in relation to each other they will vary in their position of recording depending upon the individual variation in the skull dimensions of the subject. Electrolytic gel is injected at each electrode site and the scalp is given a minor abrasion with a blunt surgical needle. An impedance meter is supplied to test the quality of electrical connection. Subjects report the procedure as relatively painless. In the current era of health hazards it is clear that any abraiding instruments must either be disposable or sterilised appropriately.

During recording, each task under investigation must be carried out for approximately 2 minutes. The recording is sensitive to motor movements so vocal responses cannot be employed and other motor responses should be minimal, e.g. finger-tip movements. It is in the selection and design of the tests to be employed that neuropsychology makes its contribution in this psycho-physiological paradigm.

The output from the electrode cap is recorded as raw EEG on microcomputer. The waveform can be retrieved from this store and transferred subsequently to other computers for data analysis which is not part of the pre-programmed package. The microcomputer conducts a linear interpolation between the electrode poles. It seems probable that the interrelationships between the poles are not in fact linear but superior methods of interpolation await better understanding of the electrical circuitry of the brain. The microcomputer divides the data into relevant frequency bands: alpha, beta I, beta II, etc. Topographical maps can display ongoing activity in any of these bands, with each frame of the display revealing 1 or 2 seconds of activity. A colour-graded scale indicates the average amplitude of the activity within each band, blue representing little activity and red representing high activity.

Averaged maps per task per subjects can also be constructed. A fixed number of 'clean' (artifact-free) frames are employed. Of necessity, the frame rejection has subjective components. In recording ERPs rejection criteria are pre-specified by fixing cut-off criteria prior to onset. With respect to ERPs, some machines record only about 500 ms of EP activity, which is too short to detect some components of cognitive interest. Other machines have been adapted to permit several seconds of recording of each EP.

Pre-programmed data analysis employs t-tests and z-tests, although some machines incorporate more sophisticated variations. Averaged maps over a group of subjects on one task can be contrasted with an averaged map for a distinct group of subjects (e.g. subjects v. controls). A difference map can be generated which gives a probability distribution, areas of maximal difference being coloured differently from areas of lesser difference. Alternatively, an individual subject can be contrasted with a control group and this technique is clearly of value in clinical applications.

Critics argue that, whereas the spatial resolution of blood flow is fairly good but its temporal resolution is poor, the temporal resolution of EEG is good but its spatial resolution is poor. Thus the topographical maps can give a misleading impression of spatial specificity. Further, the position of occipital dipoles is such that, as in all EEG work, what is recorded as left occipital activity may, in fact, emanate from the right hemisphere, and vice versa. Thus any studies attaching significance to the laterality of topographical occipital recordings should be treated with scepticism. There remains the difficulty of determining whether increased EEG activity reflects increased functional activation or increased inhibitory activity and therefore decreased functional activation. There is now some concensus that beta II activity reflects functional activation, although agreement is not universal.

On the positive side, the technology is cheap in comparison to other topographical procedures. It is non-invasive, so that large studies of normal as well as abnormal subjects are feasible. The electrode cap requires only 15–20 minutes to be attached before recording can begin, which is significantly faster than attaching electrodes individually and so potentially increases the applicability of EEG and ERP work to subjects who are limited in their ability to cooperate. Studies to date have shown it to be sensitive to both task-specific functional activity and to disabilities. The paradigm facilitates opportunities for interdisciplinary work in neuropsychology and psychophysiology.

Studies in progress employing microcomputers

In the neuropsychology laboratory at the Royal Holloway and Bedford New College there are a number of studies in progress employing microcomputers. The first of these will be described in some detail and some preliminary results given. The others will be sketched in outline.

Lateralised studies of developmental phonological dyslexia

The work of Seymour concerning microcomputer analysis of multiple cases of developmental dyslexia was discussed above. Seymour's work employs a cognitive analysis of the rapidity and accuracy of individual dyslexics on particular tasks. Another theoretical issue which recurs in the dyslexia literature is the issue of language laterality. Suggestions of atypical laterality recur but have not been convincingly established. One reason may be the heterogeneity of the disorder: only certain groups may have atypical laterality. A disproportionate number of cases of acquired phonological dyslexia have right hemispheric lesions rather than left (Temple, submitted). Thus it has been suggested that the premorbid language organisation in these patients may be atypical. The laterality of developmental phonological dyslexia has not previously been studied. Combining the methodology of Seymour, the knowledge of heterogeneity and the issue of laterality, it seems of interest to investigate such cases. Data are reported from the first in a series of cases of developmental phonological dyslexia, studied on a lateralised lexical decision and reading task in which stimulus onset, data recording and data analysis were controlled by microcomputer linked to a three-field back-projection tachistoscope.

Normal readers show a left visual field (LVF) advantage for *reading* both words and non-words. With respect to *lexical decision*, however, Leiber (1976) found that reaction times did not differ with respect to visual field when the stimuli were non-words, but a right visual field (RVF) superiority was observed when the letter strings made up a word. Axelrod et al. (1977) found that an RVF advantage was also obtained with non-words if the non-words were pronounceable and contained letter combinations which frequently occurred in English. Provided exposure durations are increased to a level at which words can be positively identified, an RVF advantage in lexical decision has also been found by Bradshaw et al. (1979). The task employed by us involves non-words which are pronounceable and which have high-frequency letter combinations, e.g. exposures are of sufficient length for words to be positively identified. Thus one would normally expect an LVF advantage on this task.

In acquired phonological dyslexia there is good reading of concrete words; poor reading of function words in text; slow reading of function words when reaction time measures are employed; and impaired reading of non-words. One might therefore expect that reaction times to concrete words would be fastest followed by function words and then non-words. One might also expect declining accuracy. However, it should be noted that the stimuli employed are only three letters in length and are thus comparatively simple function words and non-words to pronounce. This might reduce reaction time differences and accuracy score differences between conditions. If phonological dyslexics are reading with an albeit impaired left hemisphere then one would expect to see an RVF advantage with all three sets of stimulus material.

One hundred and twenty slides containing three-letter stimuli were constructed. These consisted of 20 high-frequency, concrete words (e.g. 'cat'), 20 function words (e.g. 'for'), and 20 pronounceable non-words (e.g. 'lep'). The latter were matched to the concrete words and derived from them by altering one letter. Each three-letter stimulus occurred twice: once in the left visual field and once in the right. Stimulus order was randomised except that half of each set occurred first in the left visual field and half in the right. As a control for central fixation, at the centre of each slide there was a single digit (0 to 9).

Table 7.1 Percentage correct on lexical decision

	Concrete words	Function words	Non-words
RVF	100%	95%	74%
LVF	95%	100%	79%

The stimuli were presented with a Kodak S-AV 2050 carousel slide projector operated by means of an Electronic Developments three-field back-projection tachistoscope on to a white screen behind which the subject was seated. The experiment was controlled by an Acorn Computer BBC-B microcomputer. Stimulus onset was activated by pressing the 'space' bar on the microcomputer. A trial set of ten practice slides preceded the experiment. Each stimulus appeared for 150 ms. The subject was required to decide whether the stimulus was a word or not. On the first 60 trials a word was indicated by pressing the right-hand key and a non-word by pressing the left-hand key; on the second 60 trials hands were reversed. At stimulus onset an electronic developments digital timer commenced. The clock was terminated by the subject's key press. Reaction times and key press responses were automatically stored on the BBC micro.

In addition, the subjects were required to report verbally the number which had appeared at the central fixation and then the three-letter stimulus which had been presented. They were instructed to key press bofore vocalising. Trials for which the central fixation number was incorrectly reported were deleted from further analysis. Reading responses were recorded manually.

The data presented here reflect the performance of H.M., a developmental phonological dyslexic whose performance on a range of other tasks has been previously documented (Temple and Marshall, 1983; Temple, 1984b; Temple, 1987). Table 7.1 gives the percentage correct on the lexical decision task. There was no difference in the error rate in the right and left visual fields. However, there was a significant difference between the ability to recognise words correctly and to reject non-words correctly. There was thus a significant tendency for H.M. to judge non-words as being words.

Table 7.2 Percentage correct in reading aloud

	Concrete words	Function words	Non-words
RVF	100%	100%	53%
LVF	84%	95%	56%

Table 7.3   Average reaction times (ms)

	Concrete words	Function words	Non-words
RVF	806	855	1149
LVF	906	836	1094

Table 7.2 gives the percentage correct on reading aloud the three-letter stimuli. Once again there is no significant visual field difference, although those errors that there are to words appear in the left visual field. H.M. also makes more errors on the reading of non-words than on the reading of concrete words. There was no significant difference between content and function word reading.

Table 7.3 gives the average reaction times in each of the six conditions. This indicates that there is a visual field difference in the normal direction for concrete words, with a right visual field superiority. However, function words and non-words show a visual field asymmetry in the opposite direction. Moreover, left visual field processing of function words is actually faster than its processing of content words. The reaction time data indicate the sensitivity of such measures in comparison to simple performance data. Thus employing reaction times, a distinction between content and function words appears. In text reading it is function words which generate the largest numbers of errors in phonological dyslexia (Temple, 1984b). The results suggest that for making lexical decisions about concrete words H.M. has superior left hemisphere performance and therefore left hemisphere lateralisation for language. However, there may be greater right hemisphere involvement in lexical decision procedures for short grammatical words and for non-words. This contrasts with the normal postulated language functions of the right hemisphere, where it is suggested some concrete words can be processed but grammatical items and non-words are particularly difficult (e.g. Zaidel, 1978). Replication of these results and comparison with further cases of phonological dyslexia as well as chronological and reading age controls will permit more confident interpretation.

Lateralised studies of callosal agenesis

The corpus callosum contains 20 million fibres and is the largest single tract in the nervous system. It is also the most rapidly expanding tract in brain evolution. Patients with callosal agenesis are born without the corpus callosum and provide evidence regarding its role in the development of normal cognitive function and the establishment of laterality. Previous work in this field has been hampered by the paucity of reported cases and the frequent co-occurrence of mental retardation and other brain pathology. In collaboration with Professor

M.A. Jeeves of the University of St Andrews and Dr O. Vilarroya a number of children and adults who are of normal intelligence are being studied.

Tachistoscopic studies are being controlled by microcomputer and include lateralised reading tasks; reading across the meridian; lateralised object naming; lateralised phonological processing; and lateralised spatial tasks.

Developmental prosopagnosia

Although developmental dyslexia and developmental language disorders have been much studied, developmental disorders of non-verbal function have received scant attention. These neverthless may have educational implications; they may provide information about the normal development of non-verbal skill; and may provide knowledge about normal non-verbal ability. One such abililty is face recognition. Individual differences in face recognition skill in the normal population are being studied. It is also planned to study cases of developmental prosopagnosia using methods derived from studies of normal face processing and acquired prosopagnosia. Experiments are being controlled and data recorded and analysed by microcomputer linked to the tachistoscope presentation of photographs.

For the future: multiple micros

In the future, there is the potential to link a microcomputer-controlled tachistoscopic system to a microcomputer-controlled EEG mapper. This would be most suited to ERP work, with slide stimulus onset linked to initiation of ERP recording. Decision reponses, reaction times and ERPs could then be collected concurrently. This would have potential application in a variety of theoretical and clinical areas. A trial of this sort employing a Neuroscience brain imager proved straightforward to run, and it is hoped that such work will develop in the future.

References

Axelrod, S., Haryadi, T. and Leiber, L. (1977). Oral report of words and word approximations presented to the left or right visual field, *Brain and Language*, **4**, 550–557.

Beauvois, M.-F. and Derouesne, J. (1979). Phonological alexia: three dissociations, *Journal of Neurology, Neurosurgery and Psychiatry*, **42**, 1115–1124.

Bradshaw, G. J., Hicks, R. E. and Rose, B. (1979). Lexical discrimination and letter-string identification on the two visual fields, *Brain and language*, **8**, 10–18.

Bruce, V. and Young, A. (1986). Understanding face recognition, *British Journal of Psychology*, **77**, 305–327.

Campbell, R. and Butterworth, B. (1985). Phonological dyslexia and dysgraphia in a highly literate subject: A developmental case with associated deficits of phonemic processing, *Quarterly Journal of Experimental Psychology*, **37A**, 435–477.

Coltheart, M., Masterson, J., Byng, S., Prior, M. and Riddoch, J. (1983). Surface dyslexia, *Quarterly Journal of Experimental Psychology*, **35**, 469–496.

Coltheart, M., Sartori, G. and Job, R. (1987) *The Cognitive Neuropsychology of Language*. London: Erlbaum.

Cooper, H. and Cooper, P. (1983). *Heads or the Art of Phrenology*. London: London Phrenology Company.

De Haan, E., Young, A. and Newcombe, F. (1987). Face recognition without awareness, *Cognitive neuropsychology*, **4**, 385–415.

Ellis, A. W. and Young, A. W. (1988). *Human Cognitive Neuropsychology*. London: Erlbaum.

Geschwind, N. and Galaburda, A. (1985). Cerebral lateralisation: Biological mechanisms, associations and pathology. Parts I–III, *Archives of Neurology*, **42**, 428–459, 521–552, 634–654.

Heiss, W. D. and Phelps, M. E. (eds) (1983). *Positron Emission Tomography of the Brain*. Berlin: Springer.

Heiss, W. D., Herholz, K., Pawlik, G., Wagner, R. and Wienhard, K. (1986). Positron emission tomography in neuropsychology, *Neuropsychologia*, **24**, 141–149.

Holmes, J. (1973). Dyslexia: A neurolinguisitic study of traumatic and developmental disorders of reading. Unpublished PhD Thesis, University of Edinburgh.

Leiber, L. (1976). Lexical decisions in the right and left cerebral hemispheres, *Brain and Language*, **3**, 443–450.

Marshall, J. C. and Newcombe, F. (1966). Syntactic and semantic errors in paralexia, *Neuropsychologia*, **4**, 169–176.

Marshall, J. C. and Newcombe, F. (1973). Patterns of paralexia: A psycholinguistic approach, *Journal of Psycholinguistic Research*, **2**, 175–199.

Mehta, Z., Newcombe, F. and Damasio, H. (1987). A left hemisphere contribution to visuospatial processing, *Cortex*, **23**, 447–461.

Morton, J. (1979). Word recognition. In J. Morton and J. C. Marshall (eds), *Psycholinguistic Series 2*. Cambridge, MA: MIT Press.

Newcombe, F. (1969). *Missile Wounds of The Brain*. Oxford: Oxford University Press.

Newcombe, F. and Russell, W. R. (1969). Dissociated visual perceptual and spatial deficits in focal lesions of the right hemisphere, *Journal of Neurology. Neurosurgery and Psychiatry*, **32**, 73–81.

Patterson, K. E., Marshall, J. C. and Coltheart, M. (1985). *Surface Dyslexia*. Hillsdale, NJ: Erlbaum.

Raichle, M. E., Grubb, R. L., Gado, M. H., Eichling, J. O. and Tar-Pogossian, M. M. (1976). Correlation between regional cerebral blood flow and oxidative metabolism, *Archives of Neurology*, **33**, 523–526.

Reivich, M., Kuhl, D., Wolf, A., Greenberg, J., Phelps, M., Ido, T., Casella, V., Fowler, J., Hoffman, E., Alavi, A., Som, P. and Sokoloff, L. (1979). The (^{18}F)-fluoro-deoxyglucose method for measurement of local cerebral glucose utilisation in man, *Circulation Research*, **44**, 127–137.

Risberg, J. (1986). Regional cerebral blood flow in neuropsychology. *Neuropsychologia*, **24**, 135–140.

Seymour, P. (1986). *Cognitive Analysis of Dyslexia*. London: Routledge & Kegan Paul.

Seymour, P. (1987). Development dyslexia: A cognitive experimental analysis. In M. Coltheart, G. Sartori and R. Job (eds), *The Cognitive Neuropsychology of Language*. London: Erlbaum.

Seymour, P. and MacGregor, C. (1984). Developmental dyslexia: A cognitive experimental analysis of phonological, morphemic and visual impairments, *Cognitive Neuropsychology*, **1**, 43–82.

Snowling, M., Stackhouse, J. and Rack, J. (1986) Phonological dyslexia and dysgraphia: A developmental analysis, *Cognitive Neuropsycholgy*, **3**, 309–339.

Sokoloff, L. (1975). Influence of functional activity on local cerebral glucose utilisation. In D. H. Ingvar and N. A. Lassen (eds), *Brain Work: The Coupling of Function, Metabolism, and Blood Flow in the Brain*. Copenhagen: Munksgaard.

Sokoloff, L., Reivich, M., Kennedy, D., DesRosiers, M. H., Patlak, C. S., Pettigrew, K. D., Sakurada, O. and Shinohara, M. (1977). The ¹⁴C-deoxyglucose method for the measurement of local cerebral glucose utilisation: theory, procedure, and normal values in the conscious and anaesthetised albino rat, *Journal of Neurochemistry*, **28**, 897–916.

Temple, C. M. (1984a). Surface dyslexia in a child with epilepsy, *Neuropsychologia*, **22**, 569–576.

Temple, C. M. (1984b). Developmental analogues to acquired phonological dyslexia. In R. N. Malatesha and H. A. Whitaker (eds), *Dyslexia: A Global Issue*. The Hague: Martinus Nijhoff.

Temple, C. M. (1984c). New approaches to the developmental dyslexias. In F. C. Rose (ed.), *Progress in Aphasiology*. New York: Raven Press.

Temple, C. M. (1985). Surface dyslexia: Variations within a syndrome. In K. E. Patterson, J. C. Marshall and M. Coltheart (eds), *Surface Dyslexia*. Hillsdale, NJ: Erlbaum.

Temple, C. M. (1987). The nature of normality, the deviance of dyslexia and the recognition of rhyme, *Cognition*, **27**, 103–108.

Temple, C. M. *Does Biology Matter? Cognitive Neuropsychology and the Acquired Dyslexias* (submitted for publication).

Temple, C. M. and Marshall, J. C. (1983). A case study of developmental phonological dyslexias, *British Journal of Psychology*, **74**, 517–533.

Zaidel, E. (1978). Lexical organisation in the right hemisphere. In P. A. Buser and A. Rouguel-Buser (eds), *Cerebral Correlates of Conscious Experience*. INSERM Symposium No. 6. Amsterdam: North-Holland Biomedical press.

CHAPTER 8

The investigation of clinical anxiety and cognition

MICHAEL EYSENCK AND KARIN MOGG

Introduction

The programme of research which will be discussed in this chapter was initiated by Professor Andrew Mathews at St George's Hospital in the early 1980s. It has had as its central focus the investigation of cognitive factors in clinical anxiety, especially in patients suffering from generalized anxiety disorder. The basic assumption underlying the entire research programme is that the cognitive functioning of clinically anxious patients differs from that of normal controls in theoretically and practically important ways. This is not to deny, of course, that anxious patients differ from normal controls in several other ways such as physiologically and behaviourally. However, it is a strange lacuna in research on clinical anxiety that cognitive factors have received minimal attention, and it is this lacuna which we are endeavouring to fill with the research programme.

Despite the lack of relevant research, there is an increasing recognition of the importance of cognitive factors among therapists. For example, Beck and Emery (1985) laid great emphasis on the role of cognition in clinical anxiety. According to them, 'The primary pathology or dysfunction during a depression or an anxiety disorder is in the cognitive apparatus.' They claimed that specific thoughts or images frequently precipitate anxiety states. In a study by Beck *et al.* (1974), patients with anxiety neurosis reported that the cognitive antici- pation of danger typically preceded the onset of, or increase in, anxiety level.

Beck and Emery (1985) offered several interesting speculations concerning cognitive functioning in clinical anxiety. For example, they argued that anxious patients are sensitive to many more stimuli than normal individuals: 'The range of stimuli that can evoke anxiety in generalized anxiety disorder may

Microcomputers, Psychology and Medicine
Edited by R. West, M. Christie and J. Weinman
© 1990 by John Wiley & Sons Ltd

increase until almost any stimulus is perceived as a danger.' Of particular significance and relevance to the research programme are their views on perceptual and attentional processes: 'The patient is hyper-vigilant, constantly scanning the environment for signs of impending disaster or personal harm . . . The anxious patient selectively attends to stimuli that indicate possible danger and becomes oblivious to stimuli that indicate that there is no danger.'

Although the theoretical position of Beck and Emery (1985) has not been submitted to direct experimental test, the related views of Byrne (1964) have been investigated in several studies. In essence, Byrne (1964) argued that sensitizers 'approach' threatening stimuli, whereas repressors 'avoid' threatening stimuli. While Byrne (1964) expressed his hypothesis in terms of the repression–sensitization continuum, there is very strong evidence that sensitizers are simply normal individuals who are high in trait anxiety, whereas repressors are individuals who are low in trait anxiety (Watson and Clark, 1984).

In spite of the fact that Byrne's (1964) hypothesis accords with common sense, nearly all of the relevent experimental tests in normal groups have failed to provide any support for it (see Eysenck et al., 1987, for details). What are the implications of these negative findings for research on cognitive factors in generalized anxiety disorder?

It is possible, of course, that Byrne's (1964) hypothesis would be supported if anxious patients were compared with normal controls. However, there is an interesting alternative possibility, which is based on the fact that most of the tasks used in the literature involved the presentation of only one stimulus (threatening or neutral) at a time. This would be appropriate only if there were individual differences in a metaphorical volume control, with highly anxious individuals turning up and non-anxious individuals turning down this volume control in the presence of threatening or threat-related stimuli. Instead, there may actually be individual differences in a selective mechanism. Suppose, for example, that a threatening and a neutral stimulus were presented concurrently. Anxious individuals might bias their allocation of processing resources towards the threatening stimulus, whereas non-anxious individuals might bias their allocation away from that stimulus. By definition, such individual differences in selective bias could be detected only when two or more stimuli are presented concurrently, so that previous research is irrelevant in this connection.

Beck and Emery (1985) did not make their theoretical position on this issue entirely clear. However, they did claim that anxious patients selectively attend to threatening stimuli while ignoring neutral stimuli. This suggests that they would endorse the notion that anxious patients and normal controls differ in their selective biases. These selective biases would be expected to be of importance in everyday life. The environment typically contains numerous concurrent stimuli, so that threat-related stimuli will normally occur in the presence of other, neutral stimuli.

There are numerous cognitive tasks which could have been utilized to explore the notion that anxious patients differ from normal controls in terms of selective biases. How were the tasks selected? First, it was assumed that traditional laboratory cognitive tasks are preferable to questionnaire measures as a means of assessing cognitive functioning. Questionnaires are limited to consciously accessible information, and the information that is reported can obviously be distorted in several ways. Second, it seemed essential to use tasks which provided measures reflecting the very early stages of processing. We attend to only a small fraction of the information which is presented to our senses, so that it is clear that much selection of information occurs at a pre-attentive level. Since the research programme was designed to investigate possible differences between anxious patients and normal controls in selective biases, it seemed reasonable to focus to some extent on pre-attentive processes. Third, in order to obtain a thorough understanding of individual differences in the processing of threatening stimuli, it was decided to make use of tasks permitting assessment of a variety of different cognitive processes and functions. More specifically, the research programme has included tasks measuring pre-attentive processes, attentional processes, interpretative processes and memorial processes.

An important issue in this area of research concerns the types of threat which are presented to the subjects. Patients with generalized anxiety disorder regard many different events and situations as threatening, but they tend to be especially sensitive about social-evaluative and/or physical health concerns. As a consequence, most of the experimental studies in the research programme have involved the presentation of both kinds of threat. Only relatively mild threats have been used in these studies. The reason for this is that it is almost self-evident that major threats would attract the processing resources of both clinically anxious patients and normal controls, and so there would be no group differences in the allocation of processing resources.

The final issue which needs to be considered before discussing the experiments themselves is the complex matter of causality. The basic strategy has been to use the following two-stage approach. The first stage involves a two-group design, in which the cognitive performance of patients with generalized anxiety disorder is compared with that of normal controls. This stage of research permits the identification of those aspects of cognitive functioning which are non-normal in anxious patients. However, it is not possible with these data to decide whether any non-normal cognitive functioning in anxious patients is merely a reflection of the current anxious mood state or whether it may represent a vulnerability factor playing a part in the aetiology of generalized anxiety disorder.

The most valuable information on the causality issue would be that obtained from a prospective study in which cognitive functioning was assessed in a pre-morbid sample. However, it would be extremely expensive and time-consuming to obtain such a sample, and it has not so far been possible to do this. A somewhat less satisfactory, but nevertheless informative, strategy forms the basis of the second stage of the research programme. In essence, a three-group design is used, consisting of currently anxious patients, normal controls and recovered anxious patients. If some aspect of non-normal cognitive functioning in currently anxious patients reflects anxious mood state, then recovered anxious patients should resemble normal controls rather than currently anxious patients in that aspect of cognitive functioning. In contrast, if some aspect of non-normal cognitive functioning in currently anxious patients forms part of a vulnerability factor, then recovered anxious patients should resemble currently anxious patients rather than normal controls in that aspect of cognitive functioning.

Of course, data from recovered anxious patients cannot provide unequivocal evidence on the causality issue. For example, the cognitive performance of recovered anxious patients might resemble that of normal controls because of 'faking good' rather than because cognitive functioning has genuinely become normal. Alternatively, it might be that one of the effects of therapy is to eliminate a previous cognitive vulnerability. This possibility could be explored by dividing recovered anxious patients into separate groups on the basis of the form of therapy received, focusing particularly on the contrast between cognitive and non-cognitive therapies.

The cognitive performance of recovered anxious patients might resemble that of currently anxious patients but differ from that of normal controls even if a vulnerability factor were not involved. Cognitive functioning may simply take longer to recover than standard indices of recovery (e.g. mood measures). An attempt was made to guard against that possiblity in the current research programme by requiring that all of the recovered anxious patients had been recovered for a minimum of six months prior to experimental testing.

In sum, the programme of research has two major, related aims. The first aim is to establish as precisely as possible the nature of any differences in cognitive processes between patients with generalized anxiety disorder and normal controls in their reactions to mildly threatening stimuli. The second aim is to determine which of these differences in cognitive functioning are merely consequences of anxious mood state and which reflect a vulnerability factor.

Use of microcomputers: general advantages

In principle, it is probably true that all of the experimental tasks which have been utilized in the course of the research programme could have been presented to our subjects without making any use of microcomputers. Despite this, at least three-quarters of the cognitive tasks have, in fact been presented via microcomputer. Why is this the case? Of course, microcomputers are far more versatile than any of the pieces of apparatus traditionally used in laboratory studies of cognitive processing (e.g. tachistoscopes; slide projectors; memory drums). However, perhaps the single most important reason is that microcomputers have greatly facilitated the collection of substantial amounts of data without the necessity of inordinately lengthy experimental sessions. In a typical session, we require our subjects to complete approximately four or five questionnaires (e.g. Spielberger State-Trait Anxiety Inventory; the Mill Hill Synonym Test) as well as performing three different experimental tasks. In addition, there is sometimes a standard clinical interview for the potential groups. Even with the time-saving advantages of microcomputer presentation and data collection, experimental sessions usually last approximately 90 minutes.

Of course, instead of presenting three different cognitive tasks within a single experimental session, it would have been possible to make use of two or more experimental sessions. If microcomputers had not been used to present the cognitive tasks, then the total time required for each subject to complete three tasks and the various questionnaires would probably have been about four or five hours. Since the maximum feasible length of a session (especially with patient groups) is no more than 90 minutes or so, this would have necessitated the use of three separate experimental sessions.

There are various good reasons for wanting to avoid multiple experimental sessions. Patients currently suffering from generalized anxiety disorder obviously change over time as they receive treatment. As a consequence, the use of multiple experimental sessions would (on at least some tasks) introduce unwanted additional error variance. In addition, it can be difficult to find sufficient numbers of currently anxious and recovered anxious patients who fulfil the criteria for selection. The use of multiple experimental sessions would probably have the undesirable effect of producing some attenuation of subject numbers, since it is unlikely that every subject would appear for all three sessions.

There are other general advantages associated with the use of microcomputers in experiments involving anxious patients. For example, in order to obtain sufficiently large samples, it is usually necessary to recruit anxious patients from a number of different hospitals. This often makes it desirable to conduct experiments on a multi-site basis. If precisely the same model of microcomputer is available in two or more different locations, then precisely the same computer program can be used with each machine. This makes it relatively easy to present the various cognitive tasks in essentially identical fashion in each location.

There is a final reason why the use of microcomputers is desirable when carrying out experiments with anxious patients. Most anxious patients experience anxiety in many social situations, especially those that involve evaluation or interaction with other people who are high in prestige. If the experiments had been carried out using conventional laboratory apparatus, then the experimenter would have been more directly involved with the subjects during the course of the experiments. This might very well have made the laboratory session appear threatening, especially if the element of evaluation had been relatively obvious (e.g. the experimenter looking at a timer and writing down the response latencies during task performance).

In contrast, the experimenter is usually much less prominent when microcomputers are used. He or she is not sitting there recording the subject's performance, and so the subjects are less likely to feel that their abilities are being evaluated. In general, the fact that a computerized session is less of a social occasion than is a conventional laboratory session means that the anxious patients used as subjects are less likely to experience social anxiety. However, it is not unknown for anxious patients to demonstrate a certain amount of computer phobia, at least during the initial part of the session! In our experience, this usually disappears as they become familiarized with the functioning of the computer.

Use of microcomputers: general disadvantages

So far, we have considered the advantages of using microcomputers in our research. However, their use may have some drawbacks, particularly when carrying out research with a clinical population such as generally anxious patients. None of the disadvantages has posed insurmountable problems, but they are worth noting as a warning to other researchers.

First, microcomputers can be inconvenient and cumbersome to use in clinical settings. Since patients with a specific diagnosis may be relatively uncommon and can be difficult to recruit, it may be preferable to take the apparatus to a place that is convenient for patients, rather than expecting them to travel to an unfamiliar building or institution. Thus, practical problems may arise in transporting and setting up bulky equipment in busy hospital out-patient clinics or in-patient wards. This also increases the chances of damage to, and subsquent failure of, delicate components such as disk drives. Such problems could be overcome with the use of portable microcomputers, although they may be prohibitively expensive.

Second, when planning the stimulus and response requirements of the experiment it is important to take account of the special needs and difficulties of the clinical population under investigation. Generally anxious patients are typically susceptible to distraction, and so any extraneous sources of information should be minimized. For example, if a manual response is required, it would be unwise to present an an unmodified keyboard to anxious patients and require them to respond using selected keys, since this would provide an unnecessary source of distraction and might lead to confusion. Instead, it is preferable to use simple response buttons connected to the microcomputer, so that patients do not have to operate the keyboard.

Third, it is advisable to ensure that there is flexibility in the program controlling the procedure. For example, an anxious patient may have difficulty in sustaining concentration for extended periods, or might be temporarily distracted, which could necessitate a short pause in the experiment. Thus, it should be possible to interrupt temporarily an automated sequence of stimuli without having to start again at the beginning. Although such minor variations in procedure are not ideal and should be avoided (e.g. by allowing sufficient rest breaks), they should nevertheless be anticipated so that valuable data from a patient are not lost.

Fourth, there can be problems with carrying out experiments on a multi-site basis. In particular, it is often the case that two microcomputers which are allegedly the same model and the same make nevertheless differ sufficiently from each other that programs designed for one of them will not run on the other. Care therefore has to be taken to ensure that the microcomputers to be used in a multi-site experiment are really compatible with each other.

Finally, the use of microcomputers in clinical research may require staff with a high level of programming skills, particularly in the use of 'machine code' where the computer has to make very precisely timed interventions. Unfortunately, there are relatively few research workers with such skills and even fewer who also have a background in clinical research. It is hoped that the growing interest in the application of microcomputers to research into clinical problems will encourage more workers to develop expertise in this area.

Use of microcomputers: specific experimental examples

The value of microcomputers in the research programme can probably be demonstrated most convincingly by considering some of the cognitive tasks used in some detail. The results obtained from these tasks will not be discussed in detail here because of space limitations; the interested reader is referred to work by Eysenck and Mathews (1987) and Mathews and Eysenck (1987).

One task which has been used in a number of studies is designed to assess selective biases in the early stages of processing. There have been minor procedural differences across studies, but the methodology employed by MacLeod et al. (1986) will be discussed here. In essence, pairs of words were presented concurrently, one word towards the top of a visual display and the other towards the bottom. On key trials, one of the words was a threat-related word and the other word was neutral. The subject's task was to read aloud the top word in each case, but sometimes a faint dot replaced one of the displayed words and required a rapid response. It was assumed that detection latency of the dot provided a measure of the allocation of processing resources to that part of the screen. Patients with a diagnosis of generalized anxiety disorder responded faster to the dot when it replaced a threat word than when it replaced a neutral word, irrespective of whether this was in the top or bottom portion of the screen. Normal controls showed the opposite tendency, responding faster when the dot replaced a neutral word than when it replaced a threat word. In other words, the anxious patients exhibited a selective bias in favour of threatening stimuli, whereas normal controls biased their allocation of processing resources away from threatening stimuli.

In more detail, the task involved the presentation of a total of 288 word pairs, each word pair being presented for 500 ms at a spatial separation of 3 cm. On trials without the dot, the next pair of words followed 1 s after the offset of the previous word pair. When the dot was presented, it remained visible until the subject responded. Dots were presented on 96 of the trials, and were equally likely to replace the top and the bottom words in the display. The dots were presented approximately 25 ms after the termination of the word display. There were 48 critical word pairs (i.e. one threat word and one neutral word) followed by presentation of the dot, and the microcomputer was programmed so that specific word pairs were counterbalanced across the four conditions of interest: threat in upper area, dot in upper area; threat in upper area, dot in lower area; threat in lower area, dot in upper area; threat in lower area, dot in lower area. The computer was programmed so that reaction latencies to the dots could be recorded to 1-ms accuracy.

Suppose, for the sake of argument, that it had been decided to use a three-field tachistoscope rather than a microcomputer to investigate selective biases in allocation of processing resources. It would certainly have been possible to do this: the first field would have been used as the fixation field; the second field would have presented two spatially separated words; and the third field would have presented the dot. With a timer activated by the presentation of the dot, and stopped by the subject's manual response, it would have been possible to have recorded the response latencies required to assess the allocation of processing resources.

What would have been the disadvantages of using a three-field tachistoscope in this fashion? First, the rate of presentation would have been slowed down. Response latencies would have needed to be recorded by the experimenter, and each trial would have been initiated manually. Second, it would have been a long-winded and tedious business to rearrange the stimulus materials from one subject to the next in order to provide counterbalancing. Third, it would have been time-consuming to have assigned the response latencies to the various conditions. In contrast, the computer provided virtually immediate summary data of the mean response latencies in each condition.

A second experimental task which illustrates the advantages of using microcomputers is a modified Stroop task. In essence, a threat-related or a neutral word is presented visually in one of four colours, and the subject's task is to name the colour. On the basis of earlier research (Mathews and MacLeod, 1985), it was predicted that currently anxious patients would be more likely than normal controls to allocate extra processing resources to the threat-related word. As a result, their colour naming of threat-related words should be slowed relative to the normal controls, but there should be a small or non-existent group difference in speed of colour naming neutral words. For convenience, the predicted pattern of results will be referred to henceforth as the slowing effect.

An issue of theoretical interest is whether this slowing effect is due to automatic processes operating below the level of conscious attention. This is not clear from previous research because the words were always presented supraliminally (i.e. for sufficient time that the words could be consciously recognized). Accordingly, in the more recent version of the task, the words were presented either supra- or subliminally (i.e. so briefly that they could not be consciously recognized). The argument was that the slowing effect would be present with both supraliminal and subliminal presentation if it is produced by automatic or pre-attentive processes, whereas it would be present only with supraliminal presentation if the effect depends on attentional processes.

The experimental task consisted of a total of 384 trials, half of which involved supraliminal presentation and half of which involved subliminal presentation. On supraliminal trials, there was the following sequence of events on the screen of an Acorn Computers BBC model B:

1 A forward mask was presented for 20 ms. The mask consisted of rotated letters presented in white. The letters used varied randomly, but the number of letters corresponded to the number of letters in the following stimulus word.
2 The stimulus word was presented for 20 ms. One quarter of the words were presented in red, one quarter in green, one quarter in blue and one quarter in yellow.
3 The stimulus word was presented in white, and remained visible until the subject responded.

On subliminal trials, the first two stages were as for supraliminal trials. The third stage, however, consisted of a backward mask, in which a random string of rotated letters of the same length as the stimulus word was presented in white until the subject produced a naming response which stopped the timer.

The 384 trials were divided up into 192 supraliminal and 192 subliminal trials. There were 24 threat words (12 social threat and 12 physical health threat) and 24 neutral words, and each word was presented once in each of the four colours on supraliminal and on subliminal trials. There was a 2-s inter-trial interval, and the task was divided up into four blocks of trials with a short interval between blocks.

At the end of the experiment, the 48 words presented earlier in the experiment and 48 non-words were presented under the subliminal conditions to check whether the stimuli were genuinely subliminal. The subjects consistently denied any conscious awareness of whether words or non-words were being presented. Another measure of subliminality was also used: a lexical decision task (i.e. deciding whether or not a word had been presented).

Before discussing the reasons why a microcomputer was used for this experiment, it is worth making a technical point. Especially in the subliminal condition, it is obviously imperative to have accurate and consistent timing of stimulus presentations. This is difficult to achieve with Apple microcomputers (which were used in the studies on selective attention described above). The reason is as follows. An instruction in the program to present one or more stimuli on the screen is not acted on immediately. Instead, there is a raster scan which takes approximately 20 ms to move from top to bottom of the screen, and the delay between the instruction and the appearance of the stimuli on the screen depends upon the precise initial location of the raster scan. Since the normal arrangement with Apple microcomputers is that the instruction starts the timer, this means that the actual presentation time of stimuli varies somewhat from one trial to another. In contrast, with BBC computers, the timer starts only when the raster scan is at the top of the screen. This still produces some error in timing, but the error is constant rather than variable, and so is of much less consequence.

What are the advantages of using a microcomputer in this experiment? Far and away the greatest advantage is in terms of the time required for carrying out the experiment. If one includes the lexical decision task presented after the main sequence of trials, then there was a grand total of 480 trials. Even with the benefit of microcomputer presentation and recording of the response-latency data, it still required approximately 40 minutes to run a single subject. The only realistic alternative would have been to use a four-field tachistoscope, which would probaly have necessitated an experimental session of somewhere between three and four hours.

Why would the use of a four-field tachistoscope have made the experiment so demanding of time? The reasons are very much the same as for the selective attention task. Firstly, the requirement to re-randomize the trials for each subject would have been time-consuming with so many trials. Second, manual recording of response latencies would have greatly slowed down the inter-trial interval. Third, three of the four fields would have required changing on every trial. Therefore, there would have been a substantial amount of time spent changing stimulus cards, unless a four-field tachistoscope with three automatic changers had been available. Fourth, the fact that each trial would have had to be initiated manually would almost certainly have lengthened the inter-trial interval compared to the computer-paced inter-trial interval used on the microcomputer. Fifth, the calculation of mean scores in the various conditions would have been extremely time-consuming with the hundreds of trials used in the experiment. In contrast, the computer calculated them almost immediately.

It would be possible to give other examples of experiments which have benefited from the use of microcomputer presentation of task stimuli. However, the reasons for using microcomputers in these other experiments are, in general, very similar to the reasons for using them in the two experimental tasks already described. Therefore, there would be little point in discussing these other experiments in elaborate detail. What is probably more useful is to address the issue of which cognitive tasks benefit most and least from being presented by microcomputer.

It is no coincidence that the two experimental tasks used to illustrate the merits of computer-based presentation were concerned with the early stages of processing. In both cases, very precise timing of stimuli was required, because the processes being investigated are highly time-dependent. The importance of this requirement can be seen if we consider an earlier experiment exploring a very similar selective attention paradigm to the one used by MacLeod et al. (1986). In this experiment, which is discussed by Eysenck et al. (1987), pairs of words were presented auditorily, one to each ear. A mixture of threatening and neutral words was presented on the attended or shadowed ear, whereas only neutral words were presented on the unattended ear. A measure of the allocation of processing resources was obtained by asking subjects to respond as rapidly as possible to occasional tones that could be presented to either ear shortly after the presentation of a pair of words.

The problem with this experimental approach is that it is extremely difficult to synchronize the onset and the offset of the pairs of words. Any failure of synchrony can obviously bias the allocation of processing resources. With visual, computer-based presentation, there is no problem associated with synchronous onset and offset of the pairs of words.

Another common characteristic of the two experimental paradigms discussed above was that the requirement to have reliable data in several different conditions necessitated the use of a very large number of trials. The disadvantages of using conventional laboratory apparatus typically become greater as the number of experimental trials increases. The reason is that experimental sessions of impractical length become necessary when hundreds of trials must be carried out on conventional apparatus.

The advantages of computer presentation are less obvious when other experimental tasks are used. For example, many memory tasks can be implemented quite successfully without the use of a microcomputer. There are various reasons for this. First, it is not usually necessary to have extremely precise timing of stimulus presentation when the to-be-remembered stimuli are presented for several seconds. Second, the dependent variable is typically a measure of the number of items correct on a recall or recognition test rather than a time-based measure. Therefore, the timing routines of the microcomputer are not required, and the memory test can reasonably be conducted on a paper-and-pencil basis. However, it is probably true to say that information about speed of retrieval frequently provides a useful additional source of information about the processes involved. Third, instead of the hundreds of trials involved in the experiments described above, memory experiments often involve a relatively modest number of stimuli. As a consequence, the time-consuming activities of re-randomizing stimuli and scoring data pose a manageable problem.

One of the memory tasks which has been used in the programme of research can be used to illustrate some of the above points. The main point of interest was to examine possible differences among currently anxious, recovered anxious and normal control groups in the interpretation of ambiguous sentences. These sentences were selected so that they could be interpreted in either a threatening or a neutral fashion (e.g. 'The two men watched as the chest was opened').

In order to minimize awareness of the fact that ambiguous sentences were being presented, numerous neutral sentences were presented as well. Altogether, 110 neutral and 32 ambiguous sentences were presented. Half of the ambiguous sentences necessitated the drawing of an inference to be comprehended, whereas the other half did not. Within each category (i.e. compulsory inference and optional inference), half of the sentences contained a threatening interpretation relating to social concerns, and the other sentences contained a threatening interpretation relating to physical health concerns. The sentences were presented auditorily by cassette at the rate of one sentence every 5 seconds. The only real disadvantage of using this method of presentation rather than a microcomputer was that it was not feasible to use a different random order of presentation for each subject.

The subsequent recognition test involved the presentation of 67 sentences on a BBC microcomputer at a rate of one every 10 seconds. The subjects' task on this test was to decide as rapidly as possible whether each displayed sentence had the same meaning as a sentence heard earlier, and then to decide on a five-point rating scale how confident they were in that decision. The first three were introductory filler sentences, followed by 32 sentences consistent in meaning with the unambiguous sentences presented initially randomly mixed with 32 disambiguated versions of the previously ambiguous sentences (16 threatening and 16 neutral disambiguations).

Why was it decided to use a microcomputer for the recognition-test phase of the experiment? First, this facilitated the collection of both the decision-time and confidence data. Second, the microcomputer provided the relevant summary data for each subject rapidly and effortlessly. Third, using a microcomputer facilitated the task of presenting the sentences at regular intervals while avoiding having sentences to which the subjects failed to respond in time. This was accomplished by presenting the sentences for a maximum of 5 seconds, with the offset of the sentence after that time serving as a warning that he or she should respond. If the subject did not respond within 6.5 seconds of sentence onset, then a 'HURRY UP' message was displayed on the screen. Finally, at 8.5 seconds, the five-point rating scale was presented on the screen.

In sum, it is possible to use a microcomputer as the apparatus for presenting the great majority of cognitive tasks. However, it is indisputable that microcomputers are more useful (or even indispensable) for some kinds of tasks than for others. Microcomputers are of maximal usefulness when a cognitive task has the following characteristics: (1) numerous trials; (2) precise timing of stimuli is required; (3) each trial involves a complex sequence of events; (4) there needs to be a substantial amount of re-randomization of stimuli across trials and conditions from one subject to the next; and (5) precise timing (and immediate recording) of responses is required. In contrast, microcomputers are less useful when a cognitive task involves a small number of trials, precise timing of stimuli is not necessary, the trials do not involve complex sequences of events, little re-randomization of stimuli is needed and responses do not have to be precisely timed.

References

Beck, A. T. and Emery, G. (1985). *Anxiety Disorders and Phobias: A Cognitive Perspective.* New York: Basic Books.

Beck, A. T., Laude, R, and Bohnert, M. (1974). Ideational components of anxiety neurosis, *Archives of General Psychiatry,* **31**, 319–325.

Bryne, D. (1964). Repression-sensitization as a dimension of personality. In B. A. Maher (ed.), *Progress in Experimental Personality Research.* New York: Academic Press.

Eysenck, M. W. and Mathews, A. (1987). Trait anxiety and cognition. In H. J. Eysenck and I. Martin (eds). *Theoretical Foundations of Behavior Therapy.* New York: Plenum.

Eysenck, M. W., Macleod, C. and Mathews, A. (1987). Cognitive functioning and anxiety, *Psychological Research,* **49**, 198–195.

MacLeod, C., Mathews, A. and Tata, P.. (1986). Attentional bias in emotional disorders. *Journal of Abnormal Psychology,* **95**, 15–20.

Mathews, A. and Eysenck, M. W. (1987). Clinical anxiety and cognition. In H. J. Eysenck and I. Martin (eds), *Theoretical Foundations of Behavior Therapy.* New York: Plenum.

Mathews, A. and MacLeod, C. (1985). Selective processing of threat cues in anxiety states, *Behaviour Research and Therapy,* **23**, 563–569.

Watson, D. and Clark, L. A. (1984). Negative affectivity: The disposition to experience aversive emotional states, *Psychological Bulletin,* **96**, 465–490.

CHAPTER 9

Small computers, big transformations: computers and models of perceptuo-motor performance

PATRICK RABBITT

It is now banal to say that computers have radically changed psychology. The growth of cognitive science and the study of artificial intelligence have totally transformed our models of how biological systems interpret and adapt to the world. They now provide a powerful common language in which cognitive psychologists describing hypothetical functional systems and physiologists and biochemists describing neuronal architecture can communicate. Information technology has brought applied cognitive psychologists new metaphors, insights and descriptive techniques and has also created exciting new applied problems for them to study. These large issues, and the implications of future trends, can only be profitably discussed by experts. Here we consider a much humbler theme: how, over the last fifteen years, enormous increases in the general accessibility and power of desk-top microprocessors as basic laboratory equipment used in choice reaction time (CRT) experiments have transformed the limits of feasible experiments and analysable data. Like earlier empirical tools such as microscopes and telescopes, microcomputers have radically changed what we now regard as 'data' and in the process transformed the questions we can ask and the models we use to interpret the answers we get. It is not too much to argue that this process has brought us new insights into how we, and other creatures, successfully keep up with our complex, rapidly changing environments.

It is easy to forget that before the advent of microprocessors even the best available digital timers only allowed investigators to examine reaction times (RTs) for discrete, separate events. Signals presented, responses made to them, and times (usually only with centisecond resolution) had to be logged for each trial in turn—usually by hand. This meant that models for RT, like the

Microcomputers, Psychology and Medicine
Edited by R. West, M. Christie and J. Weinman
© 1990 by John Wiley & Sons Ltd

experiments that supported them, could deal only with isolated decisions. While these were the only data available it was not feasible to model *contingencies*, to study the effects which each new event, and the response made to it, might have on interpretation of subsequent events, or to examine how individuals adapt to momentary changes in their own performance. It has always been obvious that the time characteristics of behaviour in the real world are bound up with complex interactions in which organisms anticipate events and have to evaluate and respond to the results of their own actions. The lack of any capability to study these interactive relationships was obviously a crippling limitation for scientists who realised that laboratory experiments were attempts to fractionate continuous chains of tightly articulated decisions into arbitrary discrete 'events'. The study of RTs was, quite rightly, seen as a methodological obsession and an empirical dead end.

Some creative investigators developed rough and ready techniques to overcome these limitations. When Paul Bertelson (1961) wanted to ask whether RTs when signals and responses were repeated differed from RTs when they changed from trial to trial, he could only do so by building an elaborate electromechanical switching-tree to separately cumulate response times over all repeated and all alternated trials. When he further wished to separate sequential effects between signals and between responses he had to sacrifice even the limited accuracy then possible with electronic counters and use a pen recorder marking a moving paper band (Bertelson, 1963). It is important to realise that the laboriousness and inflexibility of these techniques not only limited the kinds, and the precision, of data that could be collected. They even more severely limited the *amounts* of data which could be logged within any reasonable time, and so curtailed the periods for which experiments could be run and the amount of practice that individual subjects could reasonably be given. The effects of practice on response speed are greater than those produced by any other variable. The fact that practice was virtually ignored in all early theories of RT would be remarkable if we did not realise how very difficult it was to collect and analyse sufficient data to study practice effects; individuals still continue to improve their performance even after more than 300 000 trials of practice (Rabbitt and Banerji, in press).

It is crucial to realise that these limitations were not imposed because computer systems were completely unavailable to experimental psychologists but rather because imaginations had not yet been liberated by daily contact with friendly machines. In 1955 it would have been possible to run any RT experiment or data analysis yet carried out or planned for the early 1990s on one of the large and clumsy computer systems then available in universities. It was certainly not easy for psychologists to gain access to these machines, but it would, in principle, have been quite possible for an energetic investigator to buy or borrow time on his local large system—it would not have been strictly necessary to learn how to use it—though that would have helped.

What would have been essential was the vision to see what exciting questions it could be used to answer. The fact that people did not do this was not due to general computer illiteracy in psychology departments. Psychometricians were among the first scientists to make heavy use of large, number-crunching systems. The conceptual lag occurred because machines had not become part of most investigators' daily lives, so that they had not yet begun to imagine their possibilities as experimental tools rather than merely as aids to rapid computation of complex statistics. Limits to science are not merely set by what is momentarily feasible; they are more stringently enforced by what is currently imaginable. The importance of the microprocessor is that it is the cheapest device for liberating the empirical *imagination* which has ever been produced in the history of science.

Gradually more and more investigators began to have access to machines, though these had less than a hundredth of the memory, processing speed or user-friendliness of current desk-tops—and cost a hundred times as much, adjusting for the currency of the day. The first dedicated computer system installed in a British psychology department was an early Elliott 903 in Sheffield. From this point it becomes possible to set out case histories of how computers have advanced studies in reaction times.

Studying sequential effects and contingencies

The first great liberation was that it was not only possible to time responses in milliseconds but to record each signal, and the response made to it, as fast as any subject could carry out a task. This allowed investigators to study sequential effects between successive responses. Kornblum (1968) was one of the first investigators to seize this advantage. Models of RT based on information theory predicted that decision latencies must be inversely related to signal probability, and many experiments had shown this to be the case. However, Bertelson (1961) had also shown that RTs were much faster when the same signal and response was repeated than when different signals and responses followed each other. Thus while existing apparatus could only cumulate times for all responses to any particular signal the basic theoretical assumption of all RT models remained untestable. Because the probability that a signal would be repeated increased directly with its overall probability during a run, it remained uncertain how far subjects perceived and used signal probabilities and how far their RTs averaged across probable signals were faster than RTs averaged over rare signals merely because the former were more often repetitions than the latter. Kornblum (1968) saw that if every response could be recorded it was simple separately to examine RTs on trials when probable signals were repeated and when they were not. He did this, and showed that there were, indeed, separate effects of signal probability and of signal repetition. This moved the study of RTs out of models which predicted gross cumulated data to models which began to take account of and predict individual RTs as a function of the particular contexts in which they were made.

Remington (1969) and Kirby (1972) soon took this much further, investigating how people can estimate the local probabilities of signals in a run by breaking down very long sequences of signal and response events into all possible N-back chains. They showed that RTs vary markedly with the local structure of the chain of events in which they occur, and that to understand sequential effects it is not merely necessary to separate signal and response repetitions and alternations from the overall probabilities of individual signals and responses. The RT recorded to any given signal on any trial is affected by the precise patterning of transitions between signals and responses over at least the preceding ten events. This immediately transformed the whole field of reaction times, from a dull study based on the blatantly false assumption that each human decision is a temporally independent event with no history and no sequelae, to the study of how people continuously interact with their environment in order to find and use regularities in its temporal characteristics: in short, into the ways in which people actively interpret and cope with a rapidly mutable world.

The full range of this adaptive flexibility only gradually came to be realised, and is still incompletely investigated. The key to its analysis is another one of the micro's enormous advantage as a research tool: it can design, store and instantly present and alter displays of any desired complexity and of any required level of discrimination difficulty. When Donald Laming (1968) wished to study the effects of signal discriminability on reaction times for his PhD thesis he had to design and build a multiple-field tachistoscope to do so. Less than ten years later another research student, Stephen Fearnley (1977), was able to write a simple computer program to vary independently the discrimination difficulty of each display in a series of any required length, and to automatically record, recover and analyse the speed and accuracy with which his subjects responded to each in turn. This allowed him to show that the times which humans take to make any discrimination not only varied with its difficulty but also with the difficulty of the last several discriminations they have made. RTs to easily discriminated displays are much slower when these appear immediately after difficult discriminations have been made; and responses to difficult displays are much faster (and much less accurate) when they follow easy displays than when they follow other, quite different, difficult displays.

Because computer systems handle information so much faster than biological systems they can allow us to log enormous volumes of data during the (for them) eons of dead time while the humans using them make their slow descisions. This allows us to log subjects' performance in real time in any desirable level of detail for subsequent, off-line, analysis. This possibility of complete recording of each event in a very long series allowed investigators, for the first time, not only to study the speeds with which people make (pseudo) independent decisions, but the maximum rate at which they can prepare themselves to make one decision after they have just made another. This was done by programming a computer to time and very precisely to control the interval between the moment at which a response was made to one signal, and the moment of onset of the next (R–S interval). It was discovered that, as R–S intervals increased from 20 ms to 500 ms, subjects' RTs reduced by 30–60 ms. This reduction in RT seemed to remain identical over a wide range of decision difficulties and for either repeated or alternated responses. This suggests that we can use this experimental manipulation to measure the maximum rate at which subjects can mobilise non-specific preparation for the onset of any new event (Rabbit, 1969). Subsequent experiments have found that the index of the rate of preparation (slope of the function relating RT to R–S interval duration) remains unaltered by individual differences such as age and IQ, or by experimental treatments, such as the ingestion of alcohol, which markedly affect RTs. Other experimental treatments, such as practice, apparently slow both RTs and preparation rates (Maylor and Rabbitt, 1988). Here again microprocessors have enlarged our understanding of human decisions as processes based on active prediction and anticipation of future events rather than merely on passive, post hoc analyses of the immediate past. They have also allowed us to collect enough different kinds of data to examine dissociations between different performance indices in response to individual differences, subject treatments and experimental manipulations. These experiments also emphasise that our central nervous systems manage to cope so efficiently with the world precisely because they continually seek ways of keeping one jump ahead of it, rather than forever lagging one reaction time behind it. Later experiments have shown that even the temporal characteristics of strings of signals—e.g. repetitions and alternations of identical and different R–S intervals on successive trials—are registered and used in attempts to maximise efficiency. When long R–S intervals follow other long R–S intervals responses are faster than when long intervals follow short intervals, and vice versa (Rabbitt and Vyas, 1980). The time characteristics of sequences of events may, apparently, be automatically analysed and used to guide prediction along with all the other information which can be derived from them. RTs are determined by the local structure of the scenarios in which events occur, not simply by their nature.

These experiments which looked at RTs to signals as a function of the contexts in which they occurred began slowly to force recognition that the human cognitive system is not like a simple telephone network in which each input (perceptual event) is analysed quite independently of any that precede it. We would not be here to write about it if it were not a dynamically adaptive system which adjusts its decision criteria in order to maximise the efficiency with which it copes with a rapidly changing world. To do this it tries to use *all* the information available to it. The human cognitive system does not analyse 'signals'. It rather analyses 'scenarios' or 'contexts' of which the events arbitrarily designated as 'signals' are only one part. It was an easy move from these insights to the realisation that humans not only adapt their performance in order to adjust to environmental changes and regularities, but also to adjust to rapid fluctuations in their own efficiency.

Studying moment-to-moment control of performance

Microprocessors brought into our laboratories the capability to record each signal, response and RT as soon as it occurred, and to be able to go back at leisure to analyse and reanalyse them as often as necessary. This allowed us to locate significant events which spontaneously occurred during long experimental sessions and to study their precursors and sequelae in detail. These new techniques forced an early discovery that subjects' errors are generally much faster than their correct responses (Rabbitt, 1966). The discovery that mean RTs for responses immediately preceding errors are often faster than mean RTs for all other correct responses (Laming, 1979) suggested that errors typically occur at the end of a string of responses during which subjects progressively relax their criteria for accuracy in order to achieve greater speed (i.e. errors occur because subjects respond before they have time adequately to analyse the signals presented to them, and typically occur at the end of a run of riskily fast responses). It was also found that even when subjects are instructed to pay no attention to their errors, responses which immediately follow errors are much slower than all other correct responses (Rabbitt, 1969). This made it clear that people spontaneously, and continuously, monitor their reponses for accuracy so that they can detect errors when they occur. This also suggests that they have the necessary information actively to control their own performance, testing the limits of their ability by allowing their criteria to relax and their decision speeds to increase until an error occurs. This may allow them to identify the fastest speed at which correct responding is possible, and then, after an error, to slow down in order to try to regain and maintain that safe optimum level (Rabbitt and Vyas, 1972).

The speed and flexibility of computer-control of experiments made it possible, for the first time, to ask subjects to monitor and to respond to fluctuations in their own response output. Rabbitt (1968) asked subjects to identify and correct their errors as soon as they made them so as to discover what kinds of errors people can most rapidly and most reliably detect. It emerged that people are very good at detecting most of the errors that they make in serial CRT tasks and can spontaneously 'correct' some of them so very rapidly (14 ms or less after their commission) that we must assume that in these cases an impulsive incorrect response has only slightly preceded a correct response, which has been programmed and initiated in parallel with it. Slower detections and corrections of errors are, apparently, achieved by monitoring visual or kinaesthetic feedback. People can detect very few errors of perceptual discrimination (Rabbitt *et al.*, 1978). However, the fact that some discrimination errors can be detected and corrected must mean that incomplete perceptual analyses which have led to hasty decisions and incorrect responses can sometimes be continued beyond the moment at which the responses are produced so that a 'perceptual double-take' can initiate a new, correct response on its subsequent, more reliable termination.

Studying interactive contingencies

In the real world, the responses that humans make to their environments immediately bring about changes which they must also anticipate if they can, detect if they occur and, if necessary, respond to in turn. Biological survival demands constant, very rapid, adjustment to an environment which is reactive rather than passive. Measurements of RTs can only contribute to our understanding of the cognitive systems if we can use them to help us understand these very fast interactive transactions. This has only become possible since computer systems became fast and powerful enough to evaluate responses as soon as people make them, and accordingly to alter the events which they generate. Because microcomputers now process some kinds of information much faster than does the human CNS we can use them to study how humans contingently interact with their environments in real time.

Perhaps the simplest example of a contingently interactive CRT experiment is one in which a computer provides subjects with feedback on their performance which is different, more precise, and probably as rapid, as that provided by their own sense organs. This has been done by using the RT on each trial to continuously modulate the frequency of a 'bleep' signal which the computer emits as soon as each response is made. Thus, for example, fast responses may be immediately followed by high and slow responses by low-pitched tones. This augmented feedback, giving very rapid and very precise information about response speed, allows subjects in CRT experiments to reduce the number of slow responses which they make much more rapidly than they manage to do when only their own, unmodified, visual and kinaesthetic feedback is available to them (Rabbitt, 1981). In effect, provision of enhanced feedback of response speed accelerates practice. Techniques of studying the mechanisms by which individuals adaptively gain information from, and rapidly adjust to, the immediate consequences of their own actions are now easily available, but have hardly yet been exploited.

In contrast to this neglect of a range of simple and feasible experiments there has been some research into much more complicated interactive simulations and video games. For example, an entire special issue of the journal *Acta Psychologica* deals with a series of parallel investigations by a number of different teams of investigators of the same, very complex, video game 'Space Fortress' (Sanders, 1989). In the micro-world of this task, as in real life, signals which require very rapid responses do not occur independently of other events, but must selectively be picked out from among a multitude of other events simultaneously visible on a complex display, or held in working memory, which compete for attention with different degrees of urgency. The feasibility of intensive investigations of very complex situations takes the study of RTs out of the laboratory into real life, which never has the grace to pause to allow us to finish what we are doing before making a new demand on us. In real life the time characteristics of paced performance are determined by the range of competing demands to which a person must simultaneously attend. A signal is very seldom an isolated event such as the simple onset of a light or a tone. Signals must always be evaluated in context, and the same signal may demand radically different responses in only fractionally different perceptual scenarios. For example, a change in a traffic light from green to amber may require one to begin to brake if one is at some distance from it, but to sharply accelerate if one is very near it. In an intermediate zone one may either brake or accelerate—but must do either very much more rapidly. The precise scenario dictates not merely the choice but also the urgency of the same responses, and the concept of isolated 'signals' is a crude fiction. The real world is not made up of discrete signals, but of constantly changing scenarios. Our behaviour is not triggered by sensory events, but guided by shifting and complex interpretations. Computers have recently given us the ability to manipulate and study the time relationships of these interpretations.

Making sense of huge masses of data

The papers in the Sanders symposium illustrate that while it is an empirical triumph to be able to collect and permanently to store very large masses of experimental data, we have not yet solved the problem of making sense of such voluminous material. This is no longer a matter of computational power; the same computers that collect the data give us the means to analyse them. Large-scale 'number crunching' is probably the most generally recognised, least imaginative, and most useful new facility that computers offer us. The real problem is to develop plausible models of complex tasks against which we can test the masses of data now available to us. Computers have put us into the agonising but very fruitful dilemma that we can now answer virtually any question we can think of—if we have the imagination to ask it. The liberation of the imagination is a painful freedom.

However, the first gains from this freedom are beginning to appear in the analyses of much simpler, much more traditional, and so intellectually more transparent tasks. It has been no accident that models for CRT processes have, so far, been constructed to predict patterns of summary statistics from CRT data. Means and medians of CRTs were usually the only indices that the experimental equipment of the 1960s could yield. When measures of variations in performance, such as standard deviations, were available, these were based on data between individuals rather than within individuals. Within-subject standard deviations are sometimes punctiliously included in tabulated data, but have hardly ever been analysed to test models.

The possibility of recording the RT for every response which the subject makes during an indefinitely long experimental task has abruptly changed all this. It is now just as easy to inspect complete distributions of all CRTs, and even to segregate these into sub-distributions for various categories of response such as errors and correct responses or repetitions and alternations, as it once was to compute simple measures of central tendency. When this is done it is immediately evident that means, medians or even standard deviations are very poor descriptive statistics for CRT data because CRT distributions are very sharply skewed. Most RTs pile up towards the faster, lower limit of the CRT distribution, with a long straggling tail of slower responses.

Inspection of CRT distributions also forces us to realise that measures of central tendency or any other summary statistics are only useful indices of task performance if they make sense in terms of reasonable assumptions as to what humans are actually doing. In other words, our performance models should always determine the statistics we use and not vice versa. To allow fashionable statistical tests to determine the comparisons we make risks a considerable waste of time.

As we saw above, in serial, self-paced choice tasks mean CRTs for errors are usually much faster than mean CRTs for all correct responses. Inspection of response distributions confirms and illuminates this contrast. Error distributions are skewed in the same ways as distributions of correct responses; most error responses occur at the fast end of the error RT distribution. This suggests that the faster a response the more likely it is to be an error. This is indeed so, as we can show very simply by superimposing distributions of error RTs on their corresponding distributions of correct RTs and, by computing the percentages of errors to correct responses within successive arbitrary RT bands, derive functions which show the probability that a response will be an error given the RT band in which it occurs (see Figure 9.1). Such plots show that the probability that a response will be an error is relatively high in the fastest RT bands, and steadily declines across slower RT bands until it reaches a very low, and apparently constant, value (Pew, 1969; Pacella and Pew, 1968; Rabbitt and Vyas, 1972). Similar functions showing a gradual trade-off between response speed and accuracy can be obtained by forcing subjects to respond within increasingly brief time limits (Schouten and Bekker, 1967).

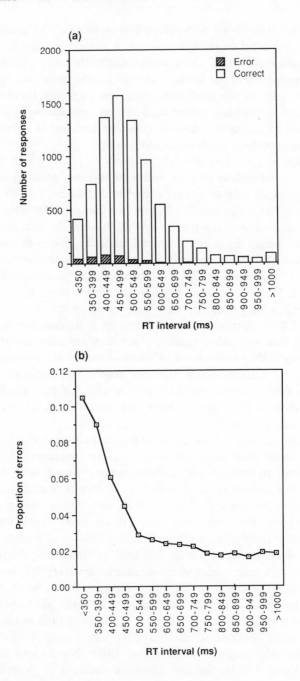

FIGURE 9.1   Computation of a speed-error trade-off function from distributions of correct and error reaction times

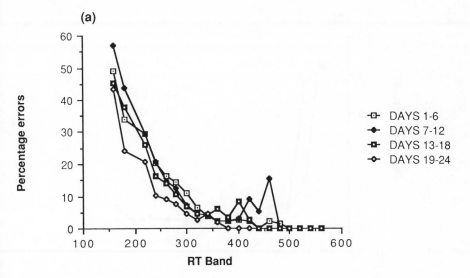

FIGURE 9.2a Speed-error trade-off functions for a single subject, MJM, alter with practice

These relationships make good sense in the context of all existing models for RTs (see Luce, 1986). All models assume that evidence from a display is continuously accumulated, or evaluated, until a decision criterion is reached. If the decision criterion is too lax, processes of evaluation will terminate prematurely and errors will become more likely. Stringent decision criteria will result in slower responses and in a very low, or zero, error rate. Thus response speed and accuracy will trade-off against each other as, in fact, we nearly always empirically observe. In the context of such models it becomes possible to answer the question as to what is the most appropriate index of the limits of a subject's efficiency at a task. Evidently measures of central tendency such as means or medians will not be appropriate because they are much influenced by the slow, but relatively very accurate, responses which make up the long tail of the skewed CRT distribution. The fastest responses which subjects make during a task are also quite inappropriate indices of the limits of their performance because, as we have seen, in these bands of the CRT distribution accuracy may be at, or only slightly above, chance. Measures of variability such as standard deviations, or measures of skew and curtosis give much more information, but are also inadequate, because they take no account of relative accuracy. However, the slopes and the intercepts of speed–error trade-off functions are, indeed, appropriate indices of limits to efficiency because they describe the fastest speeds at which any given level of accuracy is possible.

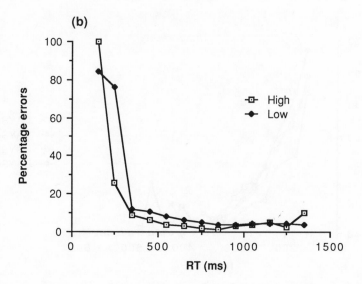

FIGURE 9.2b   Speed-error trade-off functions produced by subjects with high and low unadjusted IQ test scores (Rabbitt and Goward, in press 1989)

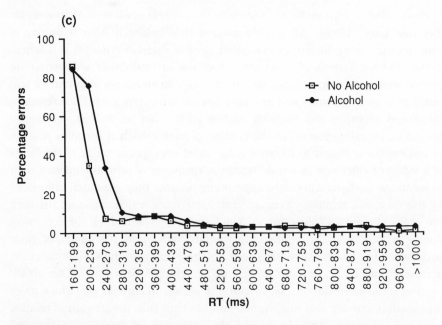

FIGURE 9.2c   Speed-error trade-off functions produced by subjects who had, and had not, recently consumed small doses of alcohol (Maylor and Rabbitt, 1988)

The discovery of an index which describes limiting levels of accuracy of performance allows us, for the first time, to give rational answers to questions as to whether, and how, within-subject factors such as practice or alcohol, or between-subject factors such as age or performance in IQ test scores affect CRT performance. All these factors are known to affect the variance and skew of response distributions, and it is seldom possible to control experiments tightly enough to control for accuracy across conditions or groups. However, when speed–error trade-off limits (SETOLs) are computed it is possible to see that all these factors do indeed affect the lower RT limits at which response accuracy is possible. Figure 9.2(a) compares SETOLs obtained from CRT distributions emitted early and late in practice by Rabbitt and Banerji (in press); Figure 9.2(b) compares SETOLs derived from age-matched groups of individuals with high and low IQs by Rabbitt and Goward (submitted); Figure 9.2(c) compares SETOLs obtained by Maylor and Rabbitt (1987) from data from individuals who had, or who had not, ingested alcohol before the task.

The great convenience of microprocesser analysis is that even very large volumes of data can rapidly be reanalysed and resorted in any number of quite different ways. This makes the interactive 'exploratory data analytic' approaches recommended by distinguished and creative statisticians (see Tukey, 1977) easily accessible to individuals who have access even to microprocessors of very modest power. Very large volumes of data can be collected, filtered to eliminate machine errors and other spurious responses, and then stored on disc. They can then, with little or no further alteration, be very rapidly and repeatedly reanalysed by suites of extremely powerful exploratory and analytic statistical programs which, in cases such as Tony Dusoir's ECDA (1988), have built-in routines which provide very convenient and informative on-line graphical display of the outcomes of categorisations and sorts. It is part of the power of these packages that they can be adapted to sort and to display data gathered on-line by computer systems and rapidly to compute new parameters to modify the programs controlling the experiments.

Some simple questions that can be asked and answered in this way may be illustrated by alternative analyses of CRT distributions collected by Rabbitt and Goward (submitted) given in Figure 9.3 (a) and (b). These are the same data-sets from which the SETOLs given in Figure 9.2 (a) and (b) were derived. Figure 9.3 (a) and (b) present alternative descriptions of distributions of all correct response times produced by groups of individuals with high and with low IQ test scores. In Figure 9.3(a) we see that distributions of correct RTs produced by high IQ test scorers are considerably less skewed than those produced by low IQ test scorers. Figure 9.3(b) makes the same point by showing plots of the 10th through 90th percentile points for distributions of correct RTs produced by these two groups. These alternative presentations of the data make it unambiguous that both practice and IQ test scores alter RT means and medians mainly because they reduce the number of very slow

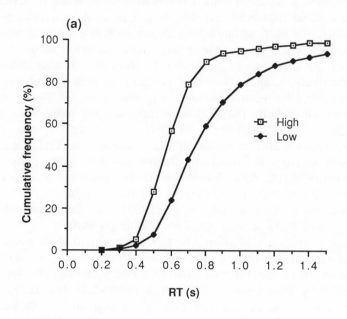

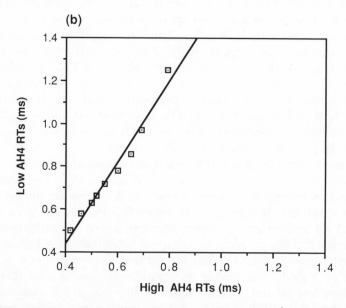

FIGURE 9.3   Ogives for distributions of CRTs produced by individuals with high and low unadjusted IQ test scores. Plots of deciles of distributions produced by high scorers against those produced by low scorers are linear, suggesting that they are simple linear transformations of each other

(a)

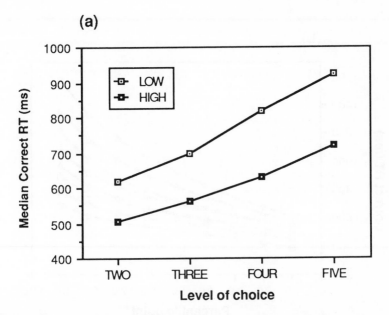

FIGURE 9.4a Low IQ test scorers are more affected by increasing informational demands than are high IQ test scorers

responses which individuals produce, but have comparatively little effect on the fastest responses which they make. These plots also point the way to the simplest statistical comparisons which can validate these conclusions, at least in the case of comparisons between groups (Rabbitt and Goward, submitted): two-way between/within analyses of variance show significant differences between groups and, of course, between percentiles; but the point of the comparison is the significant *interaction* between percentile scores and groups which establishes that IQ test scores primarily alter the shapes of RT distributions, and that their effects of means and medians are only secondary to these effects.

Exploratory analyses using alternative graphical descriptions of large volumes of data can do much more than clarify our thinking, sharpen our insights and simplify our statistical treatments of data (though this is, already, a very great deal!). Figure 9.4 plots data gathered by Rabbitt *et al.* (in preparation) from large groups of high and low IQ individuals each of whom performed an easy serial CRT task at four levels of choice (i.e four levels of difficulty). Figure 9.4(a) shows median response times for the four groups plotted as a function of level of choice. It seems that the CRTs of low-IQ groups increase faster with levels of choice than do the CRTs of the high-IQ groups. This finding is confirmed, and extended, when we compare plots of the 10th to the 90th

(b)

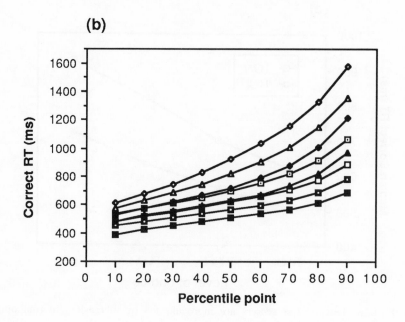

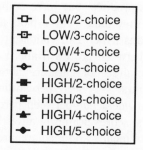

FIGURE 9.4b   Interaction between IQ test score, level of choice, and shape of CRT distribution

percentile scores for the high- and the low-IQ groups as a function of choice (Figure 9.4b). This suggests that both choice and IQ test score have their greatest effects on the slowest responses in RT distributions, where the interaction between the effects of test score and of task difficulty is much exaggerated. A three-way between/within/within analysis of variance does indeed confirm this by confirming a third-order interaction between IQ, percentile scores and condition of choice.

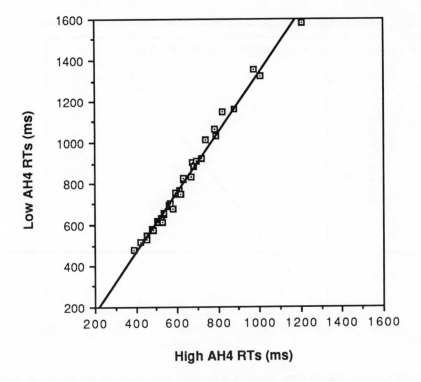

FIGURE 9.5   Deciles of CRT distributions produced by high and low IQ test scorers are co-linear, suggesting that they are simple linear transformations of each other

We now have several clear results, but how shall we interpret them? Practice, IQ test score and alcohol all have much more marked effects on the slowest than on the fastest responses in CRT distributions. From a practical point of view this is an extremely useful thing to know, because it shows that means and medians are comparatively insensitive indices for picking up small differences in performance on speed tasks which may be due to alcohol, intelligence, practice, task difficulty, and probably any combination of these variables. If we need sensitive indices to detect very small effects we should compute and compare higher percentiles of RT distributions. However, these findings raise a sharp theoretical question: do different functional processes occur to produce the fastest and the slowest responses which subjects make during serial CRT tasks? Do the variables we have studied have different effects on these mechanisms? Or is it rather the case that the same underlying functional processes produce both fast and slow responses, and that alcohol, practice, etc. only apparently have differential effects on different parts of the CRT distributions?

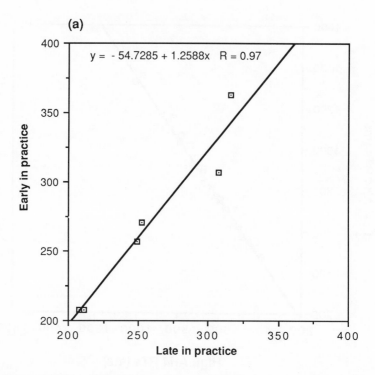

$$y = -54.7285 + 1.2588x \quad R = 0.97$$

FIGURE 9.6a Deciles from subjects with high and lower IQ scores are co-linear (Rabbitt and Goward, submitted)

We can approach an answer to this question by another re-sort and graphical re-presentation of the data. In Figure 9.5 we replot the data from Figure 9.4(b) so as to locate RTs for each percentile point from each level of choice for the high-IQ group in terms of the RT for the corresponding percentile point for the low-IQ group. As we see, all points fall on the same straight line. It follows that the algebraic expressions which generate the entire CRT distributions produced by low-IQ individuals, and at easy levels of choice, are indentical in structure to those which generate the entire CRT distributions produced by high-IQ individuals and at difficult levels of choice. The combined effects of IQ test score, and of choice, can evidently be accounted within the same algebraic expression simply by adjusting the value of a single, multiplicative, term.

Figure 9.6(a) replots in the same data from Rabbitt and Goward's (submitted) comparison between high and lower IQ test scores at a single level of task difficulty; Figure 9.6(b) replots data from subjects who had, and who had not, ingested alcohol in Maylor and Rabbitt's (1987) study. In all cases we see that percentile points maintain co-linearity, showing that the effects of IQ test score,

(b)

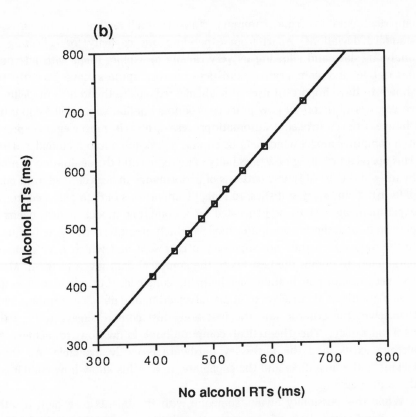

No alcohol RTs (ms)

FIGURE 9.6b   Deciles from CRT distributions obtained from Ss who had and who had not, ingested alcohol are co-linear (Mayor and Rabbitt, 1987)

of extended practice and of alcohol on RT distributions can all be described in terms of variations in the magnitude of a single multiplicative term in a common generative algorithm. This is not inconsistent with any of the existing powerful and sophisticated algebraic models contrasted in Luce's (1986) masterly review. It is not too much to say that these transforms of the data indicate that a 'general model for choice reaction times' must exist. The precise specification of the best form of this model, and the development and testing of predictions from it, is a much more formidable and exciting task.

Future prospects

We have seen that microprocessors both offer new opportunities for data collection and new facilities for data analysis. These enormously expand and improve the range of indices which we can derive and analyse. It is obviously no longer desirable, and it is certainly not necessary, to restrict our view of empirical data to crude summary statistics such as means, medians and standard deviations. Apart from expanding our capacity for collecting and analysing data and allowing us very rapidly to explore them with alternative descriptive and comparative statistics, microcomputers have recently been shown to have important uses as sophisticated aids to theoretical modelling. A very powerful theory of how practice produces qualitative as well as quantitive changes from controlled to automatic processing finds its most elegant expression in a computer model which can be run on a desk-top micro (Schneider, 1986). This opens an exciting new possibility of going beyond the evaluation of models by tests of the fits of sparse patterns of performance indices derived from pooled data using summary statistics, to global comparisons of data obtained from an experiment against those generated by a computer model. It also opens the possibility of designing computer models which are, interactively, self-adjusting to the data which they are supposed to represent and which alter their own parameters to obtain the best fits to the empirical data given to them. Models will become not pencil-and-paper heuristic constructs but adaptive structures which assimilate themselves to fit actual experimental data, and contain within themselves the criteria, and the best and most comprehensive tests of their own adequacy. The theoretical computational know-how to achieve this already exists, and the necessary hardware is easily available. All that is lacking is the incentive, and the capability, to use this know-how combined in the same person.

While this possibility awaits someone with the talents to exploit it, other, more flamboyant, lines of enquiry seem relatively unsatisfying. We have the ability to design and to run extremely complex video-games and simulations. 'Space Fortress' represents only the humble beginning of experiments of this kind. We already have the capability simultaneously to present many different signals as parts of a continuously changing scenario, and to observe how well, or poorly, humans can keep up with these complex changes. We can test how far people can simultaneously manage to analyse different patterns of information and to produce, in parallel, different kinds of responses to them. We can measure the time characteristics of the ways in which information held in long- and short-term memory is integrated with information currently presented in order to resolve complex problems. All this is very heady stuff, but will demand a fluency with computing systems, and a level of imagination in seeing and fully exploiting their capabilities, which is well beyond most of the present generation of cognitive psychologists. When this field of enquiry properly develops it will be magnificent, but it will not be the study of choice reaction times. It will have rendered obsolete the kinds of experiments which have been the modest topic of this chapter.

References

Bertelson, P. (1961). Sequential redundancy and speed in a serial two-choice responding task, *Quarterly Journal of Experimental Psychology*, **13**, 90–102.

Bertelson, P. (1963). Serial choice reaction time as a function of response versus signal-and-response repetition, *Nature*, **206**, 217–218.

Dusoir, T. (1988). *ECDA. Exploratory and Confirmatory Data Analysis*. Hove: Erlbaum Software.

Fearnley, S. (1977). Criterion changes in relative discrimination tasks. Unpublished DPhil thesis, University of Oxford.

Kirby, N. H. (1972). Sequential effects in serial reaction time, *Journal of Experimental Psychology*, **96**, 32–36.

Kornblum, S. (1968). Serial choice reaction time. Inadequacies of the information hypothesis, *Science*, **159**, 432–434.

Laming, D. R. J. (1968). *Information Theory of Choice Reaction Times*. London: Academic Press.

Laming D. R. J. (1979). Autocorrelation of choice reaction-times, *Acta Psychologica*, **43**, 381–412.

Luce, R. D. (1986). *Response Times: Their Role In Inferring Mental Oraganisation*. Oxford: Oxford University Press.

Maylor, E. M. and Rabbitt, P. M. A. (1987). Effects of practice and alcohol on performance of a perceptual motor task, *Quarterly Journal of Experimental Psychology*, **39A**, 777–795.

Maylor, E. A. and Rabbitt, P. M. A. (1988). Rate of preparation for, and processing of, an event requiring a choice response, *Quarterly Journal of Experimental Psychology* Nov. 1988 (in press).

Pacella, R. G. and Pew, R. W. (1968). Speed–accuracy trade-off in reaction-time: effects of discrete criterion-times, *Journal of Experimental Psychology*, **76**, 19–24.

Pew, R. W. (1969). The speed–accuracy operating characteristic. *Acta Psychologica*, **30**, 16–26.

Rabbitt, P. M. A. (1966). Errors and error-correction in choice-response tasks, *Journal of Experimental Psychology*, **71**, 24–273.

Rabbitt, P. M. A. (1968). Three kinds of error-signalling responses in serial choice tasks, *Quarterly Journal of Experimental Psychology*, **20**, 179–188.

Rabbitt, P. M. A. (1969). Psychological refractory delay and response–stimulus interval duration in serial, choice response tasks, In W. G. Koster (ed.), *Attention and Performance II*. Amsterdam: North-Holland.

Rabbitt, P. M. A. (1981). Cognitive psychology needs models for old age. In A. D. Baddeley and J. Long (eds), *Attention and Performance IX*. Hillsdale, NJ: Erlbaum.

Rabbitt, P. M. A. and Banerji, (in press). *Journal of Experimental Psychology*.

Rabbitt, P. M. A. and Goward, (submitted for publication).

Rabbitt, P. M. A. and Vyas, S. M. (1972). An elementary preliminary taxonomy for some errors in laboratory choice RT tasks, *Acta Psychologica*, **29**, 727–743.

Rabbitt, P. M. A. and Vyas, S. M. (1980). Actively controlling anticipation of irregular events, *Quarterly Journal of Experimental Psychology*, **32**, 435–446

Rabbitt, P. M. A., Cumming, C. G. and Vyas, S. M. (1978). Some errors of perceptual discrimination in visual search can be detected and corrected, *Quarterly Journal of Experimental Psychology*, **30**, 319–332.

Rabbitt, P. M. A., Stollery, B. and Moore, B. (submitted for publication).

Remington, R. J. (1969). Analysis of sequential effects in choice reaction times, *Journal of Experimental Psychology*, **82**, 250–257.

Remington, R. J. (1971). Analysis of sequential effects for a four-choice reaction time experiment, *Journal of Psychology*, **77**, 17–27.

Sanders, A. F. (ed.) (1989). Forthcoming special issue of *Acta Psychologica*, to be published Sept. 1989.

Schneider, W. (1986). Paper and presentation of model, Annual Meeting of the Canadian Psychology Society, November 1986.

Schouten, J. F. and Bekker, J. A. M. (1967). Reaction-time and accuracy, *Acta Psychologica*, **27**, 143–153.

Tukey, J. W. (1977). *Exploratory Data Analysis*. Reading, MA: Addison-Wesley.

Part IV

Automated Behaviour Monitoring

There are many occasions when one wishes to collect data on behaviour as it unfolds over a period of time rather than recording responses to specific discrete stimuli. Micros can greatly assist in this. The two chapters in Part IV illustrate complementary approaches to this area of application.

The first chapter warns of the dangers of substituting crude automated monitoring of movement in studies on drug effects on animal behaviour. Having decided that human observation is necessary for most purposes, it goes on to indicate how computers can be used by observers to record categories of behaviour with the facility to extract sophisticated analyses of frequencies, timing and contingencies.

The second chapter examines how micros can be used in the recording of the 'micro-structure' and 'macro-structure' of eating, both of which can help in the understanding of mechanisms underlying this behaviour. In many of the applications described in this chapter, micros are not used in isolation but rather form the heart of an integrated data recording system which might include, for example, devices for continuous measuring of weight of food eaten.

CHAPTER 10

Microcomputer-based data-logging and analysis in pharmacoethology

Colin Hendrie and John Rodgers

'Such subtlety . . .' said Slartiblartfast, 'one has to admire it.' [Douglas Adams, The Hitch-hiker's Guide to the Galaxy p. 125 (1979)]

Since the pioneering work of Grant and Mackintosh in the early 1960s (Grant, 1963; Grant and Mackintosh, 1963) many inroads have been made into our understanding of the behavioural complexities of laboratory rodents. Such an understanding is of fundamental importance in the context of the development of effective drugs for the treatment of various disorders, including mental illness. Also, without a thorough knowledge of the evolutionary, ecological and social forces influential in the development of the behavioural repertoire of these species, accurate interpretation of data derived from laboratory experiments is difficult.

For example, one of the simplest behavioural measures it is possible to record from animals is locomotor activity. Such studies typically involve placing an animal into an arena that has been marked off in squares or lines (open field; Hall and Ballachey, 1932; see Figure 10.1) and recording how many lines the animal crosses in a given period of time. As a research tool, the open field/ activity box has many of the characteristics that render it suitable for computerisation. First, the line-crossing measure is simple and unequivocal. Second, as multiple animals have to be run through each experiment, the task is repetitive. Finally, as many undergraduate and graduate students will testify, recording behaviour in this way is extremely tedious. However, within the last two decades, it has been become possible to substitute the lines in the activity box with photocell transmitters and receivers (Dew, 1953) and, more recently, to connect their output to an appropriately programmed minicomputer (e.g.

Microcomputers, Psychology and Medicine
Edited by R. West, M. Christie and J. Weinman
© 1990 by John Wiley & Sons Ltd

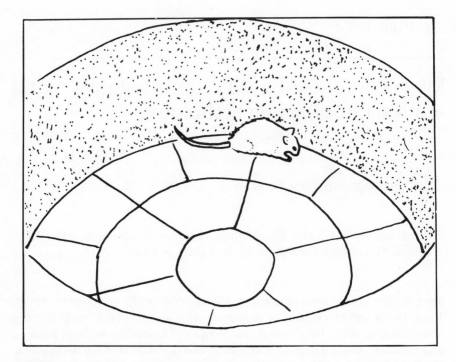

FIGURE 10.1   Open field: the animal is placed into an arena that has been marked off by lines. Behaviour is recorded by measuring how many lines are crossed in a given period of time.

Ljungberg and Ungerstedt, 1978) or microcomputer (e.g. Dourish, 1987). The experimenter's role in data collection can thus be minimised.

The utility of this approach is clearly reflected by the widespread commercial availability of automated activity boxes. Such systems also have the advantage of preventing data 'contamination' by observer subjectivity, anthropomorphisms or bias (Iversen and Iversen, 1975). Whilst this is in many respects a strength, in other aspects it is a clear weakness since the stream of behaviour exhibited by all animals is reduced to a single measure. A single measure can only be increased, decreased or unaffected by any particular drug.

One of the main uses of automatic activity monitors is to screen for the psychoactivity of newly developed drugs. The characteristics of such agents are generally unknown and they are often classified according to their effects across a range of behavioural tests. Thus, were novel agent S,M & E-$[GM]_a$-OH to increase overall locomotor activity it may well be classified as being similar to amphetamine, which also increases activity in this test situation (e.g. Taylor and Snyder, 1971). However, it is not possible to state with certainty whether the increased activity by S,M & E-$[GM]_a$-OH is a generalised increase in overall

FIGURE 10.2   Rota-rod: for this procedure an animal is trained to criterion, given a drug and retested. Motor impairments are measured by the animal's reduced ability to remain on the rod whilst it rotates.

activity (as may be the case with some anxiolytics under certain circumstances), stereotyped backward and forward ambulation (as with high doses of amphetamine) or short bursts of rapid activity followed by long periods of rest (possibly indicating anxiolysis e.g. Hendrie, in press). Similarly, were S,M & E-[GM]$_5$-OH to reduce overall activity it may be classified as having a sedative or ataxic action. In this instance additional procedures such as the rota-rod (Dunham and Miya, 1957; Figure 10.2) may be employed. In this test, an animal is trained to criterion on a rotating rod, a drug administered and the animal retested. Motor impairments are measured by the animal's reduced ability to remain on the rod whilst it rotates. A common measure used in this situation is the drug dose-effective in producing ataxia (neurotoxicity) in 50% of treated animals (NTD$_{50}$) (Rodgers, 1979). Although such procedures are commonly employed they are of only limited utility in that widely different NTD$_{50}$ estimates are produced for one and the same compound. For example, different laboratories have variously estimated the NTD$_{50}$ of chlordiazepoxide, a benzodiazepine anxiolytic, to be between 9.2 and 415 mg/kg (Rodgers and Waters, 1985). Even with these additional tests, reductions in activity in the open field or activity box may be interpreted as evidence of increased anxiety as even moderately anxious animals will freeze (Gallup and Suarez, 1980). Thus, the measurement of only one behaviour (e.g. locomotion) ignores the possibility that a reduction in one behaviour may merely reflect an increase in another (Iversen and Iversen, 1975).

The above points demonstrate that, whilst automated activity recording devices reduce the experimenter's involvement in data collection, this increases the number of experiments that must be performed and intrinsically creates difficulties in data interpretation. Thus, for many years it has been apparent (though not to all researchers) that it is after all necessary to observe animals in their test environments. In consequence, the utility of automated recording devices must be questioned.

In recognition of these difficulties, a number of groups have been arguing that the only valid method of assessing the influence of a particular drug is to determine its effects on a wide range of behaviours within the same test situation (Avis, 1974; Krsiak, 1979; Miczek and Krsiak, 1979; Rodgers, 1981). For this to be achieved successfully it has proved necessary to introduce, into the laboratory, techniques developed by ethologists in the field.

Although, as stated above, non-automated analyses may be criticised for allowing anthropomorphic/subjective interpretations to contaminate the data, one basic tenet of classical ethology is that recording methods should exclude this possibility. That is, before one can ask pertinent questions about behaviour, an essential prerequisite is the availability of precise descriptions of the behavioural repertoire of the species concerned (Tinbergen, 1963). As far as rodent behavioural patterns are concerned, such detailed descriptive information has been made available by Grant (1963), Grant and Mackintosh (1963) and Barnett (1963). Recent additions to these descriptive repertoires have been made by, amongst others, Poshivalov (1978), Dixon (1982) and Martinez *et al.* (1988). Behavioural elements used for analysis in our group at Bradford are outlined in Table 10.1 (see also Figure 10.3).

With these descriptive frameworks it has proved possible to analyse, in great detail, drug effects on animal *behaviour*. This combined use of ethological and pharmacological techniques has become variously known as ethopharmacology (Dixon, 1982) or pharmacoethology (Poshivalov, 1981). In essence, these disciplines vary very little. However, ethopharmacology has become the term applied to studying drug effects *per se* whilst pharmacoethology has more usually been applied to the technique of using drugs to implicate, by inference, the endogenous systems involved in the *mediation* of behaviour.

In the pre-microcomputer period, the manual recording of social interactions between animals proved to be difficult. First, observer concentration had to be maintained over long periods. Second, pen-and-paper recording—checklists, sociometric matrices, etc. (see Lehner, 1979 for review)—invariably required the observer to divert attention from the animals under investigation to the list itself. Consequently, data were lost, an inaccuracy that was especially acute

Table 10.1 Behavioural elements used for the analysis of murine inter-male social behaviour

Category	Element
Exploration	Cage exploration, line crossing, rearing
Investigation	Naso-anal, naso-nasal, non-specific partner investigation, approach, follow, attend
Maintenance	Autogroom, scratch, penis-lick
Offence	Tail-rattle, mincing, offensive sideways, offensive upright, chase, bite attack
Defence	Under food hopper, evade, defensive upright, defensive sideways, submissive upright, frozen crouch,dart
Residual	Forepaw digging, hindpaw digging, stretched attend, wet dog shake

with small, rapidly moving animals such as mice.

The introduction of event recorders (e.g. Eisenberg, 1963) overcame the problems inherent with pen-and-paper methods. These machines have a keyboard arranged rather like a piano keyboard, with each note corresponding to a particular behaviour. The recorded duration of each behaviour is determined by how long each key is depressed, whilst the frequency is expressed as the cumulative total of key presses relating to that particular behaviour. The one drawback with event recorders is that, as the relationship between key and behaviour is arbitrary, each observer had to be trained to recall the position of each key and its behavioural analogue. As the number of behaviours to be recorded increased so the number of arbitrary positions on the keyboard also increased. Possibly one of the largest event recorders was the 60-channel recorder employed by Hutt and Hutt (1974) in their analysis of the behaviour of squirrel monkeys.

In the mid-1970s exponents of the detailed recording of behaviour were faced with three major problems: (1) loss of accuracy due to observer fatigue or habituation; (2) loss of accuracy as a function of large arrays of arbitrarily positioned keys; and (3) time investment required to analyse the resultant data which was produced in prodigious quantities from even fairly modest experiments. For example, in this laboratory one experiment involving 40 animals required in the order of three months to analyse using a combined checklist/ audiotape commentary technique (Rodgers and Hendrie, 1982). Although some laboratories had started to exploit then state-of-the-art computer technology (i.e. Dawkins, 1971; Stephenson et al., 1975; White, 1971), this normally consisted of using such facilities for statistical analysis of data generated from event recorders. Furthermore, this type of application universally required the manufacture of expensive, highly specialised recorder/ computer interfaces. Undoubtedly this approach increased the number of experiments that could be performed in a given period; however, it was not until the widespread use of videotape recorders (VTR) that the problem of the observer habituation/fatigue was overcome. This relatively low-tech innovation produced a double advantage; first, observers were no longer required to be in close proximity to the animals under test, thereby reducing experimenter-induced disruption of ongoing behaviour; and second, as and when observers became fatigued they could stop and restart analysis at leisure (Hendrie and Bennett, 1983).

Since the late 1970s researchers have been quick to exploit the ready availability of inexpensive, relatively powerful microcomputers. Whilst early attempts to program these machines for data collection were fairly naive, most purpose-written software took advantage of the inherent flexibility of the QWERTY keyboard. By substituting the concept of event recorder key pressing for inputting codes that related to the behaviour they represented (i.e. CE for cage exploration, AG for autogroom, etc), the significant training period required for gaining proficiency with the recording technique could be reduced dramatically. One of the most elegant of these early data collection programs was provided by Depaulis (1983), who outlined a method whereby data were stored on disk, with files only being analysed for content after recording was complete. This has three advantages. First, a single program can collect data from a variety of situations without the need to change the list of otherwise pre-programmed elements to be recorded. Second, incorrect inputs can be assigned to their correct behaviour and, third, data can be analysed without repeated manual handling by linking up the disk output to a statistics program. The two disadvantages are that: (1) observers may use descriptions that have not previously been delineated, allowing for possible intrusion of subjective/anthropomorphic descriptions; and (2) resultant data must be visually scanned to remove erroneous inputs.

The approach in this laboratory has been to pre-program lists of behaviours that may be recorded and to refuse all others, thus eliminating the possibility of subjectivity (Hendrie and Bennett, 1983, 1984). This approach also removes the need to scan the data for errors as these are rejected at the input stage. The disadvantage of this method is that the data collection program must be amended for each different situation. These amendments can, however, be reduced to altering a single line within the program. In both approaches, durations of behavioural elements are recorded as the time elapsed between the onset of one behaviour and the onset of the next. A brief example of an unlined BASIC program to record frequencies and durations is given in Table 10.2.

The schematic program in Table 10.2 represents the essence of an adequate behavioural analysis program. A particular behavioural code would be entered and left on the screen until the next behaviour has begun. A separate subroutine is called to record cumulative frequencies and durations of partic-

Table 10.2

Program statement	Explanation
Let time1 = timer	Let variable 'time1'current setting of internal clock
input x$(b)	Input behavioural code; label as behaviour1, behaviour2, etc. The '$' sign indicates the variable 'x' is to be treated as text
gosub list	Instruction to send program to a subroutine called 'list' which would contain the list of behavioural codes it is permissible to record and a routine for indicating incorrect inputs. A flag would also be set to indicate to subroutine 'total' under which behaviour the next duration should be recorded and to increase the frequency count of that behaviour by 1
let time2 = timer	Let variable 'time2' = current setting of internal clock
let dur(b) = time2–time1	Duration of *b*th behaviour assigned as difference between start of timing and end of timing
gosub total	Instruction to send program to a subroutine called 'total'. This would contain the cumulative frequencies and durations of each behavioural element. Within this routine would be the instruction to print (to disk or hard copy) the cumulative frequency and duration of each behaviour should the input correspond to that used to indicate the end of a recording session. The entire list of elements from 1 to *b* would also be printed, with their associated durations in the order they were recorded
let b = b + 1	Change from recording, say, first behaviour to next behaviour. This would be followed by a statement to send the program back to the 'let time1 = timer' instruction

ular behaviours. Further refinements could easily be added such that minute-by-minute cumulative totals are recorded rather than totals across the whole test session. By simply changing the output device, it is possible to obtain hard copy (paper listing) of the data and/or soft copy (file) on disk.

Until fairly recently, the volatility of floppy disks and the limited number of individual data files that could be stored on them rendered floppy disks useful only for short-term data storage. However, with the advent of reliable high-capacity and fast-access hardisks or cards, it has been possible to use disk copy to its full potential, i.e. data storage and manipulation within a number of different program devices. The full behavioural stream may also be recorded on disk for subsequent analysis (see Figure 10.4). For example, in the program

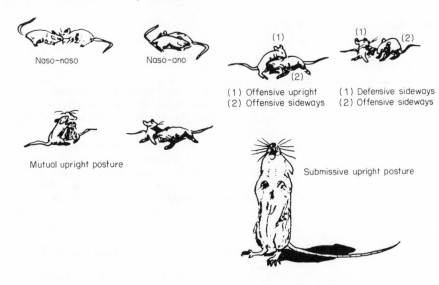

Naso–naso   Naso–ano

(1) Offensive upright   (1) Defensive sideways
(2) Offensive sideways   (2) Offensive sideways

Mutual upright posture   Submissive upright posture

FIGURE 10.3   A schematic representation of an agonistic encounter. Typically, animals spend some time in partner-oriented investigation in order to identify each other's social, sexual and reproductive status. Following this period, dominant, territory-holding animals will attack an intruder placed into their home cage (resident–intruder paradigm). In turn, the intruder will seek to defend itself with a combination of escape-oriented and defensive elements. The final defensive posture in this sequence is usually the submissive upright posture. By adopting this posture the defeated animal exposes its vulnerable ventral surface to the attacker, which may have the effect of reducing the probability of further attack.

shown in Table 10.2 output would be put to disk. Also on disk would be a number of different programs ranging from commercially available statistics packages such as SPSS PC+ to purpose-written programs for several forms of sequence analysis. Each can be called on to analyse the data in turn, either manually or under program control. Thus, the experimenter only handles the data at the input stage. In this laboratory, data-collection programs provide outputs in ASCII form (a standard code for representing data), which can be easily read by SPSS PC+ and by secondary analysis programs. The stastisics programs provide an overall analysis of the data by element or category, whilst sequence analysis provides the means by which more subtle analysis is done.

Sequence analysis can take several forms, from the most simple to the very complex (e.g. Haccou, 1987), which can require an expert understanding of mathematics. One of the most commonly used of the complex variety is continous-time Markov chain models (for review see Metz *et al.*, 1983). As each animal will begin and end a behavioural stream at different points and as individuals will not go from one behaviour to the next in exactly the same

Interactive data recording

RCE ———————————— RAG ——— RCE ———— RA — RAU — RBA — RCE ——————————

   ICE ———————————————— IDF — IDS ——— IDU — ISU ————— IAG — ICE —

RCE, ICE, RAG, RCE, IDF, RA, IDS, RAU, IDU, RBA, ISU,
RCE, IAG, ICE   = Interactive sequence

RCE, RAG, RCE, RA, RAU, RBA, RCE   = Resident sequence

ICE, IDF, IDS, IDU, ISU, IAG, ICE   = Intruder sequence

FIGURE 10.4   Interactive sequence analysis: behavioural codes recorded by direct keyboard input to a microcomputer. By prefacing each element with 'R' or 'I' to represent resident or intruder, respectively, it is possible to record the behaviour of each animal simultaneously. In the above example the continuous lines following each element represent ongoing behaviour for both interactants. With data in this format sequence analysis may be performed on elements displayed only by the resident or intruder or on the interactive behavioural stream.

order, combining sequential data from groups of animals becomes problematic. That is, for one animal it is easy to determine what behaviour is being expressed at a given time point. To delineate what is the likely behaviour to be expressed across a group of animals at this time point will probably lead to the answer: all possible behaviours that can be expressed!—descriptive but not useful.

Markovian analysis assumes that from a given behaviour A an animal can, at random, go to behaviour B or X or whatever. Should the relationship between A and B be greater than expected by chance it is concluded that there is a significant relationship between these two behaviours (for example, feeding and grooming). In experimental terms this usually means that the transition A to B has a *higher probability* than from A to C or A to D. That is, an animal can engage in one activity and choose from a number of options which behaviour to express next. By combining these probabilities across a number of animals it becomes possible to delineate sequences of behaviour that are expressed by all animals and hence investigate the actions of drugs upon these. Other examples of sequence analyses include describing transition matrices as ethograms (e.g. Brain and Poole, 1974) or utilising cluster analysis to determine relationships between groups of behaviours. One recent innovation has been to illustrate these clusters as 'dendrograms' (Brain *et al.*, 1984); however, the ability to decipher these has remained elusive to all but the initiated.

Perhaps the simplest approach to sequence analysis is to use a program to determine which sequences exist within a given behavioural stream and scan the data to calculate the incidence of each sequence and hence derive its

Sequence analysis   (a)

Behaviour	Followed by	Probability
Element 1	Element 1	0.000
Element 1	Element 2	0.000
Element 1	Element n	0.000
Element 2	Element 1	0.000
Element 2	Element 2	0.000
Element 2	Element n	0.000
Element n	Element 1	0.000
Element n	Element 2	0.000
Element n	Element n	0.000

$$p = \frac{\text{Frequency behaviour 1 followed by behaviour 2}}{\text{Frequency behaviour 1}}$$

Sequence analysis   (b)

String	Probability
Element 1 + Element 1	0.000
Element 1 + Element 2	0.000
Element 1 + Element n	0.000
Element 2 + Element 1	0.000
Element 2 + Element 2	0.000
Element 2 + Element n	0.000
Element 1 + Element 1 + Element 1	0.000
Element 1 + Element 1 + Element 2	0.000
Element 1 + Element 1 + Element n	0.000
Element 1 + Element 2 + Element 1	0.000
Element 1 + Element 2 + Element 2	0.000

etcetera, etcetera, etcetera . . .

$$p = -\frac{\text{Frequency of string}}{\text{Number of behaviours} - (\text{sequence length} - 1)}$$

FIGURE 10.5   Schematic representation of two ways to perform sequence analysis. For (a) the computer would be programmed to identify all possible two-element sequences and their frequencies and probabilities. By combining the probabilities of transition from element 1 to element 2 and element 2 to element 3 this form of data gives the false impression that it accurately represents the probability of sequence 1–2–3. This potential error may be avoided, however, by programming the computer to identify all possible sequences of length 2 through to n and hence obtaining the actual probability of sequence 1–2–3– through to n. See text for further details.

probability. As probability is a standard measure across all animals, these can be combined and statistically compared across treatments. Using this technique a further potential problem with ethograms may be avoided. That is, whilst ethograms only describe probabilities of transition from A to B, by the way they are expressed they give the impression that they accurately reflect a behavioural pathway through A, B, C, D to *n*. This false impression can lead to erroneous conclusions. For example, if the probability of transition A–B is 0.3 and the probability of transition B–C is also 0.3 the ethogram would suggest the probability of sequence A–B–C to be 0.09. By programming the sequence analyser to determine 3, 4, 5, *n*-element sequences it is possible to calculate the actual probability of any sequence. In practice, the longer the sequence, the less likely it is to be exactly repeated and hence the lower its probability of occurrence (see Figure 10.5). It is, however, unusual for the probability of any given sequence to correspond to that predicted by the ethogram (Hendrie and Rodgers, 1984).

Thus, detailed behavioural recording and analysis and the adoption of computerised ethological techniques have had a significant impact on laboratory-based studies. However, perhaps the greatest influence of ethology on behavioural pharmacology has been to change the nature of the experiments themselves. That is, on the basis of a thorough knowledge of the behavioural repertoire and social organisation of the species in question, it has become possible to avoid the use of artificial and highly aversive stimuli, such as electric shock. Rather, social histories of individual animals may be manipulated to produce the required effect. For example, individually housed mice have many of the characteristics of their dominant, territory-holding and aggressive feral counterparts. Thus, fighting may be induced by simply introducing another animal into the home cage of an individually housed conspecific (Brain and Benton, 1979). In consequence, agonistic encounters have, for example, largely replaced shock-induced fighting as a means of studying aggression in the laboratory and have also served to correct the misconception that shock-elicited fighting is, in fact, 'aggression'. Using ethological techniques it has become apparent that behaviours seen under these conditions have a large defensive component (Brain *et al.*, 1981). Thus, there is a clear and powerful impetus towards the development of 'naturalistic' laboratory models of many human disorders. Laboratory rodents cannot be viewed as having 'human' mental or behavioural characteristics in that evolutionary forces on different species are varied. However, many neurotransmitter/neurohormonal systems found in humans are phylogenetically ancient and are therefore present in many animal species much simpler than our own (e.g. Kavaliers, 1988; Pert *et al.*, 1974). For example, it should be the case that drugs effective in reducing anxiety in rodents should also be efficacious in reducing anxiety disorders in humans. Whilst the *situations* in which anxiety is produced in humans and rodents will of course be different, the mechanisms through which this mood state is mediated may be similar. The importance of developing appropriate animal models is highlighted by clinical studies which indicate some therapeutic agents developed for one purpose also to have activity in a circumstance that had not been predicted from animal studies, as has been found to be the case with sulpiride and tiapride.

Sulpiride and Tiapride are dopamine receptor antagonists that have been successfully used in the treatment of schizophrenia and movement disorders, yet were also shown in blind clinical trials to have anxiolytic action (for review, see Lepola et al., 1984). Subsequent animal studies 'confirmed' these clinical data (Costall et al., 1987). Within a framework in which drug screening has been substituted by drug design these data should be disturbing. It is clearly important to determine whether current animal models reflect true 'anxiety' or are merely sensitive to the actions of known anxiolytics. If it should be the latter, new (rather than 'me too') drug development will by implication have stopped until such time as novel, more appropriate, animal models are found. It is also clear that such models are unlikely to be developed by experimenters using introspective (and consequently anthropocentric) techniques to imagine what may make an animal anxious. Rather, situations in which animals become anxious should be used as the basis for developing laboratory models of anxiety.

Two recent advances in this area have made by Blanchard et al. (1988,1989) using wild rat/predator interactions and in this laboratory using DBA/2 mice exposed to predator calls (Hendrie, 1989). Both methods have been found to be sensitive to a variety of known anxiolytics and to be able to differentiate between these on the basis of their known models of action. Such findings are highly suggestive of the potential utility of these models in the development of novel therapeutic agents as well as their likely contribution to our understanding of the mechanisms of anxiety per se.

In conclusion, the influence of computers in behavioural pharmacology has been twofold. First, computers have facilitated the automation of many repetitive and tedious laboratory tests, with consequent problems for data interpretation. Second, computer-based data-logging techniques have enabled detailed and ethologically valid behavioural analyses to be performed on a routine basis. This possibility has led to a significant increase in the number of laboratories performing such experiments and provided an impetus for the development of new and more sensitive research tools.

As with all methodologies in their development stage, the increased number of researchers using such techniques has uncovered new problems. For example, whilst the number of rodent social behaviours originally described by Grant and Mackintosh (1963) were adequate for the technology of the time, the use of many novel and varied experimental paradigms has led to the need for further, more detailed, description. In consequence, several different names are used by various groups to equate with the same behaviour resulting in communication problems between laboratories. Similarly, with such a detailed level of analysis now available workers have had to decide on the 'fine tuning'. As such the choice of the level of analysis has become an attempt to optimise between 'lumping' and 'splitting'. That is, whether to perform data logging using only the behavioural categories or behavioural elements such as those described in Table 10.1. Using either approach exclusively may produce a level of analysis that is too coarse or too fine to detect significant effects.

Several other aspects will undoubtedly become the subject of debate as the pharmacoethological technique is further developed and refined. However, unlike traditional behavioural pharmacology, computer technology has created problems by making available a wealth, rather than a dearth, of data.

References

Avis, H. H. (1974). The neuropharmacology of aggression: a critical review, *Psychological Bulletin*, **81**, 47–63.

Barnett, S. A. (1963). *The rat: A study in Behaviour*. Chicago: Adeline.

Blanchard, D. C., Rodgers, R. J., Hendrie, C. A. and Hori, K. (1988). 'Taming' of wild rats (*Rattus rattus*) by $5HT_{1a}$ agonists Buspirone and Gepirone, *Pharmacology, Biochemistry and Behaviour*, **31**, 269–278.

Blanchard, D. C, Hori, K., Rodgers, R. J., Hendrie, C. A. and Blanchard, R. J. (1989). Attenuation of defensive threat attack in wild rats (*Rattus rattus*) by benzodiazepines, *Psychopharmacolgy*, **97**, 392–401.

Brain, P. F. and Benton, D. (1979). The interpretation of physiological correlates of differential housing in laboratory mice, *Life Sciences*, **24**, 99–116.

Brain, P. F. and Poole, A. E. (1974). The role of endocrines in isolation-induced intermale fighting in albino laboratory mice, *Aggressive Behavior*, **1**, 39–69.

Brain, P. F., Al-Maliki, S. and Benton, D. (1981). Attempts to determine the status of electroshock-induced attack in male laboratory mice, *Behavioural Processes*, **6**, 171–189.

Brain, P. F., Jones S. E., Brain, S. and Benton, D. (1984). Sequence analysis of social behaviour illustrating the actions of two antagonists of endogenous opioids. In K. A. Miczek, M. R. Kruk and B. Olivier (eds), *Ethopharmacological Agression Research*, pp. 43–58. New York: Liss.

Costall, B., Hendrie, C. A., Kelly, M. E. and Naylor, R. J. (1987). Actions of sulpiride and tiapride in a simple model of anxiety in mice, *Neuropharmacology*, **26**, 195–200.

Dawkins, R. (1971). A cheap method of recording behavioural events for direct computer access, *Behaviour*, **40**, 162–173.

Depaulis, A. (1983). A microcomputer method for behavioural data acquisition and subsequent analysis, *Pharmacology, Biochemistry and Behavior*, **19**, 729–732.

Dews, P. B. (1953). The measurement of the influence of drugs on voluntary activity in mice, *British Journal of Pharmacology*, **8**, 46–48.

Dixon, A. K. (1982). Ethopharmacology; a new way to analyse drug effects on behaviour, *Triangle* **21**, 95–105.

Dourish, C. T. (1987). Effects of drugs on spontaneous motor activity. In A. J. Greenshaw and C. T. Dourish (eds), *Experimental Psychopharmacology, Concepts and Methods*, pp. 153–211. Clifton, NJ: Humana Press.

Dunham, N. W. and Miya, T. S. (1975), A note on a simple apparatus for detecting neurological deficit in rats and mice, *Journal of the American Pharmacological Association*, **XLVI**, 208–209.

Eisenberg, J. F. (1963). The behaviour of heteromyid rodents, *University of California Publications in Zoology*, **69**, 1–100.

Gallup, G. G. and Suarez, S. D. (1980). An ethological analysis of open field behaviour, *Animal Behaviour*, **28**, 368–378.

Grant, E. C. (1963). Analysis of the social behaviour of the male laboratory rat, *Behaviour*, **21**, 260–281.

Grant, E. C. and Mackintosh, J. H. (1963). A comparison of the social postures of some common laboratory rodents, *Behaviour*, **21**, 246–259.

Haccou, P. (1987). *Statistical Methods for Ethological Data*. Amsterdam: Centrum voor Wiskunde en Informatica.

Hall, C. S. and Ballachey, E. L. (1932). The open field activity monitor, *University of California Publications in Psychology*, **6**, 1–12.

Hendrie, C. A. (1989). Hyperalgesia following agonistic encounters in DBA/2 intruder mice is not associated with recuperative behaviours, *Physiology and Behaviour*, **45**, 453–457.

Hendrie, C. A. (in press). Exposure to predator calls differentially activates opioid and non-opioidmediated endogenous analgesia mechanisms in male mice, *Psychopharmacology*.

Hendrie, C. A. and Bennett, S. (1983). A microcomputer technique for the detailed analysis of animal behaviour, *Physiology and Behaviour*, **30**, 233–235.

Hendrie, C. A. and Bennett, S. (1984). A microcomputer technique for the detailed behavioural and automatic statistical analysis of animal behaviour, *Physiology and Behavior*, **32**, 865–870.

Hendrie, C. A. and Rodgers, R. J. (1984). Microcomputer-based data logging and analysis in pharmacoethology. Paper presented at 6th International Society for Research on Aggression Turku, Finland, 12–16 July.

Hutt, S. J. and Hutt, C. (1974). *Direct observation and measurement of Behaviour* Springfield, IL: Thomas.

Iverson, S. D. and Iverson, L. L. (1975). *Behavioural Pharmacology*. New York: Oxford University Press.

Kavaliers, M. (1988). Evolutionary and comparative aspects of nociception, *Behaviour Research Bulletin*, **21**, 923–931.

Krsiak, M. (1979). Effects of drugs on behaviour of aggressive mice, *British Journal of Pharmacology*, **65**, 525–533.

Lehner, P. N. (1979). *Handbook of Ethological Methods*. New York, Garland STPM Press.

Lepola, V., Kokko, S., Nuutila, S. and Gordon, A. (1984). Tiapride and chlordiaxepoxide in acute alcohol withdrawal: A controlled clinical trial, *International Journal of Clinical Pharmacology Research*, **6**, 321–326.

Ljungberg, T. and Ungerstedt, U. (1978). A method for simultaneous registration of 8 behavioural parameters related to monoaminergic neurotransmission, *Pharmacology, Biochemistry and Behavior*, **8**, 483–489.

Martinez, M., Castano, D., Simon, Y. and Brain P. F. (1988). Ethological evaluation of behaviours shown by male mice during aggressive encounters. Paper presented at 8th International meeting of the International Society for Research on Aggression Swansea, UK, 2–6 July.

McAllister, K. and Dixon, A. K. (1988). Reappraisal of mouse ethogram according to Grant & Mackintosh: Social and aggressive behaviour. Paper presented at 8th

International meeting of the International Society for Research on Aggression Swansea, UK, 2–6 July.

Metz, H. A. J., Dienske, H., de Jonge, G. and Putters, F. A. (1983). Continuous-time markov chains as models for animal behaviour, *Bulletin of Mathematical Biology*, **45**, 643–658.

Miczek, K. A. and Krsiak, M. (1979). Drug effects on agonistic behaviour, *Advances in Behavioral Pharmacolgy*, **2**, 87–162.

Pert, C. B., Aphosian, E. and Snyder, S. H. (1974. Phylogenetic distribution of opiate receptor binding, *Brain Research*, **75**, 356–361.

Poshivalov, V. (1978). Ethological atlas for pharmacological research in laboratory rodents, *VINITI Moscou*, **31638-78**, 3–42.

Poshivalov, V. (1981). Pharmaco-ethological analysis of social behaviour of isolated mice, *Pharmacology, Biochemistry and Behavior*, **14**, (Suppl. 1), 53–59.

Rodgers, R. J. (1979). Neurochemical correlates of aggressive behaviour: Some relations to emotion and pain sensitivity. In K. Brown and S. J. Cooper (eds), *Chemical Infuences on Behaviour*, pp. 373–419. London: Academic Press.

Rodgers, R. J. (1981). Drugs, aggression and behavioural methods. In P. F. Brain and D. Benton (eds), *Multidisciplinary approaches to aggression research*, pp. 325–340. Amsterdam: Elsevier/North Holland.

Rodgers R. J. and Hendrie, C. A. (1982). Agonistic behaviour in rats: evidence for non-involvement of opioid mechanisms, *Physiology and Behavior*, **29**, 85–90.

Rodgers, R. J. and Waters, A. J. (1985). Benzodiazepines and their antagonists: A pharmacoethological analysis with particular reference to effects on 'aggression', *Neuroscience and Biobehavioral Reviews*, **9**, 21–35.

Stephenson, G. R., Smith D. P. B. and Roberts, T. W. (1975). The SSR system: an open format event recording system with computerised transcription, *Behaviour Research Methods and Instrumentation*, **7**, 497–515.

Taylor, K. M. and Snyder, S. H. (1971). Differential effects of D- and L-amphetamine on behaviour and catecholamine disposition in dopamine and noradrenaline containing neurons of rat brain, *Brain Research*, **28**, 295–309.

Tinbergen, N. (1963). On aims and methods in ethology, *Teirpsychol* **20**, 410–429.

White, R. (1971). WRATS: A computer compatible system for automated recording and transcribing of behaviour, *Behaviour*, **40**, 135–161.

CHAPTER 11

Analysing the structure and sequence of feeding in animals and man

JOHN BLUNDELL AND HASSAN ALIKHAN

One of the major reasons for using computers in the study of appetite control is to increase the resolving power of devices for measuring changes in eating and in the motivation to eat. Improving the sensitivity of detecting and quantifying changes in eating behaviour markedly enhances the comprehension of mechanisms underlying the control of appetite. Computer-assisted analysis advances theory and also improves the understanding of clinical disorders of appetite. For more than a decade microcomputers have been used in the biopsychology laboratories at Leeds University for the monitoring and analysis of feeding behaviour in animals and humans. These procedures have proved particularly useful for the analysis of changes induced by pharmacological agents. The increase in the capacity for the registration of events, and for their sequencing and analysis, afforded by the microcomputer, has made it possible to use drugs as pharmacological scalpels to finely dissect behaviour. In turn the disclosed fine adjustments in behaviour throw light upon the mechanisms involved in the actions of drugs upon appetite. These techniques have permitted the development of a new methodology for the study of appetite in the laboratory and the clinic.

Turnover of feeding behaviour

In many areas of research the assessment of behaviour is reduced to a single number. For both theoretical and experimental convenience researchers often settle for a coarse level of measurement and end up measuring the consequences of behaviour rather than behaviour itself. In feeding research this usually involves measuring the amount of food consumed in grams or calories; but these variables are not themselves behaviour—they are the results of behaviour. Of course, for a full understanding, the consequences of behaviour

Microcomputers, Psychology and Medicine
Edited by R. West, M. Christie and J. Weinman

and behaviour itself must both be analysed and interpreted conjointly. Consequences cannot properly be understood if we are ignorant of behaviour itself. This point can be readily illustrated by an example from behavioural pharmacology of anorexia (e.g. Blundell and Lathem, 1982). The fact that a chemical compound reduces the number of grams of food consumed by experimental animal does not automatically identify that compound as an anorexic drug. The animal may be rendered sick, physiologically disabled or behaviourally impaired. The manner of the expression of behaviour contributing to the suppression of intake is crucial to a proper interpretation of the action of the compound.

Behaviour has a form and structure; it is composed of elements or acts arranged in particular sequences. The analysis of this structure may take place at various levels ranging from the molecular to the molar. The structure of behaviour is not aribitrary and the structure may be regarded as functional. That is, behaviour is expressed in such a way as to achieve certain objectives. For all organisms (animals and humans) behaviour is central to the adaptive capacity of the organism. Most frequently the function of behaviour is to harmonise the physiological and environmental demands; the way in which the structure of behaviour achieves this objective reflects the operation of those physiological or environmental influences and their interactions.

The concept of behavioural structure implies the existence of temporal changes, and structure cannot be assessed by a single instantaneous measurement but only by successive or continuous measurements over time. The temporal dimension reveals the complexity and power of behavioural analysis. In the field of neurochemistry it is widely regarded that the 'turnover' of neurotransmitters provides a better indication of the functional significance of transmitters than a measure of the level or concentration. By analogy 'turnover' provides the most powerful representation of the significance of behaviour. It is the changes in the sequences of elements, or the rates of these changes, which adds power to the interpretation of behavioural consequences.

Accordingly, in feeding research it is not only the overall change in food intake (either over- or under-ingestion) that is alone meaningful. The way in which behaviour is shaped in bringing about this caloric change is important. The behavioural adjustment may result from a physiological disturbance, a pharmacological challenge or a change in environmental demands. In each case the structure of behaviour reveals something about the organism's adaptive response to new circumstances. The analysis of behaviour can therefore be used as an aid in diagnosing the causes underlying a shift in the consequences of behaviour. This principle will be particularly relevant in clinical research where abnormalities in the physiological or psychological (environment-social) domains will be reflected in altered structure of behaviour as well as in behavioural end-points.

The idea of using behavioural structure as a tool to disclose the operation of natural mechanisms as well as to diagnose pathlogical conditions (or to assess the capacity of a pathological system) places demands upon methodology. It is important that techniques and procedures can produce a valid representation of behavioural structure. Futher concepts and methods will be described below using examples from the field of behavioural pharmacology of feeding in animals to illustrate the significance of this methodology.

Contextual and temporal dimensions of behaviour

It is apparent that mammalian food intake comprises complex behaviour sequences and constitutes a discontinuous process in which periods of eating alternate with periods of non-eating. These qualitative features give character to ingestive behaviour and draw attention to the distinction between food intake—usually assessed by measuring the weight of food consumed—and feeding behaviour which can only be understood through a detailed analysis of the feeding response. Although measurement of the sheer bulk of food consumed may throw light upon certain features of energy balance, it seems likely that a more detailed analysis of the 'behavioural flux' (Blundell and McArthur, 1981) will be required to determine the way in which biopsychological processes exert a moment-to-moment control over feeding activity.

Feeding regarded as behaviour (i.e. with a definable structure in addition to mass) can be monitored along two dimensions—referred to here as the contextual and the temporal. The contextual dimension determines the nature of the elements displayed and includes all aspects of the environment, including the presence of a home area, predators, competitors, stressors and ambient temperature, together with the chemical and physical form of the available food. This last item is particularly important since in the study of feeding behaviour in the laboratory animals are usually fed a single uniform composite chow diet. However, the contextual qualities of food can be varied in a number of ways, including altering the macronutrient composition of the diet, number of choices available, sensory and hedonic aspects (embracing variety and palatability), together with the location and accessibility of food. Changing these contextual aspects may completely alter the effect of a drug (Blundell, *et al.*, 1987) or other manipulation (Collier *et al.*, 1977) upon feeding. Clearly the number of choices available, their form (liquid, powder, pellet, mash, granular, etc.) and their location will determine the type of behaviour that an animal must display in order to eat.

In addition to the nature of the actual behavioural elements involved, the structure of behaviour is revealed by the distribution of these elements over time (Wiepkema, 1971). This temporal dimension reflects the pattern of feeding and is composed of feeding and non-feeding elements. Analysis can occur at the macro- or micro-levels (Blundell and Latham, 1982). Accordingly the structure of behaviour reflects the operation of important contextual variables influencing food intake and contains the resolving power to indicate either the build-up or decay of underlaying physiological events or environmental constraints or interactions between factors in these domains.

Structure, process and mechanisms

The central theme of this chapter is the proposition that an examination of the behavioural structure of feeding can provide insights into the operation of the systems controlling food consumption. What exactly is meant by this? In a number of fields of behaviour the *structure* of a behaviour sequence can be used to indicate the occurrence of certain underlying *processes*. In turn, these processes (which guide the articulation of behaviour) are activated by specific *mechanisms*. Of course, a number of mechanisms may occur conjointly to govern the smooth running of a process. For example, in sexual behaviour of rats the copulatory sequence of mounts, intromissions and ejaculation of the male constitutes an adaptive sequence (Adler, 1969; Bermant, 1961) which reflects the operation of processes linking physiological dispositions and environmental variables. Various parameters derived from the structure of the copulatory sequence can be altered by hormonal manipulation of brain treatments. Adjustments to the structure reflect changes in the processes of sexual motivation or consummatory capacity and mechanisms involved in these processes can be inferred from the experimental manipulations (Beach, 1976, 1979). Considering feeding behaviour, the organisational structure of the behavioural sequence of feeding, grooming and resting which usually accompanies the conclusion of an episode of eating indicates the development of the state of satiety and the agency (hormonal, neurochemical, etc.) which provoked the behavioural change provides evidence for the mechanism (Antin *et al.*, 1975; Blundell and McArthur, 1981; Smith and Gibbs, 1976). Accordingly, the structure of behaviour can be used to determine whether the effect of a drug (or other physiological manipulation) on food intake is mediated by a natural process or a pathological condition. It follows from this that drugs can be used as tools to investigate the operation of mechanisms which control the articulation of natural processes. Figure 11.1 shows a representation of the structure of a behaviour sequence and illustrates the potential for using changes in behaviour structure as a dependent variable.

The differential action of chemicals on the structure of feeding can be exemplified as follows. The administration of a serotoninergic drug, *dl*-fenfluramine, which has a slightly sedative action, reduced the size of a monitored meal but kept intact the expression of behaviour (Blundell and McArthur, 1981). The increase in resting took place during the post-meal period of sedation and sleep, which was markedly extended. In contrast, the chemical lithium chloride, which produces gastrointestinal distress, reduced food

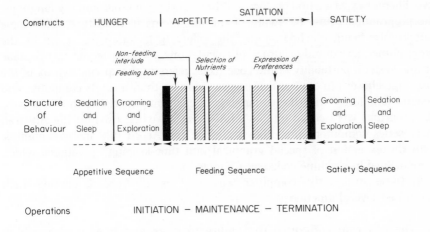

FIGURE 11.1   Schematic representation of the structure of feeding behaviour for the rat.

consumption but advanced the post-meal sedation so that it occurred prematurely, thereby disrupting the natural satiety sequence (Blundell *et al.*, 1985).

Computer-assisted analysis of feeding behaviour in animals

The argument set out above indicates the major theoretical reasons for undertaking a detailed and fine analysis of the components of feeding behaviour. The organisation of these components throws light upon factors influencing the expression of appetite. The use of computers (and microcomputers) provides a means of recording and analysing quantities of behavioural information and can be considered essential for investigating the turnover of feeding. A number of different procedures have been developed each of which discloses information about different aspects of eating or the motivation to eat. These procedures will be discussed in turn and their application will be illustrated by studies on the behavioural pharmacology of feeding. One major objective of this research is the analysis of the anorexic action of appetite-suppressant drugs.

Some notes on computing strategy

In the course of the studies where different serotoninergic drug effects were examined, several specialised programs had to be devised to fit the needs and aims of the investigation. In all cases, the depth and types of information were decided upon first and the remainder of the program designed 'from the bottom backwards'. Further, a format was adopted that allowed for modular coding to facilitate the incorporation of new features at any stage of the program execution. Two entire separate systems were designed and coded to deal with two different experimental protocols. When choosing a programming language, the programmer must be aware of the limitations of each type, with some compromise being reached among the following factors: ease of use by the programmer, speed and accuracy of calculations, memory requirements made on the system, portability of the code (code refers to the specific syntax of the language chosen) to see if it can be run on more than a single computer, and general familiarity with the commands of each language. For the most part, the programs were coded into MALLARD BASIC when used on the Amstrad PCW series computers, and BBC BASIC on the Acorn BBC microcomputers, with the exception of special graphical and time-keeping operations, which were defined in machine code (see Chapter 3).

In these studies the computer was used as a recording device which performed several functions:

1   The program contained the ability to store and later modify which behaviours are monitored. The monitoring occurred either as visually observed behavioural events recorded by pressing the appropriate key on the hand-held recorder (micro-analysis) or as the detection of a food pellet delivery (macro-analysis).
2   It automatically started and stopped recording sessions at the time desired, thus allowing for greater control of the time spent recording, and also freeing the researcher to concentrate on recording the data and not time-keeping.
3   The program recorded the time a behaviour (or event) started and terminated in a list format, so that successive behaviours occurred further on down the list. This allowed the program's data to be later examined for recurring sequences of behavioural patterns.
4   The program had a facility for noting errors and removing or editing them without losing the original file.
5   It displayed in a coherent manner all the information required, summarised and organised so that quick overviews were possible.

The computer used to record the data was a BBC Model B computer with a colour monitor, 40/80-track switchable disc drive and hand-held eight-key input device. The BBC computer has a rather limited memory (about 32K) so all the programs had to be short, specialised and squeezed into the memory available and still have room left to collect data. The result necessitated the use of many of the computer's built-in functions and all data being directly 'dumped' (i.e. transferred) to disc immediately.

Further, since the data were to be analysed on the PCW, the data had to be stored in an easily transferred format, which was achieved by storing all data in 'ASCII' (the American Standard Code for Information Interchange, a way of having data that is easily transported to another system. There are other standards, such as the IBM code, but ASCII is the more ubiquitous). Thus the PCW was fitted with a Serial Interface and Null Modem (a type of cable wiring arrangement that allows two computers to be attached to one another for the purpose of communication) to facilitate the transfer of data. The programs had to be small, so a 'suite' of programs was created so that maximum conservation of available memory space was achieved. To do this, a 'control' program was devised which would load the appropriate subprogram, run it and when finished would return to the 'control' centre.

Thus, the user was shielded from excessive computer literacy and led through the entire operation of the suite. The control program toggled through single key presses (i.e. a *menu* format was used) to the various functions. A menu format was used as this was deemed to be the easiest way of moving through the program without having to learn such meaningless commands as 'RUN*XDT11' each time there was a need to edit data. This also allowed the programs to grow and incorporate new features as each program was called separately and thus could be developed separately. In fact, in the course of writing the program, several portions were completed after the data had been encoded, but this in no way affected the running of the computer. In other words, the user was shielded from any problems requiring specialist skills.

The control menu branched into several distinct areas, as listed below briefly:

1 *Key definition*—this allows a user to define using a key word what each key press encodes for. Thus key 1 can be coded to mean 'EATING'. This also allows a user to have several definition files in stock and switch between them. The program allows a user to examine the contents of an existing file, create a new file and amend files. These can then be stored, discarded or erased as desired. When this is all decided, the definitions used for the remainder of the program are stored and then the user is returned to the control program.

2 *Data encoding*—this allows the user to collect data from the subject using the definitions so chosen. The file name is automatically prompted for, as is the duration of the session. The computer then prompts for a data diskette and it is initialised. When this is done, the user is asked to press any key to start recording. On the screen during the session, the previous behaviour and current behaviour plus time remaining in the session are displayed, although this does not affect the running of the program. At the end of the session, the computer closes the file and asks if another session will be done. If so, then the procedure is repeated. If not, then the computer asks for the record of the data diskette and then for the reinsertion of the program diskette so it can return to the 'control' program.

3 *Data manipulation*—this represents the tables produced by sorting the data into the designated categories, then displaying them either on the screen, the printer or both. There is also the option to place the table in a disc file

so the data may be examined immediately without having to recalculate everything.

4   Exit—clean, controlled exit from a computer program is important. First, it protects the files on diskette so that all are closed and set to *protected* status so that they are not overwritten. Next, the computer is reset to ensure confidentiality of information so that it is not left in limbo somewhere in the computer's RAM. Also, it allows the computer to be used immediately afterwards for another purpose without the need for a separate resetting operation.

All analysis of data was done using the commercially available 'AMSTAT' range of statistical tests for the PCW computer.

All the data were transferred using a specially designed BBC BASIC communications program sending to the commercially available 'CHIT-CHAT' program on the PCW. Error checking was done manually along with another program on the BBC which allowed the user to jump to various pieces of data which were lost or garbled.

Micro-analysis of the structure of feeding behaviour

Feeding is an episodic activity in which measures can be made of the episodes of eating (bouts), non-feeding episodes and the relationship between these variables. The procedure appears to have been first used for drug studies in animals by Blundell and Latham (1977). In this use of the technique the behaviour of rats during a one-hour period was exhaustively recorded in six categories: eating, drinking, grooming, locomotor activity, resting and others. From these records together with the weight of food it was possible to derive the following parameters: total food intake (g), duration of bouts (min) and the local rate of eating (g/min). The purpose of performing this fine analysis is to reveal certain subtle differences between the effects of drugs not revealed by a simple measure of the amount of food consumed and to disclose the action of drugs on processes underlying eating. Using this procedure differences have been observed between agents which activate post-synaptic serotoningeric receptors, block dopamine receptors, release catecholamines (see Blundell, 1982, 1987, for reviews) or act upon opioid mechanisms (Kirkham and Blundell, 1984). This type of analysis has contributed to an understanding of the role of serotonin and opioid systems in the process of satiation.

For example, naloxone—an opioid antagonist—tends to facilitate the onset of eating yet hastens the termination of an eating episode. The natural order of eating and resting is preserved (Kirkham and Blundell, 1984). During eating periods amphetamine exerts an effect on many parameters, including eating latency, total duration of eating, number of eating bouts and bout size, together with major changes in general activity and sedation. Amphetamine anorexia is characterized by a long initial delay followed by infrequent short bursts of rapid eating (Blundell and Latham, 1980). A serotoninergic drug such as fenfluramine exerts a more restricted pattern of action characterized mainly by a marked slowing of the rate of eating and a premature termination. These effects are reversed by a serotonin-blocking drug such as methergoline. Microstructural analysis has the resolving power to diagnose the effects on behaviour of different neurochemical events.

The system used in the micro-analysis of feeding behaviour is shown in Figure 11.2. The sensitivity of this procedure can be illustrated by a case study of the action of serotoninergic drugs on food intake. It has been known for more than a decade that most drugs which increase serotoninergic synaptic activity will reduce food consumption (Blundell, 1977, 1984). The disclosure of different subtypes of the serotonin receptor (e.g. Peroutka and Synder, 1979) opened up a number of possibilities for examining with greater sophistication the relationship between serotonin and appetite control. Micro-analysis provides a way of distinguishing between serotoninergic agents with action mediated via different receptor subtypes. The objective of the study described here was to distinguish between the actions of the drug d-fenfluramine, a releaser of serotonin, and RU-24969, a compound known to act via the subclass 1_B receptor. The drugs were administered in doses of 2.0 mg/kg and 0.75 mg/kg, respectively.

Prior to the start of the experiment proper, all animals were put through two weeks of simulated experimental conditions, including sham recording and injections. All animals were habituated to the glass observation tank and the food dish. On the day of testing, animals were deprived of food for 6 hours. After 5.5 hours of deprivation, the animals were injected with the appropriate drug solution and placed into the glass tank. Thirty minutes later, the animals were given a pre-weighed amount of food in a glass dish, the water bottle was weighed and the behavioural monitoring began. Each session lasted 30 minutes after the food was placed in the tank. Behaviour was logged by means of a hand-held eight-key input device attached in parallel to a BBC Model B microcomputer. The program for recording the observations was written by the experimenter, and the screen gave a running table of the observations made that could be used to check against errors. During the session, as well as for the 30 minutes prior to its start, an infrared video camera attached to a television with built-in video tape recorder was used. This recording was made to allow subsequent rechecking of any ambiguous behaviour. For analysis, the behaviour of each animal was categorised according to the definitions below:

1   *Grooming*—scratching, licking or biting of the coat, as well as cleaning of the snout and head region.

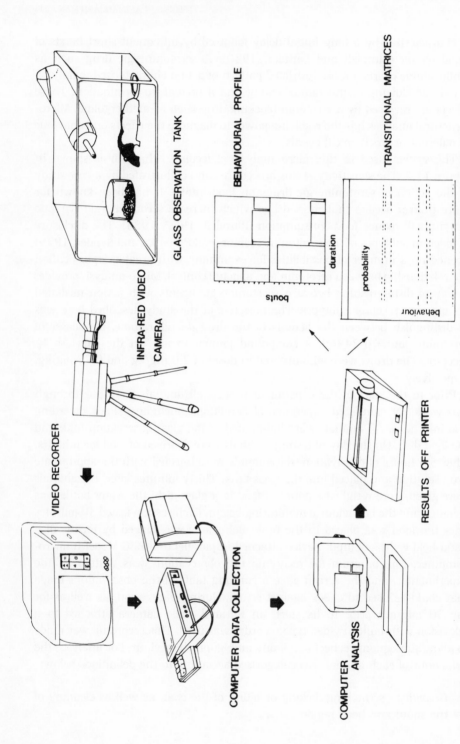

FIGURE 11.2 System for utilising hand-held keyboard and microcomputer for the coding of behavioural categories which form the basis of the micro-analysis of feeding

GLASS OBSERVATION TANK

INFRA-RED VIDEO CAMERA

VIDEO RECORDER

COMPUTER DATA COLLECTION

COMPUTER ANALYSIS

RESULTS OFF PRINTER

BEHAVIOURAL PROFILE

TRANSITIONAL MATRICES

bouts

duration

probability

behaviour

2   *Sniffing*—head movements with rear legs immobile, although small, jerky forward movements were included as sniffing rather than locomotion; twitching of the vibrissae.
3   *Eating*—biting, gnawing and swallowing of fragments. Carrying of fragments about the tank were not included as eating, but as locomotion,
4   *Drinking*—licking at the water-bottle spout.
5   *Rearing*—Front limbs raised with hind limbs extended. Not included in the rearing category were sniffing for periods longer than 2 seconds while upright. These were classed as sniffing.
6   *Locomotion*—movements involving all four limbs.
7   *Resting*—sitting or lying; sleeping with the occasional change in sleeping. Standing was included under rearing, unless the animal was engaging in copious sniffing.
8   *Other*—this included any other behaviours that did not fall under the other categories.

At the end of each session, food intake was measured by weighing the food remaining plus any detectable spillage, as well as the amount of water remaining in the water-bottle. Food was then made freely available until the next test day.

All testing was carried out under low-level red illumination with the animals in a large (1 m × 50 cm × 50 cm) glass tank, with sawdust covering the bottom and a large grill over the top. At least 48 hours separated successive treatments. Each animal acted as its own control, receiving all test solutions, with order of treatment counterbalanced to minimise order effects. Further, test solutions were administered blind; solutions were coded independently prior to the experiment. One-way analysis of variance was used to assess the differences on each parameter with all results subject to post hoc contrasts (Newman–Keuls).

The results of the micro-analysis are shown in Tables 11.1 and 11.2. Table 11.1 indicates the major effects of the drugs on eating and eating-related parameters. d-Fenfluramine and RU-24969 both reduced the total food consumed $F = 12.58$, d.f. $= 2$, $p < 0.001$ and markedly slowed the rate of eating. There was no effect on the duration of eating ($F = 1.07$, d.f. $= 2$, $p > 0.3$). Both treatments increased the latency to eat ($F = 5.29$, d.f. $= 2$, $p < 0.02$), but not latency to resting ($F = 1.07$, d.f. $= 2$, $p > 0.3$). Therefore, considering the major eating parameters, both d-fenfluramine and RU-24969 gave rise to similar changes which differ from the placebo condition.

However, differences between the two 5-HT agents were apparent on non-ingestive behaviour. For example, d-fenfluramine increased the duration of resting (Newman–Keuls, $p < 0.05$), while RU-24969 had no effect. On the other hand, RU markedly increased active behaviours, such as sniffing (Newman–Keuls, $p < 0.05$), rearing (Newman–Keuls, $p < 0.05$) and locomotion

Table 11.1   Effects of *d*-fenfluramine and RU-24969 on eating and resting over 30 minutes after 6 hours deprivation

Parameter	Saline		*d*-Fenfluramine		RU-24969	
Total food	7.84	(±1.12)*	1.89	(±0.45)*	3.80	(±0.87)*
Rate (g/min)	0.26	(±0.04)*	0.07	(±0.01)*	0.13	(±0.03)*
Eating time	592.8	(±79.0)	444.1	(±58.8)	550.1	(±81.4)
Eating bouts	70.5	(±7.7)*	35.4	(±5.5)*	55.8	(±11.6)*
Resting time	39.7	(±14.8)*	205.9	(±58.2)*	42.9	(±21.2*
Eating latency	17.0	(±5.8)*	154.0	(±44.1)*	45.9	(±31.2)*
Last eat bout	1710.9	(±59.8)	1442.0	(±290.3)	1532.2	(±379.0)
Last rest bout	1559.8	(275.4)	1718.3	(±60.8)	1436.2	(±410.8)

Figures are in seconds ($\bar{x}$±SEM for 8 rats), except for total food which is in grams, and rate of eating which is in grams per minute. All values marked * are significant at the $p < 0.01$ or better level using one-way analysis of variance and post hoc (Newman–Keuls).

Table 11.2   The effects of RU-24969 and *d*-fenfluramine over 30 minutes after 6 hours food deprivation

Behaviour	Saline Bouts	Time	*d*-Fenfluramine Bouts	Time	RU-24969 Bouts	Time
Grooming	28.5 (5.5)	226.6 (105.4)	20.8 (2.7)	200.3 (35.2)	45.8 (11.7)	190.5 (45.3)
Sniffing	161.6* (10.9)	576.6* (46.7)	107.0* (10.0)	818.6* (41.7)	218.0* (21.0)	722.0* (52.7)
Eating	70.5* (7.7)	592.8 (79.0)	35.4* (5.5)	444.1 (58.9)	55.8* (11.6)	550.1 (81.4)
Drinking	5.5* (1.2)	86.6* (34.0)	0.8* (0.4)	6.6* (5.2)	0.0* (0.0)	0.0* (0.0)
Locomotion	58.1* (5.6)	72.1* (20.3)	18.0* (3.9)	18.7* (4.7)	96.8* (15.9)	81.9* (13.9)
Rearing	66.9* (10.0)	252.0* (46.6)	20.4* (3.0)	69.3* (11.1)	65.1* (8.0)	177.3* (26.4)
Resting	11.1* (4.1)	39.9* (14.8)	34.9* (8.8)	205.9* (58.2)	7.9* (3.1)	42.9* (21.2)
Other	1.4 (0.5)	2.9 (1.5)	0.3 (0.3)	0.3 (0.3)	1.8 (0.7)	4.5 (2.3)
Total	403.6* (58.8)		237.4* (54.6)		468.6* (113.7)	

Values for behavioural parameters are means (±SEM) for eight rats. Values marked * indicate a p value of 0.01 or less, using one-way analysis of variance covarying for the effects of weight and re-examined using a posteriori tests (Newman–Keuls).

(Newman–Keuls, $p < 0.05$) (see Table 11.2 for details).

Consequently, the d-fenfluramine anorexia is characterised by a slow rate of eating followed by an increased period of resting; RU-24969 displays a very active form of anorexia, with the suppresion of food intake and slow eating embraced within a highly active state. Indeed, this specific 5-HT 1b agonist produced a marked increase in the number of switches between categories of behaviour. In contrast to d-fenfluramine, RU24969 did not increase the time spent resting. It can be seen that the two 5-HT agents gave rise to quite different patterns of activity. While both differ from the saline condition, they also differ from each other.

Does the anorexia of d-fenfluramine and RU24969 involve the same mechanisms? It seems likely that a set of receptors is part of a common substrate underlying the suppression of intake for both drugs. However, the overall impact of the drugs on 5-HT systems is likely to be different and this leads to quite different behavioural profiles; RU24969 produced a more dramatic shift in the behavioural profile than did d-fenfluramine; these qualitative changes in the pattern of activity are noticeable by visual inspection of the computer display of the micro-analysis. Accordingly this computer-assisted procedure has distinguished between the anorectic actions of two closely related, but clearly not identical, serotoninergic drugs.

Macro- or meal pattern analysis

The continous monitoring of long-term eating patterns in free-feeding animals never subjected to periods of food deprivation identifies the meal as the basic unit of feeding (Richter, 1927; Smith, 1985). From the basic variable can be computed the parameters of meal size, meal duration, meal frequency, inter-meal interval and various other measures which describe the pattern of feeding behaviour (for review see Blundell and Latham, 1982). A system for the computer-assisted monitoring and analysis of meal patterns over long periods of time is set out in Figure 11.3.

This procedure appears to have been first used in drug studies about 17 years ago (Borbely and Waser, 1966), when the active drug (amphetamine) was delivered via the rat's drinking-water. Since that time the serotoninergic drug dl-fenfluramine has been the most frequently used pharmacological tool. The initial study which compared the effects of amphetamine and fenfluramine demonstrated that these drugs displayed quite different profiles when meals were monitored continuously over 24-hour periods in non-deprived rats (Blundell and Leshem, 1975; Blundell *et al.*, 1976). Interestingly, the effect of fenfluramine was characterised by a reduction in meal size, which suggested that the drug was acting to promote the process of satiation and therefore caused an early termination of eating. This effect has now been confirmed many times in a number of separate studies (Blundell and Latham, 1978;

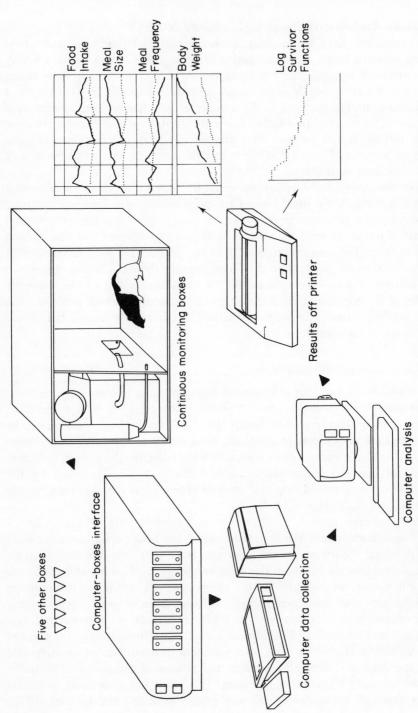

Figure 11.3 System for the computer monitoring and analysis of meal patterns in the rat.

Food
Intake

Meal
Size

Meal
Frequency

Body
Weight

Log
Survivor
Functions

Five other boxes

Computer-boxes interface

Continuous monitoring boxes

Computer data collection

Computer analysis

Results off printer

SLOT:1   ANIMAL:4   EATING   DATA FILE:FENFB 5

```
BOUT    START  END   INTERVAL  DURN        WT.    W/I-RATIO  AVE.  MDN  MDN  SIQ   QUARTER-BOUT        QUARTER-BOUT IBI'S NO.   & SECS DURN.
 NO     TIME   TIME  PRE  POST SECS   NO.  GM    PRE  POST   G/M   G/M  IPI  RNG   1   2   3   4  MDN'S    1   2   3   4         1    2    3    4

 1  N    87    95    81   233  .278   10    40     0    0    33   47   51    7     0   0   0  49    57     0   0   0   0         0    0    2   20
 2  N   328   336   233   107   312   47   188    23    8    40   42   56   11    49  53  56  57    55     1   0   0   2         0    5   21    0
 3  N   443   455   107   252   399   51   204     8   19    39   39   56   10    59  49  56  63    60     0   0   1   0        11    0   18    9
 4  N   707   721   252   152   509   66   264    24   10    42   40   70   10    59  57  70  64    64     0   0   0   0        23    6    0    9
 5  N   873   885   152   258   421   65   264    10   17    30   40   57   10    58  59  57  70    60    104   0   2   0       104   32    0    0
 6  N  1143  1149   258    32   213   67   268    17   10    38   46   61   10    58  59  61  60    49      0   1   0   2        91    0    2   20
 7  N  1181  1191    32   392   316   38   152     5   47    42   36   48    9    58  66  48  49    65      1   0   0   0        12    0    0    7
 8  N  1583  1593   392   295   347   46   184    57    4    34   43   61    8    65  51  56  61    63      0   0   1   1         7    9    8    8
 9  D  1888  1897   295   176   329   57   228     5    7    39   42   56    9    52  66  56  57    57      1   0   0   1         9   18    0   11
10  D  2073  2085   176   207   413   59   236    13   12    34   38   51   14    55  51  65  69    57     18   0   2   1         6   22    0    7
11  D  2292  2310   207   194   606   72   288    13   14    28   34   65   17    59  74  65  69    69      6   0   2   3        23   17    3   26
12  D                                    288                                       68  68  51  58    69     23                              3   76

13  N   104   120   194   101   563   28   112     5   11    11   20  115   71   104 115 288 118   118      0   2   0   3        71    0    0   58
14  N   221   230   101   108   327   12    43    11    4     8   12  191  167     0 115 288 118     0    156   1   1   1        29   48    0   35
15  N   338   341   108   387   142   12    48     4    1    20   23  102   20     0   0   0   0     0     57   1   0   0        16    0    1    0
16  N   728   737   387   233   336   17    68     1    2    12   34   67    9     0   0   0   0     0     45   2   1   0        12    0    2  184
17  N   970   978   233   243   328   24    96     2    3    18   35   70    9    81  59  52  67    67    184   1   0   1         0    6    2  148
18  D  1221  1232   243    52   431   52   208     8   40    28   32   73   24    84  69  86  70    70    101   1   1   1         8   30    0    0
19  D  1284  1291    52    42   260   27   108    40   25    24   25   96   13    86  96  97  98    98     28   0   0   0         0    0    0    0
20  D  1333  1339    42   527   206   29   116    25   27    33   32   74   15    70  74  66  53    53     10   0   0   0         0    0    0    0
21  D  1866  1876   527   245   326   41   164    27    3    30   32   75    9    77  66  75  81    81     12   0   0   0         9    0    0    0
22  D  2121  2127   245   109   222   36   144     6   13    38   38   73    5    62  67  73  60    60     14   0   0   0        14    0    0    0
23  D  2236  2244   169    77   295   37   148    13   19    30   34   69    6    69  68  69  58    58     47   0   0   3        17    0    0    0
```

```
DAY   NIGHT-TIME BOUTS        DAY-TIME BOUTS         OVER WHOLE DAY        NT:DY RATIOS
NO.   NO  WT.  AV.WT AV.RTE   NO  WT.  AV.WT AV.RTE  WT.   AV.WT AV.RTE    NO.  WT.
 1     8  1560  195   41       4  980   245   39     2540   211   41       20   15
 2     5   372   74   24       6  888   148   32     1260   114   28        8    4
```

```
UNIT   WT/GAP-RATIO
       SIZE      PRE-   POST
       40         15     13
       40          8     11
TTL RDGS   635
           315
```

MEAL-SIZE DISTRIBUTION - TOTALS & % BY WT.

```
       0-19    20-39    40-59    60-79    80-99   100-119  120-139   140+
NO WT  NO WT   NO WT    NO WT    NO WT    NO WT    NO WT    NO WT    NO WT
 1  2   1  6    4 50     4 43     0  0     0  0     0  0     0  0
 3 13   6 57    2 30     0  0     0  0     0  0     0  0     0  0
```

ERRORS= 2

FIGURE 11.4 Example of a computer printout of data from 2 days of continuous monitoring of feeding. This eating data file displays the exact start and finish of every meal, the duration and size of each meal, rates of eating during the meals, pre- and post-meal ratios and other parameters. See text for details.

Davies, 1976; Grinker *et al.*, 1980; Burton *et al.*, 1981; Davies *et al.*, 1983). In keeping with the initial observation of Blundell and Leshem (1975) it has recently been confirmed that the 'effects of fenfluramine are specific to meal size with a negligible effect upon meal initiation' (Davies *et al*, 1983). However, it is useful in a case like this to display the actual data—automatically collected and recorded—to verify the qualitative description and to explain the nature of the structural analysis. For this reason a computer printout record has been included (Figure 11.4) to allow the reader to inspect the detailed nature of the structural changes brought about by *dl*-fenfluramine. These data describe the feeding pattern of a rat over a two-day period. In this example the first day (bouts 1–12) is the control day and the second (bouts 13–23) the experimental day on which the rat received an intraperitoneal injection of *dl*-fenfluramine (5.0 mg/kg). The printout provides information about all parameters of the meal profile. Reading from left to right (Figure 11.4) we begin with the bout number (i.e. meal number). The second column indicates whether the meal was taken at night (N) or day (D). The next two columns give the actual start and end times of meals in decimal hours. The fifth and sixth columns give the pre- and post-meal interval in decimal hours. The seventh column gives meal duration and columns eight and nine the number of pellets and weight in grams consumed during a meal; the next two columns give pre- and post-meal ratios.

The remaining 16 columns of the eating data file (Figure 11.4) are devoted to an examination of intra-meal events, and are based on an analysis of the inter-pellet intervals. The major parameter derived from these data is the intra-meal eating rate. This is computed from the weight of one pellet divided by the median inter-pellet interval, which is computed from all inter-pellet intervals occurring within a meal. Quarter bout medians are also computed as there is evidence that feeding rates may be high at the start of meals and lower at the end (Wiepkema, 1971; Le Magnen, 1971). Indeed, the rate of eating, calculated from the median inter-pellet interval, is slower over the second half of the meal than the first. This is probably an indicator of the development of satiation.

It is therefore interesting that one major effect of *dl*-fenfluramine is to slow the eating rate, a phenomenon also displayed by other agents which increase serotonin metabolism (Blundell and Lathem, 1978) with the exception of tryptophan which, although it reduced meal size, appears to have no effect on feeding rate (Latham and Blundell, 1979). It should also be noted that drugs blocking dopamine receptors (e.g. pimozide and alpha-flupenthixol) also reduce eating rate but, unlike serotoninergic agents, they lead to an increase in meal size (Blundell and Latham, 1978). This indicates that the slow rate of eating brought about by 5-HT agents does not necessarily cause the reduction in food intake.

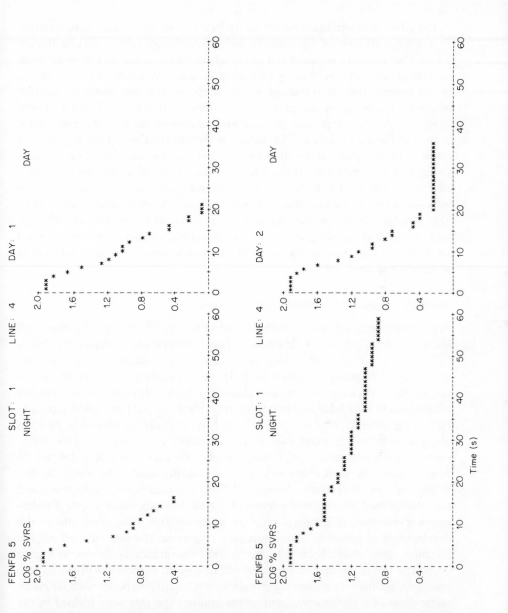

FIGURE 11.5 Example of computer printouts of log survivor plots of interpellet intervals after saline treatment (top) and *dl*-fenfluramine (bottom). The drug (injected at the beginning of the dark phase) notably increased the length of the inter-pellet intervals (reduced the rate of eating) during the night period.

The effect of *dl*-fenfluramine on eating rate can be more easily demonstrated by reference to plots of log survivor functions of inter-pellet intervals (Figure 11.5). This measure is calculated to reveal the 'break point' in the distribution of inter-pellet intervals, thereby providing an objective criterion for the choice of inter-meal interval. Changes in the slope of the log survivor function indicates a change in the probability of the event occurring (see Cox and Lewis, 1966). The slope also provides an indicator of the rate of events and it is clear in Figure 11.5 that *dl*-fenfluramine flattens the slope of the log survivor curve and therefore slows the rate of eating (during the night period). Consequently, when administered to free-feeding rats *dl*-fenfluramine displays two major effects: a reduction in meal (or bout) size and a reduction in the intra-meal rate of eating (Blundell and Latham, 1978; Burton *et al.*, 1981). This example illustrates the power of macro-analysis to describe and characterise the action of a drug on the pattern of eating, and demonstrates the need for computer-assisted monitoring procedures to achieve the required degree of accuracy and sensitivity.

Motivation measured by instrumental performance

In assessing drug action it is useful to monitor not only the act of eating itself but also the willingness to obtain food. This willingness is normally referred to as the hunger drive and it may be measured by training rats to make an instrumental response to obtain food. There is an extensive literature on the use of lever pressing in operant chambers under the control of complex reinforcement schedules as a means of measuring various motivational parameters. One other type of response which can be easily monitored is running along a straight-arm maze from a start chamber to a goal box. This device permits the measurement of a number of parameters, including latency to emerge (from the start chamber), speed of running (along the alley), latency to eat (in the goal box), amount of food consumed (on each trial) and cumulative food intake (over a series of trials). This procedure allows simultaneous monitoring of temporal changes in appetititive motivation and in the development of satiation (consummatory response). The system used for the computer-assisted analysis of instrumental performance is shown in Figure 11.6. The use of the system can be illustrated by an experiment in which two opiate antagonists—naloxone and naltrexone—were compared with equianorectic doses of *d*-fenfluramine and amphetamine. The rats were trained in the runway and given food to maintain them at 85% of normal body weight. On test days the rats were given 15 trials in the runway and allowed to eat for 2 minutes in the goal box at the end of each trial. This method was devised in order to monitor the development of satiation under control conditions and following drug administration. The technique proved capable not only of distinguishing between drugged and non-drugged rats but also of dis-

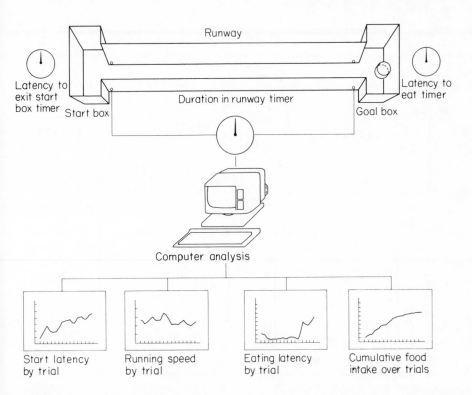

FIGURE 11.6   System for the computer monitoring and analysis of instrumental performance in the runway.

tinguishing between the actions of individual drugs. For naloxone and naltrexone levels of runway performance (latency to emerge, running speed, latency to eat) were initially quite similar to those for saline-treated animals. Initially food intake per trial was also normal. In the control conditions a typical satiation curve was demonstrated with mean intake per trial declining over time. This effect is clearly shown in Figure 11.7, which also indicates that a measure of motivational performance (overall latency to eat) changes in similar fashion. Thus the development of satiation is reflected in both runway performance and food consumed. It is noticeable that both naloxone and naltrexone facilitate the development of satiaton as it is reflected in a hastening of the decline in latency to eat and food consumed.

It is important that neither of these opioid blockers reduced the motivation to eat before feeding had been initiated. There was no evidence of any motivational deficit that might have reduced the tendency to initiate the primary instrumental or consummatory response. Consequently, the action of these opioid antagonists appears to be dependent upon food consumption; the

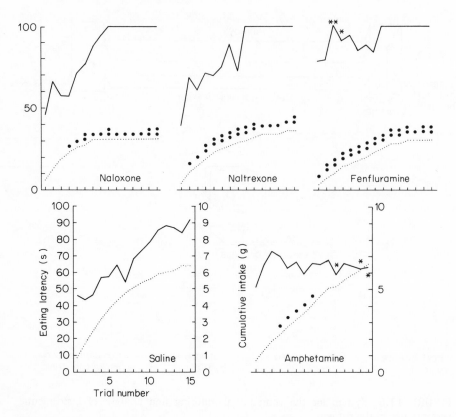

FIGURE 11.7   Overall latency to eat (—) and cumulative food intake (····) plotted from computer analysis of instrumental performance monitored in the runway.

drugs seem to augment the feedback resulting from ingestion and this results in an intensification of the process of satiation (Kirkham and Blundell, 1986). This study illustrates how instrumental performance analysed in this manner can help understanding of the mechanisms of action of anorectic compounds, and shows the essential role of the microcomputer in generating the temporal profile of effects.

Clincial implications

To the casual observer behaviour often appears simple, coarse and undifferentiated. However, a systematic, close inspection reveals that behaviour is complex, with a well-organized structure composed of sequences of components. The concept of turnover of behaviour draws attention to the way in which behaviour unfolds with time and illustrates the organisation of the behavioural components which contribute to the organism meeting some demand. Measuring this turnover of behaviour gives an opportunity to measure parallel changes occurring in the physiological domain or the environment and to assess precipitating, synchronising or consequential events.

It is worth noting that the principles applied above to the study of the behavioural pharmacology of appetite in animals are equally relevant for the study of natural and disordered eating in humans. The micro-structural analysis of human eating using a hand-held keyboard for coding aspects of the human eating pattern have shown that different types of drugs exert differing effects upon the profile of behavioural components (Rogers and Blundell, 1979). The macro-structure of human eating patterns is also adjusted by serotoninergic manipulation (Blundell and Hill, 1987), and the use of the microcomputer for the nutritional analysis of food diaries has revealed differences in the intake of nutrients with meals of different sizes (Hill and Blundell, 1986). Accordingly computer-assisted methodology provides a means for upgrading the analytical power of studies on human feeding and nutrition. Wherever knowledge about the structure and organisation of feeding behaviour can aid understanding of mechanisms and causes then the microcomputer can provide the researcher with additional resolving power.

References

Adler, N. T. (1969). Effects of the male's copulatory behaviour on successful pregnancy of the female rat, *Journal of Comparative and Physiological Psychology*, **69**, 613–622.

Antin, J., Gibbs, J., Holt, J., Young, R. C. and Smith, G. P. (1975). Cholecystokinin elicits the complete behavioural sequence of satiety in rats. *Journal of Comparative and Physiological Psychology*, **89**, 784–790.

Beach, F. A. (1976). Sexual attractivity, proceptivity and receptivity in female mammals, *Hormones and Behaviour*, **7**, 105–138.

Beach, F. A. (1979). Animal models for human sexuality. In: *Sex, Hormones and Behaviour*, Ciba Foundation Symposium 62 (new series), pp. 113–132. Amsterdam: Excerpta Medica.

Bermant, G. (1961). Response latencies of female rats during sexual intercourse, *Science*, **133**, 1771–1773.

Blundell, J. E. (1977). Is there a role for serotonin (5-hydroxytryptamine) in feeding? *International Journal of Obesity*, **1**, 15–42.

Blundell, J. E. (1982). Neuroregulators and feeding: Implications for the pharmacological manipulation of hunger and appetite, *Reviews in Pure and Applied Pharmacological Sciences*, **3**, 381–462.

Blundell, J. E. (1984). Serotonin and appetite, *Neuropharmacology*, **23**, 1537–1552.

Blundell, J. E. (1987). Structure, process and mechanism: case studies in the psychopharmacology of feeding. In L. L. Iversen, S. D. Iversen and S. H. Synder (eds), *Handbook of Psychopharmacology*, Vol. 19, pp. 123–182. New York: Plenum.

Blundell, J. E. and Hill, A. J. (1987). Serotoninergic modulation of the pattern of eating and the profile of hunger—satiety in humans, *International Journal of Obesity*, **11**, (Suppl. 3), 141–155.

Blundell, J. E. and Latham, C. J. (1977). Pharmacological modification of eating behaviour. *Proceedings of 6th Int. Congress on Physiology of Food and Fluid Intake*, Paris.

Blundell, J. E. and Latham, C. J. (1978). Pharmacological manipulation of feeding behaviour: possible influences of serotonin and dopamine on food intake. In S. Garattini and R. Samanin (eds), *Central Mechanisms of Anorectic Drugs*, pp. 83–109. New York: Raven Press.

Blundell, J. E. and Latham, C. J. (1980). Characterisation of adjustments to the structure of feeding behaviour following pharmacological treatment: effects of amphetamine and fenfluramine and the antagonism produced by pimozide and methergoline, *Pharmacology, Biochemistry and Behaviour*, **12**, 717–722.

Blundell, J. E. amd Latham, C. J. (1982). Behavioural pharmacology of feeding. In T. Silverstone (ed.) *Drugs and Appetite*, pp. 41–80. London: Academic Press.

Blundell, J. E. and Leshem, M. B. (1975). Analysis of the mode of action of anorexic drugs. In A. Howard (ed.), *Recent advances in Obesity Research I*, pp. 368–371. London: Newman.

Blundell, J. E. and McArthur, R. A. (1981). Behavioural flux and feeding: Continuous monitoring of food intake and food selection and the video-recording of appetitive and satiety sequences for the analysis of drug action. In S. Garattini (ed.), *Anorectic Agents, Mechanisms of Action and of Tolerance*. New York: Raven Press.

Blundell, J. E., Latham, C. J. and Leshem, M. B. (1976). Differences between the anorexic actions of amphetamine and fenfluramine: possible effects on hunger and satiety, *Journal and Pharmacy and Pharmacology*, **28**, 417–477.

Blundell, J. E., Rogers, P. J. and Hill, A. J. (1985). Behavioural structure and mechanisms of anorexia: calibration of natural and abnormal inhibition of eating, *Brain Research Bulletin*, **15**, 371–376.

Blundell, J. E., Hill, A. J. and Kirkham, T. C. (1987). Dextrofenfluramine and eating behaviour in animals: action on food selection, motivation and body weight. In A. Bender and L. J. Brooks (eds), *Human Body Weight*, pp. 233–239. London: Pitman.

Borbely, A. and Waser, P. G. (1966). Das fressverhalten der Ratte. Haufigkeit und Gewicht der Mahlzeiten unter dem Einfluss von Amphetamin, *Psychopharmacologia*, **9**, 373–381.

Burton, M. J., Cooper, S. J. and Popplewell, D. A. (1981). The effect of fenfluramine on the microstructure of feeding and drinking in the rat, *British Journal of Pharmacology*, **72**, 621–633.

Collier, G., Hirsch, E. and Kanarek, R. (1977). The operant revisited. In W. K. Honig and J. E. R. Stadden (eds), *Handbook of Operant Behaviour*. Englewood Cliffs, NJ: Prentice Hall.

Cox, D. R. and Lewis, P. A. W. (1966). *The Statistical Analysis of Series of Events*. London: Methuen.

Davies, R. F. (1976). Some neurochemical and physiological factors controlling free feeding patterns in the rat. PhD Thesis, McGill University, Montreal.

Davies, R. F., Rossi, J., Panksepp, J., Bean, N. J. and Zolovick, A. J. (1983). Fenfluramine anorexia: a peripheral locus of action, *Physiology and Behaviour*, **30**, 723–730.

Grinker, J. A., Drewnowski, A., Enns, M. and Kissileff, H. (1980). Effects of d-amphetamine and fenfluramine on feeding patterns and activity of obese and lean Zucker rats, *Pharmacology, Biochemistry and Behaviour*, **12**, 265–275.

Hill, A. J. and Blundell, J. E. (1986). Model system for investigating the actions of anorectic drugs: effect of D-fenfluramine on food intake, nutrient selection, food preferences, meal patterns, hunger and satiety in healthy human subjects. *Advances in Biosciences*, pp. 377–389. Oxford: Pergamon Press.

Kirkham, T. C. and Blundell, J. E. (1984). Dual action of naloxone on feeding revealed by behavioural analysis: separate effects on initiation and termination of eating, *Appetite*, **5**, 45–52.

Kirkham, T. C. and Blundell, J. E. (1986). Opioid antagonist effects on feeding observed in the runway, *Neuropharmacology*, **25**, 649–651.

Latham, C. J. and Blundell, J. E. (1979). Evidence for the effect of tryptophan on the pattern of food consumption in free feeding and food deprived rats. *Life Sciences*, **24**, 1971–1978.

Le Magnen, J. (1971). Advances in studies on the physiological control and regulation of food intake. In E. Stellar and J. M. Sprague (eds), *Progress in Physiological Psychology*, pp. 203–261. London: Academic Press.

Peroutka, S. J. and Synder, S. H. (1979). Multiple serotonin receptors: differential binding of ^{3}H-5-hydroxytryptamine, ^{3}H-lysergic acid diethylamide and ^{3}H-spiroperidol, *Molecular Pharmacology*, **16**, 687–699.

Richter, C. P. (1927). Animal behaviour and internal drives, *Quarterly Review of Biology*, **2**, 307–343.

Rogers, P. J. and Blundell, J. E. (1979). Effect of anorexic drugs on food intake and the micro-structure of eating in human subjects, *Psychopharmacology*, **66**, 159–165.

Smith, G. P. (1985). The physiology of the meal. In T. Silverstone (ed.), *Drugs and Appetite*, pp. 1–21. London: Academic Press.

Smith, G. P. and Gibbs, J. (1976). Cholecystokinin and satiety: theoretic and therapeutic implications. In D. Novin, W. Wyrwicka and G. Bray (eds.), *Hunger: Basic Mechanisms and Clinical Implications*, pp. 349–355. New York: Raven press.

Wiepkema, P. R. (1971). Behavioural factors in the regulation of food intake, *Proceedings of the Nutritional Society*, **30**, 142–149.

Part V

Computerisation of Questionnaires

It is easy, though not necessarily fruitful, to take standard psychological questionnaires and computerise them. Questions appear on the computer screen, usually one at a time, and responses are made using a set of buttons, or are typed in on the keyboard. The chapters in this section illustrate how questionnaires can be usefully adapted for computerised presentation and indicate what benefits this form of presentation has to offer. The first chapter shows that computerisation permits valuable information to be recorded about the timing of responses. It also greatly eases the process of data analysis. Third, it provides a form of interaction which subjects can find interesting and rewarding. The second chapter shows how the technology of micros can dramatically enhance and expand the technology of questionnaire administration. Empirical results indicate that response latency can be a useful guide to an item's reliability. If the respondents take a long time to respond, there is a high chance that if the question is presented again, perhaps in a slightly different form, different responses will be given. This knowledge can be used both in questionnaire design, as a means of weeding out problematic questions, and also in administration by monitoring response latencies and, when these are longer than usual, making sure that different versions of the question are presented later on to try to improve reliability.

CHAPTER 12

Holistic assessment of mood states in field trials of psychoactive drugs

MARGARET CHRISTIE, ALI MEHMET AND MATTIJS MUIJEN

Introduction

In 1984—when the work in this chapter was at the planning stage—Ancill and Carr had just reported on their five years' experience of microcomputerised assessments (MCAs) in clinical research with psychiatric patients. They had, for example, modified the Hamilton Depression Rating Scale for self-rating by patients, and suggested that MCAs in clinical trials could provide a *more thorough understanding* of the benefits and risks involved in treatment with new medication. New *antidepressant* medications currently available may vary considerably in the degree of their *side effects*, while varying little in their efficacy for the treatment of depression. Broader views of *side effects* are apparent in papers discussing the 'quality of life'—social functioning as well as psychomotor activity—of patients receiving psychoactive medication (Feighner, 1987; Diamond, 1985) and these broadening of perceptions may themselves be set within the current resurgence of 'holism' in medicine (Christie, 1987; Christie and Mellett, 1986). Against this background we were invited to explore the extent to which a new antidepressant might be '... better to live with for working patients': 'we' at that point being M.J.C., A.M. and—for a short time—Mark Pitkethly (M.A.P.). All three had psychophysiological expertise—M.J.C. within a background of 'whole person' research, A.M. with computing skills and M.A.P. as a potential clinical psychologist. All were at that time associated with a department in which the 'Dentest' (MCA) had been developed by Bennett *et al.* (1981) to examine the after-effects of relative analgesia with nitrous oxide in the 'field' situation of dental surgeries. But none of us were psychopharmacologists and from this starting point of relative ignorance we embarked on a two-phase exploration, progress through which

Microcomputers, Psychology and Medicine
Edited by R. West, M. Christie and J. Weinman
© 1990 by John Wiley & Sons Ltd

is charted below—largely for readers who, like M.J.C., A.M. and M.A.P., may be about to launch into uncharted waters. Our concluding section aims to set the exploration and its findings within the context of contemporary developments in psychoactive therapy.

Phase 1: development and evaluation of the MCA for mood profiles and response times

If our concern was to be with well-being of *ambulant* patients treated over a number of weeks with antidepressant medication we had to move away from laboratory-based assessments and toward the 'field' situations of general practice or day centre. MCAs offered the possibilities of:

1   Relatively autonomous functioning and minimal human intervention.
2   Storage and subsequent analysis of data by statistical packages such as SPSSX and MINITAB (see Chapter 1).

We opted for the comprehensive assessment of *mood profiles* offered by the Nowlis Mood Adjective Check List (MACL), which was initially developed for use in a psychopharmacological context (Nowlis and Nowlis, 1956) and had, in its original pencil-and-paper (PP) version, proved to be a sensitive and comprehensive indicator of mood profile in normal subjects, during investigations of diurnal variation and post-prandial change in dimensions relevant to performance efficiency (Christie and Venables, 1973; Christie and McBrearty, 1979). The MACL depends on the use of certain adjectives to complete the sentence 'I feel . . .'. Subjects are asked to rate on a four-point scale the extent to which their present mood is described by the 45 adjectives which are *listed* in Table 12.1, though are *presented* in a randomised sequence for MACL completion.

Subsequent summation of the individual scores—grouped into appropriate clusters such as drowsy + sluggish + tired for Deactivation—offers assessment of mood along 13 dimensions ranging from Deactivation, through Pleasantness, Anxiety, etc., to Clinical Depression. The MACL offered scope for MCA of mood profiles, not least because computerisation reduced the human time and possible error associated with the substantial amount of scoring and data reduction.

Additionally, however, *timing* of responses would be possible—times for responding to each *adjective*, for each mood *dimension* and for the *total* completion of the MACL assessment—as an adjunct to the simple (SRT) and choice (CRT) reaction time measurement for which we used software from Bennett *et al.*'s (1981) 'Dentest'. We also constructed a four-button console to replace a computer keyboard for subject responses—and embarked on the first

Table 12.1   The 13 mood dimensions of the MACL, with contributory adjectives

	Dimension		Adjectives		
1	Aggression	Angry	Defiant	Bold	Rebellious
2	Concentration	Concentrating	Earnest	Engaged in thought	Serious
3	Deactivation	Drowsy	Sluggish	Tired	
4	Social affection	Affectionate	Forgiving	Kindly	Warm-hearted
5	Anxiety	Apprehensive	Fearful	Tensed up*	Insecure
6	Depression	Blue	Lonely	Regretful	
7	Egotism	Boastful	Egotistic	Cocky	Self-centered
8	Pleasantness	Elated	Lighthearted	Overjoyed	Pleased
9	Activation	Active	Energetic	Vigorous	
10	Nonchalance	Nonchalant	Playful	Witty	
11	Scepticism	Sceptical	Suspicious		
12	Startle	Shocked	Startled		
13	Clinical depression	Worthless	Helpless	Hopeless	Empty Sad

* American version: Clutched up.

study, with normal subjects, after software had been developed for the CBM Commodore PET by our colleague, Colin Hendrie (see Chapter 10).

Study 1

Forty subjects were recruited from non-academic university staff: these had age and sex distributions similar to those reported as characteristic of depressed patient populations—14 males; 26 females; age range 19–51, mean 34.6 years. Subjects were assigned to one of the four groups shown in Table 12.2 and completed the MACL on two occasions, a week apart, using the PP or MCA (PET) method as indicated in Table 12.2.

As there is variation in the numbers of adjectives comprising each mood dimension, scores were converted to percentages before being summed over

Table 12.2   Design and subjects of study 1: MACL presentation using PET and/or PP

Group	Order of presentation		No. of Subjects		Age	
	1st	2nd	males	females	mean	range
1	PP	PP	3	7	33.7	25–21
2	PP	PET	4	6	33.2	22–47
3	PET	PET	4	6	36.1	19–51
4	PET	PP	3	7	35.4	22–47

Table 12.3   Group mean percentage from normal subjects of study 1: 13 MACL dimensions presented by PP and PET

Dimension	PP	PET
1	19.37	17.29
2	62.35	69.67
3	28.05	29.44
4	58.53	56.67
5	27.08	31.46
6	18.05	18.33
7	13.54	13.54
8	37.71	40.82
9	59.94	61.1
10	40.55	40.27
11	33.75	39.16
12	4.17	6.25
13	10.83	12.72

the PP and PET groups, to produce the normative data of Table 12.3, which shows no significant differences in the main scores for either group. Preliminary discussion of the method, however, revealed a clinician's scepticism about the possibility of obtaining cooperation and computerised data from severely *depressed patients* so a limited study was undertaken with several such patients, by M.A.P., in the Airedale District Hospital. Cooperation and data were forthcoming, but we began to consider possible ways of maintaining interest during completion of the MACL test, which can, with retarded performance, take 10 minutes.

Study 2

Software was generated for a BBC (model B) and a 14-inch colour TV was used for presentation (see Figure 12.1). In a pilot trial a split-half comparison of MACL scores from PP and BBC versions was carried out. A computer record of response latencies for each adjective was stored, together with summed times for response to all adjectives of each mood dimension and for total test time.

Data were collected from 40 normal subjects—13 males, 27 females; age range 19–61, mean 36.4 years; randomly assigned to the four groups as shown in Table 12.4. After reducing the 45 adjectives to 40 by removing one from the five dimensions having an uneven number, a split half presentation of the MACL was undertaken: the four groups of 10 subjects completed both halves (A and B) sequentially using PP or BBC versions, as shown in Table 12.4.

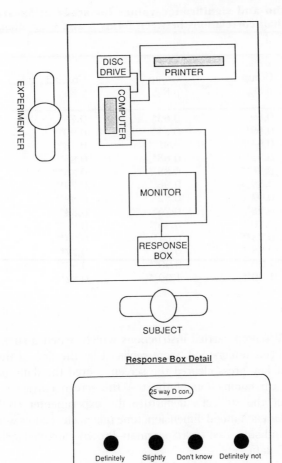

FIGURE 12.1   System used in Phase II MCA.

Table 12.4   Male (M) and female (F) subjects and design for study 2: split-half (A and B) MACL using PP and/or BBC presentation

Group	F	M	Age range	A	B
1	7	3	22–59	PP	PP
2	7	3	18–57	PP	BBC
3	6	4	19–51	BBC	PP
4	7	3	25–61	BBC	BBC

Table 12.5   Rho and significance values for study 2: Spearman–Brown corrected split-half correlations between forms A and B for dimensions 1–13 of the MACL

MACL dimension	Group 1 ρ Sig.	Group 2 ρ Sig.	Group 3 ρ Sig.	Group 4 ρ Sig.
1	0.69*	0.63*	0.76*	0.76*
2	0.69*	0.84**	0.90**	0.70*
3	0.94**	0.96**	0.73*	0.82**
4	0.92**	0.68*	0.85**	0.89**
5	0.96**	0.88**	0.86**	0.80**
6	0.39	0.96**	0.79**	0.81**
7	0.02	0.82**	0.89**	0.95**
8	0.98**	0.76*	0.83**	0.84**
9	0.80**	0.90**	0.85**	0.78*
10	0.83**	0.64*	0.94**	0.94**
11	0.88**	0.25	0.77*	0.91**
12	1.00**	0.90**	0.93**	1.00**
13	1.00**	1.00**	0.82**	0.93**

*$p \leqslant 0.05$; **$p \leqslant 0.01$.

The colour TV screen carried instructions which, when a subject indicated that these had been understood, were replaced by the first of the adjectives. Each subsequent key press cleared the screen, stored the data and displayed the next word. On completion of the test the screen carried a message of thanks and after the subject's departure the experimenter could scan the summed scores for each mood dimension, time taken, etc. Scores were converted to percentages and subjected to a Spearman–Brown corrected split half correlation of PP/BBC data.

Results are summarised in Table 12.5 showing that some 70% of correlations reach an 0.01 level of significance, some 20% an 0.05 level, and the remaining three of the 52 correlations do not reach statistical significance.

We concluded, at this point, that the BBC version of the MACL was a viable alternative to the original paper form for use with *normal* subjects; the next stage was evaluation of its potential for work with *ambulatory patients*, within Phase 2, in the East Ham Day Centre.

Phase 2: the East Ham study

The East Ham Centre was established in 1983 within the Newham health district in London: this is an inner city catchment area which has large Asian and Afro-Caribbean communities. Referrals of depressed patients were mainly from general practitioners, with some from psychiatric out-patient clinics and day hospitals.

Table 12.6   MACL study within East Ham trial: patient/treatment details

	Fluoxetine	Mianserin	Placebo
N total	13	11	14
N males	6	4	5
N females	7	7	9
Age range	24–53	22–65	22–54
Mean age	37.31	37.91	34.64

In this setting a comparative clinical trial of a new antidepressant was being mounted: fluoxetine—a selective serotonin reuptake inhibitor—was being compared in a randomised, double-blind placebo-controlled study with an established antidepressant (mianserin) and placebo and we felt that this offered a challenging opportunity of evaluating the computerised MACL. Details of the trial are available in Muijen *et al.* (1988), but a brief description is needed here to set the scene for our account of the Phase 2 appraisal.

Approximately 30% of referred patients were assessed as being appropriate for inclusion in the clinical trial, meeting the research diagnostic criteria for major depressive illness (Spitzer *et al.*, 1977), having a score of greater than 17 on the Hamilton Depression Rating Scale (HDRS: Hamilton, 1967) and being within the age range 18–65. Two patients did not wish to take part: 83 out-patients gave informed consent and participated in at least some aspect of, and 52 completed, the double-blind trial. Patients were randomly allocated to one of the three treatment groups: fluoxetine, mianserin or placebo (medication being in identical 20-mg capsules) and were seen weekly by the same psychiatrist (M.M.), when the HDRS and the Montgomery–Asberg Depression Rating Scale (MADRS; Montgomery and Asberg, 1979) were administered alongside clinical and patient assessments of depressive state.

Of the 52 patients who completed the clinical trial there were 38 who:

1   agreed to participate in the computer study;
2   had sufficiently fluent English to understand the MCA instructions;
3   had a complete set of mood assessment data from week 0 through to the fourth week of treatment.

Details of this set of patients are given in Table 12.6.

The MCA testing procedure was as described in Study 2, supervised by A.M. on most occasions and by M.M. on the remainder: this aspect of the trial took some two years to complete.

Data storage

The MCA data were stored for analysis on completion of the clinical trial. All data were stored in a serial file with the format: subject number, name, age, sex, and week of treatment. These data were recorded at the beginning of each test session by means of an interactive program operated by the researcher. Once this had been done and the test battery commenced, data from the current test session were stored in memory until the end of the test, when they transferred to the serial file. Each test session gave rise to the following data.

MACL. Scores for each of the 45 adjectives presented were stored along with each individual response time, then were condensed such that the totals for each of the 13 mood dimensions were stored along with their mean response time: finally the total time taken to complete the MACL test was stored. In addition to examining changes in its individual dimensions these have also been grouped into *clusters* of mood state: Christie and Venables (1973), for example, summed scores from the Activation/Deactivation/Concentration dimensions in a study of mood variation during working days, while Handlon (1962) in explorations of individual responses to '. . . stresses and easements of everyday living . . .' grouped euphoric and dysphoric mood dimensions. We followed this lead, and in addition to scores for the 13 dimensions of Table 12.1 also computed scores for clusters of 'efficiency', 'pleasant' and 'dysphoric' mood.

Simple reaction time (SRT). Each of ten simple visual response times was stored along with the total SRT and mean response time.

Choice reaction time (CRT). Each of ten choice response times was stored along with the number of correct and incorrect responses. The mean response times for correct and for incorrect responses were also stored, along with time taken for the CRT test and the mean time for all responses.

In a seperate 'Clinical Data File' data from the psychiatrist's assessments were stored: these consisted of: the HDRS total score, the ten subscores of the Montgomery–Asberg Depression Rating scale, the three Clinical Global Impressions (CGI) and the two Patient Global Impressions (PGI).

Each subject who took part in the MCA produced five complete sets of the above data set from week 0 before treatment through to the fourth treatment week.

The organisation of the above data files enabled retrieval of any of the data from weeks 0 to 4 into a separate file which could be transferred directly to a mainframe (VAX 780) for subsequent analysis with either SPSSX or MINITAB.

Data analysis

Several types of question might be asked of the MACL data:

1   How much improvement in the patients' depressive state is there *after* four weeks' treatment?
2   What insights into aspects of the patients' 'quality of life'—their social functioning and performance efficiency—can be gleaned *during* the treatment period?
3   How much agreement is there between *mood states relevant* to performance efficiency—specifically activated mood states—and indices of *performance efficiency* such as reaction times and MACL response times?
4   How much *agreement* is there between information derived from the MCAs and that derived from the more traditional clinical tools of HAMD, MADRS, and CGI?

The ease with which answers to these questions could be sought in the data was, of course, greatly increased by the use of desk-top computers for data reduction and analysis, as indicated in the previous section.

Turning then to the four questions and first, the appraisal of improvement after 4 weeks' treatment, using *change* scores which were computed by taking the difference between week 0 and 4 percentage scores and analysing for between-group (F, M, P) differences using the Mann–Whitney 'U'.

The summary in Table 12.7 indicates the extent of changes in what can be designated as the *negative* mood dimensions of 'Clinical Depression' and 'Anxiety' and compares these with the *positive* dimensions of 'Pleasantness' and 'Nonchalance'. Turning to the *grouped* mood clusters seen in Table 12.8 we derived three: Group A relevant for performance efficiency; Group B, the negative moods of anxiety and depressive state; and Group C, our positive moods of 'Pleasantness', 'Nonchalance' and 'Social Affection'.

Table 12.8 summarises some comparisons of the three treatments' effects on these three mood clusters, including both an appraisal of change at the end of 4 weeks' treatment and an attempt to answer question 2—to evaluate patients' well-being *throughout* treatment. This approach is reflected in the third column of Table 12.8, the results there being derived by summing the differences on scores for week 0/week 1, week 1/week 2, week 2/week 3 and week 3/week 4:

Summarising here we suggest that the MCAs of mood have provided information about changes *after* 4 weeks and discriminated between the three drug treatments; they have provided information about both negative and positive mood states *during* the 4 weeks' treatment, together with some information about subjective aspects of performance efficiency. How these *subjective* feelings of activation meshed with *objective* evaluation of response and reaction times in the F and P groups is indicated by Table 12.9, which

Table 12.7 Changes in mood from week 0 (pre-treatment) to week 4 of treatment: fluoxetine (F), mianserin (M) and placebo (P) groups' mean percentage change scores

MACL dimension	Week 0			Week 4			0–4			Direction and significance of change
	F	M	P	F	M	P	F	M	P	
Negative mood states (positive difference = improvement)										
'Clinical depression'	75.4	89.6	747.7	50.8	66.7	71.4	24.6	22.9	3.3	F>M—NS F>P—$p \leqslant 0.05$ M>P—NS
'Anxiety'	82.7	87.1	79.7	57.7	70.4	78.0	25.0	16.7	1.7	F>M—NS F>P—$p \leqslant 0.01$ M>P—NS
Positive mood states (negative difference = improvement)										
'Pleasantness'	9.6	12.1	11.9	37.2	17.4	11.9	−27.6	−5.3	0.0	F<M—$p \leqslant 0.01$ F<P—$p \leqslant 0.01$ M<P—NS
'Nonchalance'	15.4	4.0	16.3	39.3	15.1	14.3	−23.9	−11.1	2.0	F<M—NS F<P—$p \leqslant 0.01$ M<P—NS

Table 12.8   Summary of patients' state: week 4 data, week 0–4 differences, and 4 weeks' treatment period, for combined mood dimensions of group A (efficiency), combined mood dimensions of group B (dysphoria) and combined mood dimensions of group C (euphoria) in patients treated with fluoxetine (F), mianserin (M) and placebo (P)

Mood group	Week 4	Week 0–4	Well-being throughout treatment

A: Efficiency
  Activation
  Deactivation
  Concentration
	F better than M
	$(p \leqslant 0.05)$
		F better than M
		$(p \leqslant 0.025)$
			F better than M or P
			$(p \leqslant 0.05)$

B: Dysphoria
  Anxiety
  Depression
  Clinical
  Depression
	F better than P
	
	$(p \leqslant 0.05)$
		F and M better than P
		
		$(p \leqslant 0.025)$
			F and M better than P
			$(p \leqslant 0.05)$
			
			$(p \leqslant 0.025)$

C: Euphoria
  Pleasantness
  Nonchalance
  Social Affection
	F better than M
	or P
	$(p \leqslant 0.025)$
		F better than M
		or P
		$(p \leqslant 0.025)$
		$(p \leqslant 0.01)$
			F better than P
			$(p \leqslant 0.01)$

suggests that while the F group both *feels* activated and performs better, the P group is demonstrating a placebo response in that it may *feel* activated, but it *performs* less well. This type of placebo response may, perhaps, reflect to some extent the clinician/patient interaction: this leads us into consideration of the *clinician's* evaluation of patient's progress—based on the *structured* information gathered via HAMD, MADRS and the CGI—and comparisons of this with the information gathered from patient/microcomputer interaction.

Table 12.9   Relations between subjective experience of activation and objective assessments of reaction and response times: comparisons between F and P groups (M results all NS)

	Fluoxetine	Placebo
Correlation of Activation change scores (week 0–week 4) with correct choice reaction time	$\rho = -0.65$ $p = <0.025$	$\rho = +0.61$ $p = <0.025$
Reduction in total response time for MACL completion: (week 0–week 4))	$t = 2.12$ $p = <0.025$	

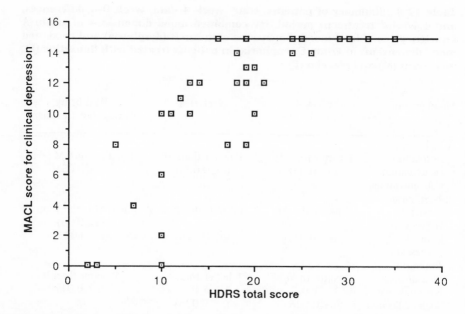

FIGURE 12.2 Comparison between MACL scores for 'clinical depression' and the total score for HDRS.

The first comparison of clinician and microcomputer was reported by Muijen *et al.* in 1986 and based on the data of Figure 12.2. The total HAMD score was correlated with the MACL score for 'Clinical Depression', across all 38 subjects sampled at week 3. The correlation of 0.72 reflects reasonably good correspondence, though there is evidence of a possible ceiling effect due to the highest scorers on the MACL. Moving beyond this preliminary analysis we turned to *week by week* comparisons of the MACL's 'Clinical Depression' scores and those for the psychiatrist's CGI, which records his impression on a seven-point scale of the extent to which a patient is depressed at the time of the consultation. Table 12.10 suggests that there is close agreement of assessments on this weekly basis.

The CGI also provided for a clinician's assessment of *change* in depressive state: at each weekly visit the patient's condition was compared with the psychiatrist's recalled assessment of their week 0 state. When we compared these assessments of change with the change scores for MACL 'Clinical Depression'—the difference between week 0 and each week's score—the agreement, shown in Table 12.11, was less close than in Table 12.10 and less close than similar comparisons by the *patient*, for which the correlations are, on successive weeks: $\rho = -0.42$ $(p \leqslant 0.005)$; $\rho = -0.42$ $(p \leqslant 0.005)$; $\rho = -0.51$ $(p \leqslant 0.001)$; $\rho = -0.30$ $(p \leqslant 0.05)$.

Table 12.10   Comparison of depressive state from week 0 through 4 weeks' of trial: correlation of CGI score with MACL score for 'clinical depression' ($N=38$)

Week	0	1	2	3	4
ρ	0.37	0.55	0.58	0.69	0.51
p	$\leqslant 0.025$	$\leqslant 0.001$	$\leqslant 0.001$	$\leqslant 0.001$	$\leqslant 0.001$

Table 12.11   Comparison of change in depressive state since week 0: correlation of psychiatrist's impression with MACL change scores for 'clinical depression'

Week	1	2	3	4
ρ	−0.35	−0.30	−0.44	−0.28
p	$\leqslant 0.025$	$\leqslant 0.05$	$\leqslant 0.005$	$\leqslant 0.05$

Table 12.12   Correlation of MADRS item 8 with grouped MACL scores for positive mood

Week	0	1	2	3	4
ρ	0.19	−0.16	−0.12	−0.41	−0.39
p	NS	NS	NS	<0.005	<0.01

Table 12.13   Week by week comparison of total MADRS scores with scores from MACL clusters of positive and negative mood

		0	1	2	3	4
'Clinical depression' 'Anxiety' 'Deactivation'	ρ:	0.35	0.46	0.41	0.65	0.59
	p:	<0.025	<0.001	<0.005	<0.001	<0.001
'Nonchalance' 'Pleasantness' 'Social Affection'	ρ:	−0.31	−0.21	−0.10	−0.36	0.36
	p:	<0.05	NS	NS	<0.025	<0.26

All in all we were pleasantly surprised by the reasonable levels of agreement within the triad of patient/psychiatrist/computer when the *negative* mood state of clinical depression was being assessed, but what of more *positive*, pleasant mood?

The MADRS does give some scope for assessing more positive mood state: its item 8 asks about the ability to feel pleasure. So MACL scores for positive mood were correlated with those for item 8 of MADRS; the results are shown in Table 12.12, where there is much less agreement, until the third week of treatment. Our suggestion is that the positive mood states are less clearly perceived until the point in treatment where placebo responses carry less weight than the active drug effects which are more evident at the third week. We examined this aspect of the trial by comparing *total* MADRS scores week by week, with both negative and positive mood clusters: the results are shown in Table 12.13.

Again there is less good agreement for *positive* mood, and evidence of a week 3 effect: at which point we conclude our explorations into the MCA data and attempt a stocktaking in our concluding overview.

Overview

Up to this point we have offered a baldly pragmatic account of our explorations. But like Severe (1987b), who reported on the experience of setting up microcomputerised monitoring of a clinical trial, we feel that our saga might be more aptly titled 'Jumping in head first: one year later'. We did indeed jump in head first, but now, some five years later, feel that we've surfaced through the sea of data and can look around us, asking ourselves both 'What *did* we do with our MCAs?' and also 'What *could* we do with them?'

What did we do?

First, we could be said to have 'enriched' a Phase III clinical trial—an evaluation of a new drug's effects on 'patients who are representative of *routine clinical practice* and in *circumstances* more closely allied to it' (Royal Society of Medicine Medico-pharmaceutical Forum Report, 1987). Thus we worked in a clinical 'field' situation, testing subjects over several weeks of treatment, but using an MCA; and these are more typically seen in Phase I trials, with healthy volunteers, given single doses and tested in laboratory environments. Chapter 4 of the present volume exemplifies such Phase I work: Hindmarch has published widely in the area and papers such as his 1988 report of fluoxetine have relevance for our findings on the psychomotor effects of antidepressant medication in the East Ham trial.

That we used MCAs in a clinical trial is fairly innovative: we noted the pioneering efforts of Ancill and Carr (1984) in our introductory paragraph, but a recent issue of *Psychopharmacology Bulletin* (1987) reviews developing applications of microcomputers to clinical trials under three headings: (1) data management; (2) statistical analyses; (3) computer-based patient assessments— described as '. . . an area of microcomputer use in which one is bound only by one's own imagination' (Severe, 1987a). Examples of such assessments included the Minnesota Computer Assessment (using the Apple IIc) of response to methylphenidate in the treatment of attention deficit disorders (ADDs) (Greenberg, 1987); a delayed response task, also for ADD, and using a program written in Applesoft BASIC (Solanto and Lewitter, 1987); a picture memory test administered by a Mackintosh computer (Corwin and Snodgrass, 1987); a neuropsychological assessment battery employing and IBM XT microcomputer (Rappaport, *et al.*, 1987); and a microcomputer-based system for studying motor and cognitive function, called the Rehabilitation Workstation (Maulucci *et al.*, 1987). Severe (1987) observes that applications of computer-based assessments seem to occur more often in clinical populations of children and the elderly.

As we have indicated, however, our MCAs were aimed at '. . . a more thorough understanding . . .' of effects, in the Phase III stage of drug evaluation, and in ambulant patients treated with antidepressant medication who were at home and at work. To what extent *did* we, by using our MCAs, achieve a more thorough understanding than was available via the clinician's global impression and the HDRS and MADRS? We would suggest that the evidence of changes in psychomotor response available from the reaction time and response time data supplements and possibly confirms impressions. Further, the response time data can be parsimoniously collected during the mood profile assessment *and* offer scope for the interesting comparisons of *subjective* reports of activation and *objective* assessments of performance efficiency referred to on page 241.

We regard the evidence of changes in the *positive* mood state (see Table 12.8) as a useful complement to the assessment of ability to feel pleasure which might be available from item 8 of the MADRS, and viewed with interest the possible interactions of placebo and drug response in the first two weeks of treatment. This is not the place to expand on the problems of placebo response in depression (Brown, 1988) or on the complexities of clinician/patient interactions. That the latter have obvious relevance in areas other than clinical trials has been described by (the author of Chapter 13) Skinner and his colleagues working with lifestyle assessment (Skinner and Allen, 1983; Allen and Skinner, 1987); in Canadian family practice (Skinner *et al.*, 1985a, 1985b); while Fava *et al.* (1986) advise the combined use of both self-rating and observer scales for optimal assessment of patients with affective disorders.

Our preliminary exploration into comparisons of information about affective disorder derived from patient/clinican and patient/computer interactions suggested that there was good concordance for the dysphoric mood dimensions—for depression and anxiety—but less agreement about the positive, pleasant aspects of mood. Why? Is the interaction between patient and clinician seen by the former as an activity dedicated to the discussion of depression—and maybe also anxiety? Does the clinician have a dearth of tools for exploring positive mood—with the exception of the MADRS item 8? Is it, perhaps, another manifestation of the phenomenon highlighted in a psychophysiological review of 'Pleasure' (Stern *et al.* 1975)? The authors reported a dearth of articles on the psychophysiology of pleasure in comparison with pain or unpleasantness. Maybe we regard pleasure as a subject less relevant than the dysphoric aspects of life? Certainly there have been very few empirical studies, with the exception of work on erotic stimuli, and while it is difficult to administer and quantify non-sexual stimuli and responses, the psychophysiological equipment is available: motivation appears to be absent, in contrast to the interest in pleasurable emotion at the end of the nineteenth century!

Having moved to a somewhat speculative plane, we would like to conclude with some speculative glances at the future possibilities of MCAs in the holistic assessment of drug effects.

What might we do?

If our concern is primarily with the functional efficiency and general well-being of *ambulant* patients, in their work and home environments, when being treated with psychoactive medication, we could look toward primary health care situations; here some 80% of the UK National Health Service drug prescriptions originate (Royal Society of Medicine Medico-pharmaceutical Forum Report, 1987) and the treatment of affective disorder has expanded significantly in recent decades (Edwards, 1981; Tyrer, 1981). We have in mind not only the possible participation of general practitioners in Phase III trials but also their role in post-marketing surveillance of reactions to medicines.

Before looking more closely at the latter role, however, it would be advisable to ask whether MCAs in general practice are likely to be *acceptable*. Questions about *microcomputer* usage in general practice were asked and answered within two reports of surveys funded by the UK Department of Health (1985, 1986). It was evident from these sources that their potential for administrative tasks was recognised—but their use as an adjunct to drug surveillance is much less evident. Warnings about possible prejudice *from clinicians* have been sounded by Skinner and Pakula (1986), who suggest that if computers *appear* to encroach on the domain of clinical judgement then may be perceived as a threat. Skinner and his colleagues have, however, also reported (1985a) that computerised lifestyle assessment in Canadian family practice was not unacceptable to *patients*: 77% of their population agreed to participate—and found they liked the MCA. These figures are comparable with the East Ham data: 73% of the appropriate trial patients agreed to participate.

Assuming that MCAs *would* be acceptable in general practice environments, what scope might there be for assessment packages such as the timed MACL? Returning to the theme of post-marketing surveillance (PMS) and its various aspects, described briefly in sources such an Inman (1987), in the UK the Department of Health administers its 'yellow card' system for voluntary reporting by doctors, of suspected *adverse* drug reactions. Inman, however, has argued for a broader-based system of prescription-event monitoring (PEM: Inman *et al.*, 1986) which facilitates a more 'holistic' appraisal of the *costs and benefits* to the patient or both new and some older established drugs: his data, for example, provide for a better informed and hopefully more objective evaluation of the risk and benefit associated with non-steroidal anti-inflammatory drugs. Inman (1987) reported that his PEM scheme is supported by up to 70% of the 23 000 general practitioners in England, with the potential for providing up to 10 000 case-reports each month. One can readily appreciate the positive response of clinicians to PEM of drugs to treat chronic conditions such as arthritis or high blood pressure, but what of the ubiquitous psychoactive medications?

Our first page noted the growth of concern with the 'quality of life' for patients receiving psychoactive medication and the issue of side-effects from antidepressant drugs. But it is, perhaps, unrealistic to expect a general practitioner with '. . . six minutes for the patient' (Balint and Norell, 1973) to explore, in a more 'holistic' manner, and beyond its impact on dysphoric mood, the effects of an antidepressant drug. At which point we suggest the possible value of MCAs, though the software which served the East Ham study would require reappraisal: there we had human aid for administration and response to patients' questions, in the form of AM and MM, whereas the typical environment of a UK general practice is such that any MCA would undoubtedly have to be more autonomous and independent—a stand-alone system with user-friendly software to deal with any patient's queries. That said, it does seem possible to envisage a role for MCAs in those environments of community care where the computer is seen as offering promise rather than threat!

Acknowledgements

Without the helpful support of Dr David Roy and the East Ham Centre staff this project would have been impossible.

Funding for the work described in this chapter was provided by Lilly Industries: their financial support, and the encouragement of Dr John Hall, was much appreciated, as was the statistical advice within phase I of Dr Spencer Bennett, Airdale Health District.

The first author acknowledges with grateful thanks the generous response of Professor V. Nowlis to an earlier request for permission to use the MACL.

References

Allen, B. and Skinner, H. (1987). Lifestyle assessment using microcomputers. In J. Butcher (ed.), *Computerised Psychological Assessment: A Practitioner's Guide*. New York: Basic Books.

Ancill, R. J. and Carr, A. C. (1984). Using microcomputers to measure effects of psychoactive drugs, *Acta Therapeutica*, **10**, 393–400.

Balint, E. and Norell, J. S. (eds) (1973). *Six Minutes for the Patient*. London: Tavistock Publications.

Bennett, S., Davies, P. and Payne, I. (1981). Psychomotor deficits contingent upon relative analgesia in a dental situation: implications for drivers. *International Conference on Road Safety*, Cardiff.

Brown, W. A. (1988). Predictors of placebo response in depression, *Psychopharmacology Bulletin*, **24**, 14–17.

Christie, M. J. (1987). The semantics of whole-person care. In G. N. Christodoulon (ed.), *Psychosomatic Medicine: Past and Future*. New York: Plenum.

Christie, M. J. and McBrearty, M. T. (1979). Psychophysiological investigations of post lunch state in male and female subjects, *Ergonomics*, **22**, 307–323.

Christie, M. J. and Mellet, P. G. (eds) (1986). *The Psychosomatic Approach: Contemporary Practice of Whole-Person Care*. Chichester: Wiley.

Christie, M. J. and Venables, P. H. (1973). Mood changes in relation to age, EPI scores, time and day, *British Journal of Social and Clinical Psychology*, **12**, 61–73.

Corwin, J. and Snodgrass, J. G. (1987). The picture memory and fragmented pictures tests: use with cognitively impaired populations, *Psychopharmacology Bulletin*, **23**, 286–290.

Department of Health and Social Security (1985). *General Practice Computing—Evaluation of the Micros for GPs' Scheme: Final Report*. HMSO, London.

Department of Health and Social Security (1986). *Micros in Practice—Report of an Appraisal of GP Microcomputer Systems*. HMSO, London.

Diamond, R. (1985). Drugs and the quality of life: the patient's point of view, *Journal of Clinical Psychiatry*, **46**, 29–35.

Edwards, G. (ed.) (1981). *Psychiatry in General Practice*. University of Southampton: University of Southampton Press.

Fava, G. A., Kellner, R., Lisansky, J., Park, S., Perini, G. I. and Zielezny, M. (1986). Rating depression in normals and depressives: observer versus self-rating scales, *Journal of Affective Disorders*, **11**, 29–33.

Feighner, J. P. (1987). Impact of anxiety therapy on patients' quality of life, *American Journal of Medicine*, **82**, (Suppl. 5A), 14–19.

Greenberg, L. M. (1987). An objective measure of methylphenidate response: clinical use of the MCA, *Psychopharmacology Bulletin*, **23**, 279–282.

Hamilton, M. (1967). Development of a rating scale for primary depressive illness, *British Journal of Social and Clinical Psychology*, **6**, 278–296.

Handlon, J. H. (1962). Hormonal activity and individual responses to stress and easements of everyday living. In R. Roessler and N. S. Greenfield (eds), *Physiological Correlates of Psychological Disorders*, University of Wisconsin Press, Madison.

Hindmarch, I. (1988). A pharmacological profile of fluoxetine and other antidepressants on aspects of skilled performance and car handling ability, *British Journal of Psychiatry*, **153**, (Suppl. 3), 99–104.

Inman, H. W. (1985). Risks in medical intervention: balancing therapeutic risks and benefits. In M. Cooper (ed.), *Risk: Man-made Hazards to Man*. Oxford: Oxford University Press.

Inman, W. H. W. (1987). *PEM News*, No. 4, Southampton: Drug Safety Research Unit.

Inman, W. H. W., Rawson, N. S. B. and Wiltin, L. V. (1986). Prescription-event monitoring. In W. H. W. Inman (ed.), *Monitoring for Drug Safety*, 2nd edn. Lancaster: MTP Press.

Maulucci, R. A., Eckhouse, H., Jr and Herman, R. M. (1987). A microcomputer workstation for assessing function, *Psychopharmacology Bulletin*, **23**, 294–297.

Montgomery, S. A. and Asberg, M. (1979). A new depression rating scale designed to be sensitive to change, *British Journal of Psychiatry*, **134**, 382–389.

Muijen, M., Roy, D. H. and Mehmet, A. (1986). Application of a computerised test battery in the assessment of response to treatment after depression, *15th CINP Congress*, Puerto Rico.

Muijen, M., Roy, D., Silverstone, T., Mehmet, A. and Christie, M. (1988). A comparative trial of fluoxetine, mianserin and placebo in depressed out-patients, *Acta Psychiatrica Scandinavica*, **78**, 384–390.

Nowlis, V. and Nowlis, M. (1956). The description and analysis of mood, *Annals of the New York Academy of Sciences*, **65**, 345–355.

Psychopharmacology Bulletin (1987). Applications of microcomputers to clinical trials in psychopharmacology, **23**, No. 2.

Rappopport, H. K., Kirschner, N. M. and Fishburne, F. J., Jr (1987). Computerised neuropsychological assessment, *Psychopharmacology Bulletin*, **23**, 291–293.

Royal Society of Medicine Medico-pharmaceutical Forum (1987). *Report of the Working Party on Clinical Trials*. London: RSM Services.

Severe, J. B. (1987a). Editorial introduction, *Psychopharmacology Bulletin*, **23**, 259–260.

Severe, J. B. (1987b). Computers in coordination of a multicenter clinical trial, *Psychopharmacology Bulletin*, **23**, 261–263.

Skinner, H. A. and Allen, B. A. (1983). Does the computer make a difference? Computerized versus face to face versus self-reported assessment of alcohol, drug and tobacco use, *Journal of Consulting and Clinical Psychology*, **21**, 267–275.

Skinner, H. A. and Pakula, A. (1986). Challenge of computers in psychological assessment. *Professional Psychology: Research and Practice*, **17**, 44–50.

Skinner, H. A., Allen, B. A., McIntosh, M. C. and Palmer, W. H. (1985a). Life-style assessment: applying microcomputers in family practice, *British Medical Journal*, **290**, 212–214.

Skinner, H. A., Allen, B. A., McIntosh, M. C. and Palmer, W. H. (1985b). Life-style assessment: just asking makes a difference, *British Medical Journal*, **290**, 214–216.

Solanto, M. V. and Lewitter, M. (1987). The delayed response task for ADD children, *Psychopharmacology Bulletin*, **23**, 283–285.

Spitzer, R. L., Endicott, J. and Rolbins, E. (1977). *Research Diagnostic Criteria for a Selected Group of Functional Disorders*, 3rd edn. New York: State Psychiatric Institute, Biometrics Research.

Stern, R., Farr, J. A. H. and Ray, W. J. (1975). Pleasure. In P. H. Venables and M. J. Christie (eds), *Research in Psychophysiology*. London: Wiley.

Tyrer, P. (1981). The treatment of anxiety and depression in general practice. In G. Edwards (ed.), *Psychiatry in General Practice*. Southampton: University of Southampton Press.

CHAPTER 13

Innovative use of microcomputers for measuring the accuracy of assessment

MARGO GEORGE AND HARVEY SKINNER

Introduction

The widespread availability of inexpensive yet powerful microcomputers has stimulated conversion of traditional assessment procedures to computerised administration, scoring and interpretation. Unquestionably, the speed and accuracy of computers has justified their importance in assessment. The significance of computers in assessment, however, goes beyond merely mimicking established clerical procedures. Rather, computers are a medium for researchers to investigate more advanced scientific questions and use of answers as they relate to assessment. For example, instead of waiting until the end of a computerised assessment to ask why a person responded inaccurately to an item, a more useful approach would be to determine what type of system could be developed to take remedial action during the course of an assessment to investigate and improve the accuracy of responses.

The focus of this chapter is on an innovative application of microcomputers for measuring the accuracy of computerised assessment. Specific reference is made to using response latency information (i.e. time between item presentation and a person's response) for real-time detection and reduction of inaccurate responses. The concept of measurement accuracy is outlined in general, and then specifically as it relates to computerised assessment. Future directions for measuring assessment accuracy are provided.

Measurement accuracy

Measurement accuracy is one of the long-standing concerns in assessment. It is fundamental to the validity or dependability of assessment outcomes, yet to

Microcomputers, Psychology and Medicine
Edited by R. West, M. Christie and J. Weinman
© 1990 by John Wiley & Sons Ltd

a certain extent all assessments are inaccurate due to errors of measurement. An important goal of measurement specialists is to reduce these errors, or at least to estimate the extent to which they constrain the interpretation and use of assessment information.

Errors of measurement are either random or systematic (Crocker and Algina, 1986). *Random errors* are chance fluctuations in an individual's score due to a multitude of factors not controlled in the measurement procedure (e.g. guessing, distraction, scoring errors). By definition, random errors are not expected to be repeated over testing occasions. Classical true-score theory is a model that illustrates how random errors can affect observed scores (Allen and Yen, 1979). The model assumes that an observed score (X) is the sum of a stable true score (T) plus a random error score (E), i.e. $X = T + E$. The smaller the error score, the more the observed score approximates the true score. Neither true nor error scores are measured directly. However, from a conceptual level the notion of true score is beneficial because it implies measurement that is perfectly accurate.

Systematic errors, on the other hand, consistently influence an individual's score due to some particular characteristic of the person, the test item or both. These errors persist across repeated testing occasions of a given instrument without affecting consistency scores; however, they are a source of response bias which lowers the content interpretation or construct validity of measurement. Systematic errors have been estimated through measures of response styles, such as social desirability or acquiescence (Wiggins, 1973), and deviant response tendencies, such as always endorsing an extreme response regardless of the item content (Sechrest and Jackson, 1967).

Reliability is the consistency or reproducibility of scores obtained using an assessment instrument and is dependent only on random errors of measurement: the greater the errors, the less consistent the assessment; the smaller the errors, the more consistent the assessment (Kerlinger, 1964). There are three types of reliability estimates or coefficients. Stability is one type of reliability coefficient referring to the degree to which responses remain constant over repeated administrations of the same instrument to the same sample. The coefficient of equivalence measures the correlation between scores on at least two forms or two halves of a test. Finally, the coefficient of internal consistency estimates the extent to which item scores from a single test administration correlate with the total test score, in the kinds of discriminations made among respondents.

The relationship between reliability, construct validity, systematic error or bias, and random error is depicted in Figure 13.1. In this example, reliability (0.80) is decomposed into (a) systematic error or bias (0.20), as measured by response style, e.g. social desirability, and (b) construct saturation (0.60), as determined by construct validity or the extent to which an operation measure conforms to the construct being measured. Random error (0.20) is estimated

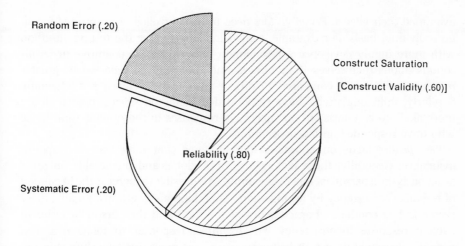

FIGURE 13.1 Reliability can be decomposed into systematic error and construct saturation.

by subtracting obtained reliability (0.80) from perfect reliability (1.00). The objective of an assessment instrument is to maximize the content saturation of an assessment instrument, through scientific construct validation methods (Wiggins, 1973), and to minimize the error components which reduce the consistency of assessment scores.

Components of response inconsistency

There are a number of reasons for examining the components of response inconsistency. First, response inconsistency is a reliable phenomenon. Glaser (1952), in an article entitled 'The reliability of inconsistency', reported a stability of inconsistent responses as indicated in patterns of intercorrelations on three administrations of a mathematics, space relations and vocabulary test. Second, many factors reliably contribute to response inconsistency. For instance, Kuncel and Fiske (1974) reported a tendency of respondents to use similar inappropriate response processes when responding to items from personality questionnaires, which in turn resulted in reliably unstable responses on retest (e.g. difficulty understanding the meaning of an item on the first test increased the likelihood of applying a different meaning to that item on retest). Third, it is important to identify the factors which contribute to response inconsistency, because, once identified, these factors can be manipulated to make responses more consistent and reliable. The latter point is perhaps the most crucial concern of assessment developers and users.

There are at least three possible types of factors contributing to response inconsistency. Table 13.1 presents a list of some of the most reliable factors contributing to response inconsistency and references of authors who have examined their effects. *Person factors* need to be controlled or accounted for on an individual basis. For example, some individuals enter the testing situation with more highly developed self-schemata or well-defined cognitive generalizations about themselves than others, and this may be reflected in greater response consistency compared to others with less developed self-schemata. Similarly, individuals who have responded to items on several occasions are more likely to be consistent on successive responses to those items than those who have responded on fewer occasions.

Item factors focus on characteristics of items that may lead to response instability. Generally, these factors are more global and predictable on an a priori basis than person factors. For example, it is possible to increase the likelihood of response consistency by asking short, unambiguous questions. Finally, *item/ person factors* combine characteristics of the item and the person in order to explain response inconsistency. For example, responses to items nearer a person's threshold on a trait being measured are more unstable than those to more distant items.

Accuracy in computerised assessment

One of the more compelling aspects of computerised assessment is the possible reduction in measurement errors and consequent increase of assessment accuracy. Random errors may be reduced through the constancy or objectivity of computerised assessment, e.g. systematic question wording, sequence, timing and scoring (Greist *et al.*, 1973; Rezmovic, 1977). The impartiality or non-judgemental characteristic of computerised assessment has the potential of reducing systematic errors, particularly when soliciting more sensitive information, such as sexual difficulties or alcohol and drug abuse (Skinner and Pakula, 1986; Erdman *et al.*, 1985).

Evidence of the greater accuracy of computerised assessment over conventional methods is supported by respondents' admissions of more negative characteristics to the computer. As early as 1969, Evan and Miller reported that respondents were prepared to admit to higher levels of anxiety and sociocultural anomie when using a computer, as compared to paper-and-pencil methods. Results from comparing psychiatrists and a computer as interrogators of patients with alcohol problems indicated a 30% higher level of alcohol consumption from the computerised method of assessment (Lucas *et al.*, 1977). Greist and Klein (1980) compared responses from sensitive questions with more neutral questions and found that female respondents were significantly more likely to indicate sexual problems to the computer than to a psychiatrist. Carr *et al.* (1983) found that a computerised method of eliciting psychiatric histories from patients resulted in an average of five and one half more 'discoveries' of facts unknown to clinicians. These included respondents' reports of a marked concern over masturbation (30%), criminal record (26%) and

Table 13.1 Components of response inconsistency

Component	Mark of inconsistency	Reference
	A. Person factors	
Response latency (time between an item presentation and response)	Longer latencies	Fekken and Jackson (1983) Fekken (1986)
Prior item responses (number of times a person has responded to an item)	No prior responses to items	Schubert and Fiske (1973) Schubert (1975)
Self-schemata (degree to which an item refers to self)	Poorly developed self-schemata	Markus (1977) Fekken (1986)
Estimated stability (degree of estimated item consistency)	Low estimated stability	Payne (1974)
Items placed in a 'don't know' category or left blank (items which are not answered by respondent)	Unanswered items	Kuncel and Fiske (1974) Fekken and Holden (1987)
Item meaning (degree to which an item meaning is changed or reinterpreted)	Change in item meaning	Kuncel and Fiske (1974) Kuncel (1977)
	B. Item factors	
Item time reference (reference of an item to time of event, e.g. past)	Items dealing with the recent past	Payne (1974)
Ambiguity (degree to which an item is rated as ambiguous or unclear)	High estimated ambiguity	Payne (1974) Kuncel and Fiske (1974) Kuncel (1977)
Endorsement frequency (proba-bility of an item being endorsed)	Moderate endorsement frequency	Payne (1974) Kuncel (1977) Fekken and Jackson (1983)
Item difficulty ratings (degree to which an item is rated as difficult to answer)	High estimated difficulty	Kuncel and Fiske (1974) Kuncel (1977)
Social desirability ratings (degree to which an item is rated as socially desirable)	Moderate social desira-bility ratings	Payne (1974) Kuncel (1977) Fekken and Jackson (1983)
Item length (length of item, e.g. number of letters)	Longer items	Payne (1974) Kuncel (1977)
	C. Item/person factors	
Subject–item distance (distance between scale position of item and scale position of subject)	Responses nearer to a person's threshold	Kuncel and Fiske (1974) Kuncel (1977) Fekken and Jackson (1983)

amnesic blackouts after drinking heavily (23%).

Contrary to these findings, Skinner and Allen (1983); Skinner *et al.* (1985a) collected histories of alcohol, drug and tobacco use and found no significant differences in level of problems or consumption patterns reported in face-to-face interviews, computerised assessments or self-report formats. Similarly, Millstein (1987) found no differences in behaviour (e.g. sexual behaviour) or symptomatology (e.g. gynaecological) among subjects interviewed face-to-face, by the computer, or by self-administered questionnaire. However, those subjects using the computer reported a significantly greater number of positive feelings (e.g. relaxation).

Additional support for the better accuracy of computerised assessment is found in the reduction of response bias indicators. Evan and Miller (1969) reported lower scores on a personality lie scale for groups receiving computerised assessment as opposed to paper-and-pencil methods. Stockwell and Jackson (1983) compared the effect of response styles and factor content for computerised and traditional test administration of personality scales. Results suggested that, compared with the paper-and-pencil procedure, the acquiescence factor was stronger, the social desirability factor was weaker, and the factor structure was more succinct in results from the computerised administration. In contrast, no significant differences were found in response bias (honesty and defensiveness) scores among subjects responding by computer, personal interview, or paper-and-pencil tests of threatening and disturbing items (Koson *et al.*, 1970).

Thus, although there is evidence supporting the increased accuracy of computerised assessment over more traditional methods, other findings are inconclusive. Further research is needed to clarify the content areas and assessment contexts where one could expect computerised assessment to make a difference. Deciding on whether the computer is more accurate than traditional methods should not be the only criterion. Instead, the focus should be on possible ways of improving assessment accuracy by using the computer in an *interactive* testing environment.

Real-time detection and reduction of inaccurate responses

Beyond passive approaches of merely collecting and analysing data related to assessment, the computer can function in an active capacity by detecting potential sources of inaccuracy during an assessment and taking remedial action. Stout (1981) argues that:

> the best time to investigate a potential problem is right after it happens, and only a system that can react to problem signals during an interview can initiate such an investigation and, if necessary, take corrective action. (pp. 441–442)

His hypothetical version of such a system is called an 'interviewee behaviour assessment monitor' (IBAM). Once a potentially inaccurate response or pattern is detected the computer could then: (1) insert additional questions in order to assess the reliability of previous answers; (2) recommend that the respondent rest before completing the assessment; (3) branch to a more appropriate alternative form; or (4) recommend to the researcher that the respondent cooperate more fully and re-answer previous questions for which the answers were deemed unreliable.

How can inaccurate responses be detected in real time? Jackson (1984) suggests several means of appraising accuracy by monitoring: (1) the consistency of responses to redundant or highly correlated items, such as repeated items from the Minnesota Multiphasic Personality Inventory (MMPI) (Graham, 1977); 2) answers to implausible or rarely endorsed items, such as items from the Personality Research Form (Jackson, 1984) Infrequency Scale; (3) unique or inconsistent profile patterns, evidenced, for example, by someone obtaining a high score on Extroversion and a low score on Sociability; and (4) response bias indicators, such as standard MMPI validity scales, L, F and K.

Inconsistent responses could also be detected and remedial action taken by flagging factors listed in Table 13.1. For example, item responses associated with low self-schemata, low estimated stability, high estimated ambiguity or moderate social desirability ratings could prompt the computer to ask more appropriate questions for the particular respondent, which would increase the likelihood of consistency in responding.

Response latency

An innovative way of detecting and reducing inaccurate and inconsistent responses is through the utilization of response latency information within an interactive computerised approach (Butcher *et al.*, 1985; Hofer and Green, 1985). Research in the area of personality assessment suggests that response latency is one of the best predictors of stability of individuals' item responses.

Fekken and Jackson (1983) used four models, namely Social Desirability, Threshold, *P*-Value, and Response Latency, to predict the stability of an individual's responses to a personality assessment. Although a significant effect was found for the combined models' ability to predict instability of responses, the response latency model was found to be the best predictor of item change. Results suggest that individuals are most likely to change their responses on retest to items which have relatively long latencies. A second study examined similar relationships among the models, with the inclusions of the Individual Social Desirability Model and the Individual Threshold Model. Again, results indicated that the Response Latency Model performed significantly better than the other five models in predicting item response changes.

More recently, Fekken (1986) reported that mean latency across items of a personality measure was significantly correlated with mean item instability; however, mean latency across individuals was not significantly correlated with total item change. Furthermore, Holden and Fekken (1988) used response latency information to differentiate between dissimulated (fake good/fake bad) and honest self-report to a computerised test of psychopathology. Results suggest that response latency is a useful indicator of invalid or inaccurate responding, with respondents who fake good having faster responses than honest self-report or fake bad groups.

Current research

A study is currently under way to examine the use of response latency information to increase consistency in Computerised Lifestyle Assessment (CLA). This instrument provides health-care professionals and their clients with a 175-item assessment of 18 health-risk behaviours, including areas such as: Nutrition, Sleep, Family Interactions, Smoking, Alcohol Use and Sexual Activities (Allen and Skinner, 1987). The CLA was selected because of its proven accuracy, acceptability and reliability (Skinner *et al.*, 1985a, 1985b, 1987), and also due to its variability in the sensitivity of questions.

The study consists of two parts. In study one, individuals' item response latencies are recorded to establish latency cut-off points for each question. Any response latency falling outside the cutting point (i.e. extremely short or long) will be labelled as deviant. It is assumed that deviant latencies are associated with inconsistent item responses. In the second study, the computer is used interactively to probe the meaning of latency responses in two or three CLA sections, and to measure test–retest consistency as a function of probing interventions. (Consistency will be measured by the first score taken after probing and the second score at retest, 1–2 weeks later). Respondents ($N = 180$) will be randomly assigned to one of the following groups: (1) systematic probing based on extreme latency responses; (2) systematic probing based on moderate latency responses; (3) random probing; and (4) no probing. The design is outlined in Figure 13.2.

Depending on the group, latency response will prompt the computer to further question each individual about that particular item. For example, if an individual hesitates while answering the question 'How often have you had at least one drink of beer, liquor, wine or any other alcoholic beverage?' then the individual will respond to the same item again, only this time it will have a more elaborate preamble than the first time it was asked: 'you might have drunk alcohol to increase your appetite, before dinner, along with your meal, to celebrate a special occasion, or for any other reason. How often have you had . . . alcoholic beverages?' In addition, respondents will rate (1–7) the degree to which items associated with deviant latencies are ambiguous and personal, and the expected degree of consistency on retest. Item length, item response polarity, number of response alternatives and reading speed are other important factors to be considered. These represent some of the most important

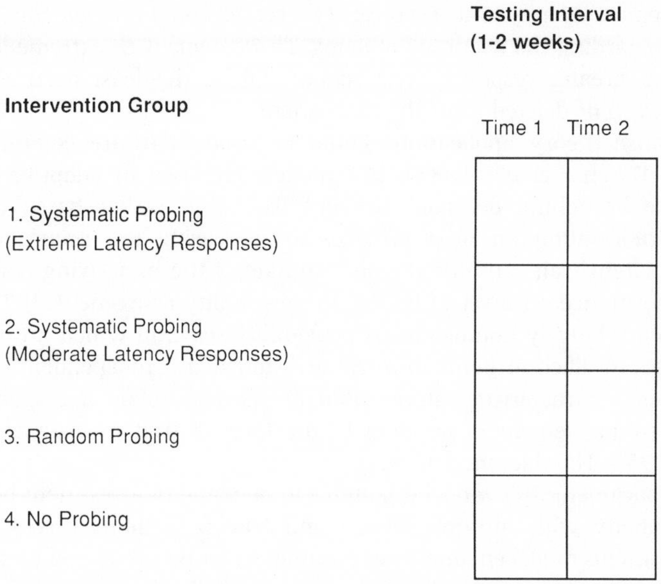

Testing Interval
(1-2 weeks)

Intervention Group

Time 1   Time 2

1. Systematic Probing
(Extreme Latency Responses)

2. Systematic Probing
(Moderate Latency Responses)

3. Random Probing

4. No Probing

FIGURE 13.2 Design of study evaluating effect of systematic probing of responses according to response latencies.

factors in predicting response latency and in predicting consistency of responses (Dunn *et al.*, 1972; Holden *et al.*, 1985; Kuncel and Fiske, 1974; Payne, 1974; Fekken, 1986; Rogers, 1974).

It is expected that participants in the systematic extreme probe group will be more consistent because, unlike the other groups, they will be probed on items deemed most likely to be inconsistent. According to Sudman and Bradburn (1982), probing with longer questions provides better memory cues than shorter items and consequently aids in recall and response accuracy. Response latency is expected to be predicted from factors identified as important in the literature (e.g. item length). Also, response latency should be one of the most reliable predictors of consistency.

Future directions for measuring assessment accuracy

Two significant directions for measuring assessment accuracy are the use of computerised-accuracy markers in the development of assessment instruments and the application of item response theory (IRT) in tailored assessments. Instruments are now being developed exclusively for the computer and a variety of computerised-accuracy markers can be used to validate item selection (e.g. response latency). Multiple accuracy markers should provide more valid information than unitary measurements of accuracy (Lanyon, 1987). For example, response latency and response style scores could provide convergent information regarding the accuracy of items. Those items with extreme latency responses and greater response style scores will be the least accurate and should be revised or deleted from the assessment.

Item response theory applications could be used in future computerised assessments (Butcher *et al.*, 1985). IRT models are used in adaptive ability testing where branching decisions are not fixed, but rather based on the amount of information an item provides in increasing the accuracy of a respondent's latent trait estimate (i.e. an estimate of the underlying construct affecting performance on a set of items). In personality assessment, IRT could be applied to a relatively homogeneous personality scale, in which an individual's responses to different items in a test are statistically independent, and in which an item characteristic curve could be used to relate a respondent's probability of endorsement of an item to the level of trait measured by the item (Lord, 1953; Hambleton, 1979).

The three-parameter IRT model is suitable in personality assessment because of its applicability with multiple choice and true–false items (Crocker and Algina, 1986). This model encompasses parameters found in the one-parameter (difficulty) and two-parameter (discrimination and difficulty) models and also includes the pseudo-guessing parameter. In ability testing, the pseudo-guessing parameter indicates the probability of an individual with a low ability getting a response correct. Response latency information could serve as an IRT psuedo-guessing parameter in personality assessment, to measure the probability of an individual with a low degree of a personality trait endorsing an item. Relatively quick response latencies are associated with the tendency to fake good (Holden and Fekken, 1988). In tailored personality assessments using IRT, items with aberrant response latencies could provide one source of information to initiate a branching sequence to items with more appropriate information power.

In conclusion, the computer is more than an assessment tool. It can serve as a catalyst for initiating creative and innovative approaches to improving assessment accuracy. Accurate assessments are essential for assuring that test results contain minimal error and may be used to make decisions concerning, for example, a student's placement or a client's treatment. The challenge to researchers is to go beyond passive approaches of measuring accuracy, and to examine accuracy in real-time through the use of on-line computerised monitoring and correction devices. Response latency is a promising computerised accuracy and consistency marker with the potential of improving the accuracy of assessment.

References

Allen, B. and Skinner, H. (1987). Lifestyle assessment using microcomputers. In J. Butcher (ed.), *Computerized Psychological Assessment: A Practitioner's Guide*. New York: Basic Books.

Allen, M. and Yen, W. (1979). *Introduction to Measurement Theory*. California: Brooks/ Cole.

Butcher, J., Keller, L. and Bacon, S. (1985). Current developments and future directions in computerised personality assessment, *Journal of Consulting and Clinicial Psychology*, **53**, 803–815.

Carr, A., Ghosh, A. and Ancill, R. (1983). Can a computer take a psychiatric history? *Psychological Medicine*, **13**, 151–158.

Crocker, L. and Algina, J. (1986). *Introduction to Classical and Modern Test Theory*. Toronto: Holt, Rinehart & Winston.

Dunn, T., Lushene, R. and O'Neil, H. (1972). Complete automation of the MMPI and a study of its response latencies, *Journal of Consulting and Clinical Psychology*, **39**, 381–387.

Erdman, H., Klein, M. and Greist, J. (1985). Direct patient computer interviewing, *Journal of Consulting and Clinical Psychology*, **53**, 760–773.

Evan, W. and Miller, J. (1969). Differential effects on response bias of computer vs. conventional administration of a social science questionnaire: An exploratory methodological experiment, *Behavioral Science*, **14**, 216–227.

Fekken, G. (1986). *Conceptualizing the difficulty of responding to a personality test item*. Paper presented at the annual meeting of the Canadian Psychological Association, June, Toronto, Canada.

Fekken, G. and Holden, R. (1987). Assessing the person reliability of an individual MMPI protocol. *Journal of Personality Assessment*, **51**, 123–132.

Fekken, G. and Jackson, D. (1983). Predicting consistent psychological test item responses: a comparison of models. Unpublished manuscript, Queen's University, Department of Psychology, Kingston, Ontario, Canada.

Glaser, R. (1952). The reliability of inconsistency, *Educational and Psychological Measurement*, **12**, 60–64.

Graham, J. (1977). *The MMPI: A practical guide*. New York: Oxford University Press.

Gresit, J. and Klein, M. (1980). Computer programs for patients, clinicians, and researchers in psychiatry. In J. Sidowski, J. Johnson and T. Williams (eds), *Technology in Mental Health Care Delivery Systems*. Norwood, NJ: Ablex.

Gresit, J., Klein, M. and Van Cura, L. (1973). A computer interview for psychiatric patient target symptoms. *Archives of General Psychiatry*, **29**, 247–253.

Hambleton, R. (1979). Latent trait models and their applications. *New Directions for Testing and Measurement*, **4**, 13–32.

Hofer, P. and Green, B. (1985). The challenge of competence and creativity in computerised psychological testing. *Journal of Consulting and Clinical Psychology*, **53**, 826–838.

Holden, R. and Fekken, G. (1988). *Using Reaction Time to Detect Faking on a Computerized Inventory of Psychopathology*. Paper presented at the annual meeting of the Canadian Psychological Association, Montreal, Canada.

Holden, R., Fekken, G. and Jackson, D. (1985). Structured personality test item characteristics and validity, *Journal of Research in Personality*, **19**, 386–394.

Jackson, D. (1984). *Personality Research Form Manual*. Port Huron, MI: Research Psychologists Press.

Kerlinger, F. (1964). *Foundations of Behavioural Research*. Toronto: Holt, Rinehart & Winston.

Koson, D., Kitchen, M., Kochen, M. and Stodolosky, D. (1970). Psychological testing by computer: Effect on response bias, *Educational and Psychological Measurement*, **30**, 803–810.

Kuncel, R. (1977). The subject–item interaction on itemmetric research, *Educational and Psychological Measurement*, **37**, 665–678.

Kuncel, R. and Fiske, D. (1974). Stability of response process and response, *Educational and Psychological Measurement*, **34**, 743–755.

Lanyon, R. (1987). The validity of computer-based personality assessment products: Recommendations for the future, *Computers in Human Behavior*, **3**, 225–238.

Lord, F. (1953). The relation of test score to the trait underlying the test, *Educational and Psychological Measurement*, **13**, 517–548.

Lucas, R., Mullin, P., Luna, C. and McInroy, D. (1977). Psychiatrists and a computer as interrogators of patients with alcohol-related illnesses: A comparison, *British Journal of Psychiatry*, **131**, 160–167.

Markus, H. (1977). Self-schemata and processing information about the self, *Journal of Personality and Social Psychology*, **35**, 63–78.

Millstein, S. (1987). Acceptability and reliability of sensitive information collected via computer interview, *Educational and Psychological Measurement*, **47**, 523–533.

Payne, F. (1974). Relationships between response stability and item endorsement, social desirability, and ambiguity in the MMPI and the CPI, *Multivariate Behavioral Research*, **9**, 127–148.

Rezmovic, V. (1977). The effects of computerised experimentation on response variance, *Behavior Research Methods and Instrumentation*, **9**, 144–147.

Rogers, T. (1974). An analysis of two central stages underlying responding to personality items: The self-referent decision and response selection, *Journal of Research in Personality*, **8**, 128–138.

Schubert, D. (1975). Increase of personality response consistency by prior response, *Journal of Clinical Psychology*, **31**, 651–658.

Schubert, D. and Fiske, D. (1973). Increase of item response consistency by prior item response, *Educational and Psychological Measurement*, **33**, 113–121.

Sechrest, L. and Jackson, D. (1967). Deviant response tendencies: Their measurement and Interpretation. In D. Jackson and S. Messick (eds), *Problems in Human Assessment*. Toronto: McGraw-Hill.

Skinner, H. and Allen, B. (1983). Does the computer make a difference? Computerised versus face-to-face versus self-report assessment of alcohol, drug and tobacco use. *Journal of Consulting and Clinical Psychology*, **51**, 267–275.

Skinner, H. and Pakula, A. (1986). Challenge of computers in psychological assessment, *Professional Psychology: Research and Practice*, **17**, 44–50.

Skinner, H., Allen, B., McIntosh, M. and Palmer, W. (1985a). Applying microcomputers in family practice, *British Medical Journal*, **290**, 212–214.

Skinner, H., Allen, B., McIntosh, M. and Palmer, W. (1985b). Lifestyle assessment: Just asking makes a difference, *British Medical Journal*, **290**, 214–216.

Skinner, H., Palmer, W., Sanchez-Craig, M. and McIntosh, M. (1987). Reliability of a lifestyle assessment using microcomputers, *Canadian Journal of Public Health*, **78**, 329–334.

Stockwell, R. and Jackson, D. (1983). *Response styles and the computerized administration of personality tests*. Paper presented at the annual meeting of the Canadian Psychological Association, Winnipeg, Canada.

Stout, R. (1981). New approaches to the design of computerised interviewing and testing systems, *Behavior Research Methods and Instrumentation*, **3**, 436–442.

Sudman, S. and Bradburn, N. (1982). *Asking Questions: A Practical Guide to Questionnaire Design*. London: Jossey-Bass.

Wiggins, J. (1973). *Personality and Prediction*. Reading, MA: Addison-Wesley.

Part VI

Therapy and Training

Part VI

Therapy and Training

The final part of this book examines the use of micros in therapeutic interventions. These range from the novel idea of training chronic psychiatric patients in basic computing skills with a view to improving their employment prospects, to the development of a 'patient-centred' computer network in a hospital for mentally handicapped people, in which the management of patients is of less concern than their environment and assisting with rehabilitation.

We have seen earlier that micros have tended to be used as substitutes for other pieces of apparatus, whether these be simple questionnaires or complex dedicated performance-monitoring systems. The micros have offered advantages of increased flexibility, power and speed coupled with dramatically reduced cost. In the case of therapy, there is an added dimension. The micro can be conceived of as to some extent taking over the role of the human therapist. For example, in the chapter on use of micros in a hospital for mentally handicapped people, patients are encouraged to interact with computer programs which are both entertaining and informative. The patients find this rewarding and helpful. The chapter on use of micros in aphasia therapy similarly conceives of patients interacting directly with software packages. The therapist may or may not supervise the session.

In addition to describing the specific benefits of implementing micro-based systems in different therapeutic contexts, these chapters also illustrate some of the broader practical issues, such as the cooperation between institutions, the role of other staff and the sharing and development of appropriate software. They also provide interesting insights into the way in which micros can effect important changes in the attitudes of patients and staff and in the relation between them.

CHAPTER 14

Training in microcomputing for chronic psychiatric patients

ANGELA SUMMERFIELD AND MAURICE LIPSEDGE

In this chapter we describe an innovatory project with the teaching of basic computing skills to day hospital patients who mostly have a diagnosis of schizophrenia, with the aim of their rehabilitation into employment.

Although the rehabilitation of psychiatric patients has long history in the UK (e.g. Hawkins, 1871), recent changes in psychiatric practice have had fundamental effects on the potential employability of chronic patients. The introduction of major tranquillisers has greatly aided the discharge of patients from in-patient units and the trend towards community care has resulted in a shift of emphasis among mental health professionals with respect to what they envisage as a possible future for their clients. Despite this, Lipsedge and Summerfield (1987a) noted that no official records are kept of the participation of such patients in employment. In a survey of inner city, urban and rural areas in south-east England (Lipsedge and Summerfield, 1987b) they reported an overall unemployment rate of 62% amongst psychiatric out-patients as against a national figure of 10% for the general population. The Manpower Services Commission currently regard 15% employment rehabilitation of such unemployed patients as an achievable target.

In planning rehabilitation schemes for psychiatric patients, certain issues need to be taken into account. First, overall levels of unemployment and indeed of general economic well-being have a significant influence on outcome. Warner (1985) noted that the number of psychiatric hospital beds is related to unemployment levels, and Morgan and Cheadle (1975) found that local unemployment conditions were paralleled by degree of success in placing patients. The employment prospects of psychiatric patients cannot be divorced from those of the population as a whole. Declining industries are unlikely to provide many jobs, a factor not always taken into account by National Health

Microcomputers, Psychology and Medicine
Edited by R. West, M. Christie and J. Weinman
© 1990 by John Wiley & Sons Ltd

Service rehabilitation workshops in which the more routine skills traditional in British manufacturing industry have typically been taught. Service industries (such as catering and tourism) have become increasingly significant in the British economy and developments in new technology are exerting an important influence on how these are organised. Lemond (1987) predicts that as a result of current software developments, radical changes in computing will result in a far wider range of possible applications, accessible to commercial and industrial users, as new software systems, suitable for use on small machines, are released. Some knowledge of basic computing skills is therefore likely to become necessary for many employees in these contexts, even at quite low levels.

A knowledge of employment requirements is, however, insufficient on its own for the successful training and placement of patients. Due regard needs to be given both to the social skills required for functioning in the workplace and the limitations, if any, placed on the individual's performance by his or her type of illness and associated treatment, particularly long-term medication. A distinction needs to be made between diagnosis and degree of impairment. Diagnosis is not on its own a particularly good predictor of rehabilitation outcome. Residual symptoms may cause distinctive types of difficulties: for instance, anxiety may reach an intolerable level in the context of learning a complex new skill. Type and level of impairment will necessarily interact with the nature of work or retraining, and selectivity in allocating patients needs to be exercised accordingly. Motivation is an important factor in determining whether a particular patient will successfully complete training and enter employment. Quite apart from internal aspects of motivation such as damaged self-esteem as a result of a long illness, psychiatric patients like everyone else are influenced by the status, financial rewards and intrinsic interest of the work they undertake (Dick, 1983). Furthermore, as Olshansky and Unterberger (1963) suggest, the fact of being employed reassures many patients that they are 'normal'. The feeling of many rehabilitation workers that psychiatric patients are somehow better suited to simple repetitive work is not supported by the evidence. Bennett (1978) has suggested that the intellectual capacities of schizophrenic patients are frequently underestimated and that more demanding work can be appropriately provided.

It was in the context of these considerations that we decided to introduce training in basic computing skills to Speedwell Day Hospital, Deptford, southeast London. We chose computer skills for two reasons. First, information technology based industries were experiencing severe staff shortages. In *Personal Computer World*, March 1986, it was reported that 12 000 jobs were vacant because of lack of appropriately qualified staff. The Department of Trade and Industry has made strenuous efforts to encourage training initiatives and has repeatedly expressed concern about shortfalls in training targets. Second, our research group has an established record in industrial contract work for the

computer industry and as a consequence an appreciation of industrial requirements of staff and the state of the art in relation to both hardware and
software. We believe this to be critical in achieving a style and standard of
training which is likely to lead to employment.

Despite the many positive indications in favour of the introduction of
computer training, new technology can meet with a mixed reception from
users and indeed from members of the public. A frequent misconception is that
all training necessarily involves instruction in programming, whereas many
opportunities exist for skilled workers with expertise in handling standard
packages or data entry, but who have no programming background. Attitudes
to new technology are complex. Chapanis (1982) explored the ambiguities in
attitudes of employees generally. Hopes of social and financial benefits deriving
from such innovations were mingled with anxieties about redundancies as a
consequence of automation. Breakwell *et al.* (1986) have observed that women
have fewer opportunities for training in new technology than men and may
be more apprehensive about it. On the other hand, Turkle (1985) has described
the feelings of personal enhancement and creativity which many users of
home computers report and the ease with which many hours of time can be
devoted to this hobby.

The introduction of information technology training for patients is necessarily an educational process. Such considerations should therefore inform the
design of any training course. In their review of the influence of computers on
education, Underwood and Underwood (1987) comment on the lack of impact
of computers on practice in the twenty years since Suppes (1966) predicted
they would change the face of education. Computers offer flexibility and
interactive capabilities which in principle could be turned to good effect in
achieving educational objectives. However, as Clark (1984) has observed,
sophisticated technologies do not necessarily ensure sophisticated learning.

Underwood and Underwood (1987) point out that in computer based
learning the person who actually uses the computer gets most out of it and
that the user should not be entirely, or even mainly, the teacher. In using
computers to teach computing, as in any other educational context, the learner
must have sufficient opportunity to interact with the machine. They also report
studies by Amarel (1984) and others in which teachers found it necessary to
the maintenance of their authority to restrict students from acting as informal
tutors to other students. Students are also not easily controllable in other ways
when working with computers. Assigned tasks are quite often put aside in
favour of the delights of writing one's own programs or hacking into other
people's. Teachers may also be required to demonstrate their expertise in front
of students by methods other than delivering a previously prepared lecture or
lesson. All this can be extremely threatening to the student.

Learning with computers also offers students opportunities for learning to
relate to other people in small groups. In their own work, Underwood and

Underwood (1987) found that such groups generated experts who were consulted by the other students. However, they report that while in groups of young children a male and a female expert emerged in each group and were consulted by others, older children ignored female group experts in their groups. Computers tend to shift the balance from individual learning to learning in groups and by discussing one's ideas with others who drop by. However, this may enhance the gap between more gifted students who acquire the additional role of expert with the social standing this brings and their less talented colleagues. Issues of this kind are of particular importance when working with chronic psychiatric patients, because of the low self-esteem and hesitancy in social situations which many of them display, either as a result of the demoralising effect of a long illness or because deficiencies in this respect had made them vulnerable to psychiatric breakdown in the first instance. On the other hand, a genuine work-oriented reason for collaborating with others in a small group situation may help patients who find group therapeutic situations too threatening.

The Speedwell Day Hospital project

This project was initiated in January 1986, and a description of the early stages of it is given by Lipsedge *et al.* (1987). Speedwell Day Hospital is situated in Deptford, south-east London, an inner city area which suffers from considerable blight as a consequence of the closure of the London docks and the very high local unemployment level. The day hospital was opened in 1981, and caters for about 60 psychiatric patients with a National Health Service professional staff of psychiatrists, nurses, occupational therapists, a clinical psychologist and a social worker. Because of its connection with the Guy's Hospital group (a large teaching hospital) it is also a base for research workers, including the social psychology team from Birkbeck College, London University, who for many years collaborated with the medical school in applying social psychology and new technology to psychiatry. Speedwell offers a comprehensive range of therapeutic approaches to its clients, who are drawn from the local community. Many Speedwell clients have previously been in-patients at Guy's or elsewhere and have been referred to Speedwell for rehabilitation. Like other day hospitals, Speedwell has been impeded in this work by rising unemployment. In the 1960s day hospital clients would typically stay a few weeks before returning to work, and their psychiatric care would thereafter take place on an out-patient basis. This is hardly a feasible option at present since most patients either have no job to start with or lose it as a result of being ill. Furthermore, the very poor local job prospects sap patients' motivation to move on, since the range of activities offered by the day hospital programme is much more enjoyable than a life of being unemployed without such a centre to go to.

The client population at Speedwell consists mainly of people with few or no formal educational qualifications and substantial psychiatric histories, often with multiple in-patient admissions. Most patients have a diagnosis of schizophrenia. About half the patients are of ethnic minority origin, almost all Afro-Caribbean. Slightly less than half are women. In short this is a group which is multiply disadvantaged and might be expected to have difficulties in obtaining employment even without problems of mental illness. It is known that in the London Borough of Lewisham where Deptford is situated, the unemployment rate among black school leavers is twice as high as among their white peers. Furthermore, few Speedwell clients have been exposed to educational and training opportunities of a good standard involving small classes and highly qualified staff. Nor have they had the advantage of expert vocational guidance. Their capacity for making use of such opportunities was therefore unknown. Such clients do nevertheless express a consistent ambition to be employed. They are only too aware of the poverty and humiliation which follow from existing on state welfare benefits. A willingness to live in such a way is, we suspect, much less common than has been claimed and can be more frequently observed among the children of the privileged, whose relations will support them in the event of any real emergency. The poor have no desire to be poor.

In order to attack the employment rehabilitation problems of Speedwell clients it was decided to introduce pilot courses in which patients would be introduced to the fundamentals of computing. At an early stage the authors made contact with the nearby Outset Information Technology Centre. This centre is part of a chain of centres sponsored by the Department of Trade and Industry. All centres in this programme specialise in training unemployed young people with few educational qualifications in information technology skills. The training is carefully designed to meet modern commercial and industrial requirements in a realistic office environment. Office standards of punctuality, reliability and other aspects of good practice are required. Trainees may specialise in work with particular packages or in microelectronics and are trained on current office systems. They also receive training in job-related social skills. In the country as a whole the ITeC chain places 80% of its trainees in jobs and the Outset ITeC achieves a 60% placement rate in an area where 30% of white males and 60% of ethnic minority males are unemployed. The ITeC has a substantial representation of ethnic minority and female trainees and about half of the total are physically disabled. Like other ITeCs, Outset had no previous experiences of running courses for psychiatric patients. As a consequence of our contact with the Outset ITeC we decided to offer an initial package which would consist of a three-month familiarisation course at Speedwell, followed by a nine-month course at Outset. Each course would consist of one half day of instruction per week, together with opportunities for practice.

The pilot study: familiarisation courses at Speedwell

The aim of the initial study was to test the feasibility of teaching basic computing skills to psychiatric patients within the day hospital itself (as well as at the Outset ITeC). This study ran for one year and nine months.

Twenty-three patients took part in the study, of whom 17 completed their course. (Three further trainees went straight to the ITeC course because of previous computing background.) Virtually all the patients had a history of psychiatric illness, mainly schizophrenic, but the group included one manic-depressive. In addition two had severe personality disorders, one of whom had a long history of substance abuse. All the psychiatric patients had been receiving neuroleptic medication for many years, and many had been admitted to mental hospital on a compulsory basis. One patient had a physical handicap.

No attempt was made to select entrants on the basis of education, familiarity with computers, psychiatric history or indeed any variables other than willingness to participate and sufficient freedom from primary symptoms to allow the individual to concentrate on the task in hand. Since patients with acute psychosis are not normally admitted to Speedwell, the entire client population formed a potential pool of entrants. We established this non-selective policy on the grounds that teaching computing to psychiatric patients had not been attempted before, to our knowledge, so we were in no position to lay down guidelines for entry. Applying general educational criteria would have been pointless since the vast majority of the clients had no formal educational qualifications. In any case we were committed to the idea that the clients should have access regardless of formal intelligence level.

Each class was organised as a group of between five and ten individuals, depending on availability of candidates at the point at which the group was scheduled to start.

For research, rather than selection purposes only, before beginning each familiarisation course, on completion and after the ITeC Course, each group of trainees completed the AH4 test of general intelligence (administered once at the beginning), the Rotter Locus of Control Scale, the Rosenberg Self-Esteem Scale, the Beck Depression Inventory and the Breakwell, Fife-Shaw, Lee and Spence scale of attitudes to new technology. In order to avoid experimenter expectancy effects, these tests have not yet been scored. Scoring will take place when the final pilot group of ITeC graduates have been placed in employment.

Limited initial resources restricted the way in which the courses were organised. Most of the teaching of the familiarisation courses at Speedwell itself was carried out by two part-time mature students from the Department of Psychology at Birkbeck College who had substantial professional experience in computing. A third mature student with similar experience who was on placement from California State University, Dominguez Hills, also participated (as did the first author). All the university students were unpaid. None had been trained as a teacher, although all had some experience of instructing other staff. In retrospect we believe that the involvement of such commercially experienced people was critical in determining the success of the programme, since they were fully familiar with office practice and imposed a task-oriented regime on the trainees of a kind that staff with a more academic background might have hesitated to institute. Equipment presented another problem. The research team used Apple IIe microcomputers for scientific computing and therefore had a range of available software and access to additional machines for back-up in case of machine failure. One such machine was therefore purchased for use in the pilot courses. We believe this to have been a less than satisfactory arrangement because of the lack of an adequate number of workstations. The documentation for the IIe is, in our opinion, of superior quality, although the machine itself presented some difficulties for naive users. Speedwell was able to provide us with its general clerical room for holding the classes and some electric typewriters were also made available. Because the room was used for other purposes it was not possible to set it up as a commercial office. The day hospital staff were also able to have access to the Apple and some basic training was given to them as well. This was carried out by the first author and a senior member of the research team. Day hospital patients spend much time in individual and group work with the regular staff and it is therefore most important that the staff should have some under-standing of the rather distinctive problems of learning computing as well as having the advantages of personal access to the computer.

The instructional programme had two aims. The first was to familiarise the patients with the use of the microcomputer and the second was to reduce their levels of anxiety about unfamiliar technology. The emphasis of the training was practical, of the 'hands-on' type, rather than theoretical, although in the final course of the pilot series rather more emphasis was placed on the learning of theoretical concepts such as the nature of operating systems. Good practice in standard start and end of day and other routines was emphasised from the beginning. Trainees learned the names of different parts of the system, how to turn the computer off and on, the layout of the keyboard and how to set up the printer. Instruction in disc usage included how to care for discs, how to format and copy them and how to load and save software. File creation and management were also taught. Apple introductory packages were used to aid the trainees. These included 'Introductory Apple', 'Inside Story' and 'Applesoft Tutorial'. As an introduction to standard packages, 'Format 80', the Apple word processing package was used together with examples of spreadsheets, databases and graphics packages. The aim of the instructors was to give the trainees some individual familiarity with each of these packages, rather than to achieve an exhaustive knowledge of them. Each trainee personally attempted to carry out every main operation that was being taught. Computer games were deliberately not included, since it was thought that these might result in a particular mental set which might later prove unhelpful. No intensive training in keyboard skills was given, because of the unavailability of sufficient workstations, but trainees were encouraged to practise on a typewriter where possible. Only the most basic elements of programming were demonstrated. All trainees who completed the familiarisation courses were able to start up the computer, load the word processor and enter, format, change and save a document. Most learned to type-in a program in BASIC, correct it, list, run, save and load it. Some trainees acquired real expertise with certain packages which particularly interested them.

Completion rates for the familiarisation courses were good. Of 23 trainees who started, only six dropped out, most doing so within the first one or two weeks. As the courses progressed the trainees became less worried about damaging the computer and were more inclined to experiment. While substantial differences in speed of learning soon became apparent, this was not as detrimental as might have been expected. Trainees helped each other and cross-connections between fast and slow learners worked to the benefit of both.

Staff were waylaid in the corridors by trainees who wanted to complain about the deficiencies of software engineers, rather than about their mental-health problems, as had previously been the case.

The pilot study: follow-on course at Outset ITeC

Thirteen trainees transferred to courses at the Outset ITeC after satisfactory completion of the Speedwell familiarisation course. The ITeC is set up to replicate an office environment and high standards of adherence to office behaviour and practice are required. The Speedwell trainees were assigned to a special group, separate from the other trainees, but in every other respect their training was of the same type. Every person was assigned an Olivetti/ AT&T IBM-compatible personal computer and after initial instruction was encouraged to specialise in either databases (dBase II), spreadsheets (Multiplan) or word processing (Wordstar). Additional practice opportunities were provided and trainees were also allowed access to the Apple at Speedwell, thus allowing some cross-training to occur.

At the end of each course trainees sat for the Royal Society of Arts Certificate in Computer Literacy and nine out of nine passed—two with distinction. Of the nine trainees who have so far completed the entire training (four others being still in progress), three have obtained computer-related employment, one was offered a job in computing but chose a different occupation and three have gone on to advanced study—two at university level. This represents a success rate greatly in excess of the 15% rehabilitation rate regarded as realistic for such patients by the Manpower Services Commission, even without allowing for the particularly disadvantaged nature of this group compared with the nationwide psychiatric population.

The main study

Initial promising results from the pilot study enabled us to obtain funding for a much more substantial two-year project with appropriate evaluation. Specially adapted premises will allow an accurate simulation of an office environment with a full range of office equipment, and a network of ICL PC Quattros will allow each trainee access to an individual workstation. Custom-built teaching materials are in preparation and it is proposed to add desk-top publishing to the present range of skills taught. Trainees will continue to receive further training at the Outset ITeC on a revised syllabus. There will be more emphasis on keyboard skills at all levels, as well as an integrated programme of job-related social skills to include preparation of applications, the job interview and the first day at work. An evening support group for graduates of the course who are at work is to be introduced.

Conclusions

The initial stages of the Speedwell computer project have adequately demonstrated the feasibility of instructing chronic psychiatric patients with little educational background in the basics of computing. A significant fraction of trainees from a population with a record of long-term unemployment have, as a consequence of this training, been able to find work or access to higher education.

Other benefits of the scheme are more subtle. The computer classes have acted as a vehicle for group cohesion and have boosted the trainees' self-perceptions. There have also been implications for their mental health in that, despite their histories of relapses leading to repeated hospital admissions, only one experienced a major exacerbation of symptoms while participating in the project.

We feared that psychotropic medication might lead to impairment of psychomotor skills and learning ability. The instructors thought that some patients were rather slow in their reactions, but a satisfactory standard of performance was eventually achieved.

In summary, this study confirms that with quite modest amounts of training chronic psychiatric patients with long histories of unemployment are able to obtain skilled work on the open job market.

Acknowledgements

We should like to thank Marijke van Beesten not only for her contribution to the teaching of the original courses but also for her substantial role in the current project. We should also like to thank Gabriele Lazzari and Rita Marmolejo for teaching the trainees and the staff of the Systems Strategy Centre, International Computers Ltd, for their interest and support. We are greatly indebted to the European Social Fund, the London Borough of Lewisham and the Lewisham and North Southwark Health Authority for funding our work. We are grateful to Sister Lynny Turner and the staff of Speedwell Day Hospital for the great support they offered the patients throughout the project and to Edna Howard for her administrative skills. We are also grateful to Brian Aviss for technical assistance and the Greta Cason, Susan Godfrey and Daphne Ring for secretarial assistance.

References

Amarel, M. (1984). Classroom and computers as instructional settings, *Theory into Practice*, **22**, 260–266.

Bennett, D. H. (1978). Social forms of psychiatric treatment. In J. K. Wing (ed.), *Schizophrenia: Towards a New Synthesis*. London: Academic Press.

Breakwell, G. M., Fife-Shaw, G., Lee, T. and Spence, J. (1986). Attitudes to new technology in relation to social beliefs and group memberships. Unpublished paper, University of Surrey.

Chapanis, A. (1982). Computers and the common man. In *Houston Symposium, 3, Information Technology and Psychology, Prospects for the Future*. New York: Praeger.

Clark, R. E. (1984). Learning from computers: Theoretical problems. Paper presented to AERA, New Orleans.

Dick, D. (1983). Occupation or work: the real issue. In K. G. Herbst (ed.), Rehabilitation the way ahead or the end of the road? London: Mental Health Foundation.

Hawkins, H. (1871). A plea for convalescent homes in connection with asylums for the insane poor, *Journal of Mental Science*, **17**, 107–116.

Lemond, F. (1987). Breakpoint year for the computer industry. *The World in 1988*. London: Economist Intelligence Unit.

Lipsedge, M. and Summerfield, A. B. (1987a). The Employment Rehabilitation Needs of the Mentally Ill. Unpublished report to the Manpower Services Commission.

Lipsedge, M. and Summerfield, A. B. (1987b). Psychiatric Employment Rehabilitation: The Client Population and its Occupational Characteristics. Unpublished report to the Manpower Services Commission.

Lipsedge, M., Summerfield, A. B., Lazzari, G. and van Beesten, M. (1987). Jobs and computers: information technology training for long-term day hospital patients. *Bulletin of the Royal College of Psychiatrists*, **11**, 84–86.

Morgan, R. and Cheadle, A. J. (1975). Unemployment impedes resettlement. *Social Psychiatry*, **10**, 63–67.

Olshansky, S. and Unterberger, H. (1963). The meaning of work and its implication for the ex-mental hospital patient. *Journal of Mental Hygiene*, **45**, 139–149.

Suppes, P. (1966). The uses of computers in education, *Scientific American*, **215**, 207–2201.

Turkle, S. (1985). The psychology of personal computers. In T. Forester (ed.), *The Information Technology Revolution*. Oxford: Blackwell.

Underwood, G. and Underwood, J. D. M. (1987). The computer in education: a force for change? In F. Blackler and D. Oborne (eds), *Designing for the Future: Information Technology and People*. Leicester: British Psychological Society.

Warner, R. (1985). *Recovery from Schizophrenia: Psychiatry and Political Economy*. London: Routledge & Kegan Paul.

CHAPTER 15

Use of a microcomputer network for people with a mental handicap

VEENA PARMAR AND MONICA LAWLOR

Introduction

People who live in hospitals which provide long-term care for those with a mental handicap suffer limitations because levels of staffing are not high enough to provide adequate individual stimulation and enrichment. Adults with a mental handicap are, by definition, slow learners who require a great deal of time and help to learn skills which more able people easily acquire in childhood. For this reason effective work with these clients is very labour-intensive. It is not realistic to suppose that funds will ever be available to raise staffing ratios to a level which everyone agrees would be optimal. It is therefore necessary to think of ways in which resources in terms of staff, money and plant can be used to improve the quality of life of residents within existing budgets. The recent advances in microcomputer network systems seemed to us to offer an opportunity for providing individual opportunities for learning and personal enrichment for a comparatively small capital outlay and low continuing cost.

With these considerations in mind, an Econet microcomputer network for the use of the residents was set up in 1986 in the Royal Earlswood Hospital in south-east England with a grant from the Hospital Trust Fund; it is also used by other people with a mental handicap who come to the hospital during the day to use the facilities. The primary purpose of the network was therapeutic; it was to provide an additional resource for skills training, but it has also served as a useful means of assessment as well as a source of entertainment in leisure time. The hospital has 450 resident patients (because these people live permanently in the hospital we normally refer to them as 'residents' rather than patients, and for that reason we have used the term in

Microcomputers, Psychology and Medicine
Edited by R. West, M. Christie and J. Weinman
© 1990 by John Wiley & Sons Ltd

this chapter where it is appropriate); of these 450 people, about 300 could probably make some use of the network. So far 402 programs have been installed on the network; these vary in difficulty so that at least some programs are available for those with most and for those with the least severe handicaps.

The network

This is an Acorn Computers Econet system with six individual networks, one main net serving the main building and five sub-nets serving individual buildings in the grounds. Additional sub-nets can be spurred off, via a bridge, from any point on the system main net or sub-nets; it is planned to connect the network to the Local Authority Social Education Centre and to a recently opened day unit.

A 'file-server' is dedicated to the task of managing the system storage, which is currently of 20 Mb (20 million characters) capacity. One file-server can have its store upgraded to 40 Mb and beyond that additional file-servers can be connected.

A central printer is connected to the file-server and is available to all users; material (text or graphics) awaiting printing is stored so that a user is not kept waiting while the printer deals with a large volume of print-out.

Each terminal station is trolley-mounted, consisting of a BBC Master Computer and a colour monitor, both of which are fully secured to the trolley by an enclosure.

Items which may be connected to a terminal station include the usual printer and disc drive, in addition to which we have a number of more specialised input devices, among which are the following:

A concept keyboard—a flat board with 127 squares, each of which may be employed as a touch key or which can be combined in blocks to give 1, 2 or more touch key areas, up to 127.

A touch screen—a frame mounted over the VDU which allows the user to activate the program by touching the relevant area of the screen.

A voice key—a switch which can be activated either by voice or by blowing into it.

A light pen—this gives a beam of focused light which can be used as a switch when directed at the chosen area of the visual display on the screen; this device can either be hand-held or mounted on the user's head.

Pressure pads—these act as a switch when pressed on with the hands, feet or other parts of the body.

A rocker switch—this is a largish double-pole switch which is set over a central bar and can be activated by depressing either end, like small seesaw.

A joystick—a simple four-position switch operated by a large ball on a stem mounted in a frame with four slots presented as a cross.

A variety of other single and multiple switches—using relatively large hand or body movements.

Programs available to the users cover a wide range of abilities from visual/audio response to a simple switch, to primary school level educational software and commercial computer games. Software has been obtained from commercial suppliers—organisations like SEMERC (a government-sponsored agency making educational software)—and some has been specially written for the network. Software has been installed on the network in such ways as to allow program selection to be driven by menus which can be tailor-made to each user.

The system keeps a record of each person's use of the computer and the programs they have used; it also stores their pictures and documents in their own area on the file-server.

Who makes use of the system?

So far we have records of at least 90 residents (out of 450) who are or have been using the network—probably another 200 or so can, over time, be brought into the 'user group'. Of the 90 residents, 15 have a marginal or mild mental handicap, all with behavioural problems or a degree of mental illness. A further 20 residents have a severe mental handicap; the remainder (who are the majority) have a moderate degree of mental handicap with IQs in the range of 20–50. A few of the users have a degree of mental handicap which would normally be classified as profound, but with mental ages over 1 year. In addition to their mental handicap, many of the residents have some degree of physical or sensory handicap. Most of the users are adult, but some children living in the surrounding community have used the system as visitors and clearly enjoy it, so that we aim to bring children's homes into the network as soon as we can get the funds.

Computer-based learning (CBL)

The network provides conditions which favour learning far more than most learning situations which our clients encounter. As a group our clients are characterised by learning disability. It is therefore extremely important for us to be able to create situations which maximise the probability that learning will take place. The way in which microcomputers favour learning can be summarised as follows:

1   The learning can be self-paced.
2   The feedback is immediate.
3   It is possible to program very small increments in task difficulty controlled by the client's progress.

4   The cost per trial in terms of effort to the client is low (it may be no more than a single key press or puff of breath).
5   Large numbers of massed trials are possible.
6   The task can be initially matched to the client's functional level.
7   The rate of reinforcement can be automatically maintained at optimal levels and on schedules chosen to meet the client's needs.

Many of the difficulties attendant upon classroom learning are therefore absent; in a classroom, task difficulty is often haphazard with respect to any individual, feedback is delayed or absent and learning is paced by the teacher or other learners; even in one-to-one teaching situations, the teacher may force the pace or fail to respond immediately to the client, leading to a degree of mismatch between what the client needs and what it is actually possible to offer. These principles are familiar to anyone involved in teaching; the difficulty is not to describe optimal conditions for learning but to find a means of offering them to our clients.

Many of our clients are described as very distractable or as having little capacity for concentration; these attentional defects which our clients are reputed to possess are much less in evidence when they are using the computer programs. The ability to concentrate may thus have more to do with the situations in which our clients usually find themselves than in the clients themselves.

CBL for people with a mental handicap

There is very little in the literature about the use of computers to aid learning in people with a mental handicap. There are few programs available on the market which are suitable for use with people with a developmental age below 5 years, and those designed for use in primary school are often unsuitable for adults with learning difficulties. It was therefore difficult to draw upon other people's experience to find the best way to use our network. We were necessarily guided by general clinical principles and educational practice. We have worked with our clients to teach them to use and control the computers, to get reward from their own skill; if they did not enjoy the experience no attempt was made to thrust it on them—they were free to stop when they wanted. This point is made because Aitken (1988) has argued strongly that CBL is unsuitable for those with learning difficulties and lacks all the qualities which are to be found in a good teacher. These comments were provoked by reports by Lancioni and Oliva (1988a, 1988b) describing the use of a computer to control the behaviour of multiply handicapped clients. In their experiments the clients were required to do simple domestic chores and material rewards were available from the computer on a contingent basis—a model which derives from operant training of caged animals rather than the mainstream of normal education. The critical difference is whether the computer is set up to control the client or the client encouraged to control the computer. Most of Aitken's objections disappear if the client is taught to use the computer, but they could discourage clinicians from attempting to introduce people with a mental handicap to computers and thus deprive them of a valuable source of learning and stimulation.

We have no plans to use the network to gain compliance from clients in return for sweets or food. There may be a place for such a strategy, which would after all only be a mechanisation of operant conditioning techniques which have proved very successful in helping clients with difficult behaviour. The point we wish to make here is that this is not the only way in which microcomputers can be used and that their value should not be judged on the basis of only one of a number of possible uses.

Living skills training

The computers have a role in skills training. Many of our clients have difficulty in understanding and using money because their experience of money use is limited. We have successfully used money training programs (one using the touch screen) with residents who are likely to move out of hospital. For this purpose we have taken groups of two or three clients who live together and encouraged them to work through these programs together, so that they can pool their resources of understanding both within and between the training sessions. The programs are comprehensive—they range from coin recognition (see Figure 15.1) to using a shopping list and working out change.

Other clients are severely hampered in life by having failed to gain basic literacy skills during their schooling. Computer training in this area has the advantage that with this age group it does not go over ground on which they have previously failed, and they are motivated by the ease with which they can make perfect letters with minimal manual dexterity. However clumsy and hesitant the touch on the key, the letter which appears on the screen in bold and perfectly formed; the client can then be further reinforced by having his work printed out and given to him to keep.

Other programs which aim to teach living skills are those which deal with safety in the home, teaching the user to identify hazards and correct them. Yet others deal with simple cooking, going through the stages required to prepare a slice of toast or a simple meal. Such programs help to fix both the necessary steps and the critical sequences in the client's mind and act as a supplement to the hands-on training provided by the occupational therapy department.

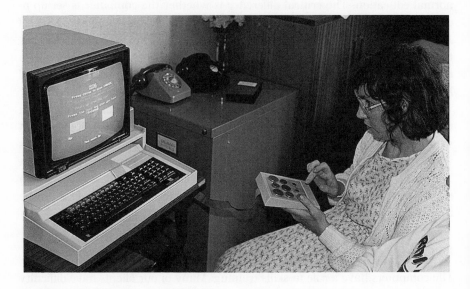

FIGURE 15.1   A client, using a special response box with real coins, working on a coin recognition program

Sensory motor skills

For less able clients the programs described above are too complex but they can benefit from programs which are designed to promote sensory and motor discrimination. Object or part-naming and other skills which are within the reach of people who suffer a severe or even profound level of handicap. This type of work can best be illustrated with reference to a program that constructs the features of a human face which has proved both popular and useful. The program starts with an oval on the screen (Figure 15.2), to which eyes, ears, hair, a mouth and a nose are added by pressing the appropriate marked area on a concept keyboard. When the face is completed it enlivens, the hair changes colour and a tune plays. Besides teaching simple cause and effects this program can be used to help the client to learn the names of facial features by encouraging them to point the features out on their own face as well as getting them onto the 'face' on the screen.

Social motivation for computer work

Individual exceptions apart, the computers have proved very popular with clients, especially those with a mild or moderate handicap. One patient has gone so far as to insist on placing the ward computer terminal by his bed at night in order to maintain physical contact with it even in his sleep! Of course not all clients enjoy the computers or find them an aid to learning; some much

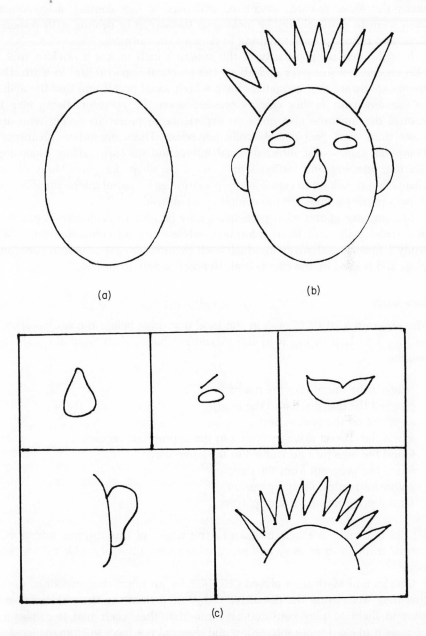

(a)

(b)

(c)

FIGURE 15.2 The FACE program showing the state of the screen (a) at the beginning of the program and (b) when the face has been completed, and (c) the layout of the concept keyboard by the client.

prefer the social rewards associated with face to face contact; a few others even seem to positively dislike looking at the screen or dealing with response keys, and refuse to have anything to do with the network.

It is the general popularity of the system which makes it obvious that it offers social rewards over and above the practical opportunities to learn. Our clients are aware that computers have a high social profile and that the ability to use one with facility confers prestige upon the operator, Being able to control the machine also gives an experience of power to people who are, more than most people, habitually powerless. There are other advantages. Computer games offer directed social interaction (in turn taking, modelling, sharing, winning and losing) which are a paradigm for play. Many of our clients find it difficult to create such opportunities for social interaction because many ordinary games are too complex and abstract.

In computer games each participant may be able to demonstrate practical and social skills and learn informally while enjoying companionship. Case study 1 illustrates the way in which such an interactive session moves beyond play, and is used by the clients both to practice and acquire skill.

Case study 1

The program 'CHUCKIE' was in the local disc drive before the session started as they had been using it in the morning. Charles then went through this routine:

plugged the micro into the mains
plugged the disc drive into the micro
switched on the system and
found the correct drive by typing in the appropriate request
found the directory he wanted in the same way
found the program from the directory
entered a request for the program
set the program up for four players

He did not make a single mistake in the whole of this routine, which was carried through in an easy and practised manner. Charles is able to read and write.

Charles and Mark then played CHUCKIE for an hour; they explained to me that they were using the disc drive rather than than the network because it allowed them to play continuously, and that they each had two 'players' because it made it more interesting and they did not have to change places so often. They took turns without fuss and appeared to be following their respective scores quite easily, although only Charles could read. The game is a progressive one and the increasing difficulty of the task gives an indication of success as well as the written score. Mark displayed considerable manual dexterity and good hand–eye coordination while playing, but his strategy was more haphazard than that used by Charles, who was less quick and well coordinated but made moves with a better pay-off. Both players could recall their degree of success on the previous game after each turn and could say which of their 'players' was doing best.

At the end of an hour they were asked to select another game. They decided to use one on the network; Mark obtained it by carrying out the following routine:

plugged in the connection to the network,
logged himself on to the system
selected the game he wanted from the 'default' menu
typed in the appropriate number and obtained the program

As he is unable to read and write he was evidently using some kind of pattern recognition and matching. He had been taught this routine by Charles over a period of several weeks.

(Note: Charles is in his late twenties, he has a mild mental handicap and some emotional difficulties; Mark is in his late teens, has a moderate mental handicap and a record for delinquency.)

The level of skill which Charles has reached in his use of the microprocessor and the network is considerable. Most jobs involving the use of computer terminals, for such purposes as seat booking or stock checking, would demand no greater skills. In order to operate the system successfully the operator cannot rely entirely on inflexible routines; some generalisations and some selective judgements have to be made, therefore the cognitive processes are relatively complex. Mark's ability to use the network is more limited: he has learnt a single routine, but he has learnt it to a high level of efficiency and is able to restart it if he makes an error, but he can vary it only within very narrow limits. The fact that Mark is unable to read makes it improbable that he will become as skilled as Charles until he has overcome that handicap.

Examining what each of these men has learnt and the way in which they use that knowledge throws considerable light on their cognitive capabilities which it might be hard to obtain in any other way. It also suggests what further training is likely to prove helpful to each of them.

Assessment of cognitive function

Mental handicap is not a unitary condition. In order to help our clients we need to know not only the overall extent of the handicap (such as would be represented by an IQ or a Mental Age score) but also the exact nature of the cognitive deficits which contribute to the handicap and also the cognitive strengths upon which we can build to enhance the client's functional skills.

The microprocessor allows one to study a number of critical aspects of cognitive function such as simple and disjunctive reaction times, delayed response, visuospatial skills, factors affecting stimulus discriminability as well as short- and long-term memory. We can also look at a client's coping strategies and modes of problem solving. To illustrate the way in which the computer can serve to illuminate the cognitive resources of a client the second of the cases to be presented is described below.

Case study 2

Emma is a deaf-mute woman in her twenties, who has a mental handicap and associated behavioural disturbance (she has severe mood swings, and an inability to tolerate frustration which leads to attacks on others and to self-injury). She is unable to speak and apparently unable to use sign language, but she is able to read simple sentences and write one- or two-word replies. The speech therapist assessed her comprehension of written language at below the 3-year equivalent level for spoken speech. This level is grossly discrepant with her score on a non-verbal psychological test which gave her a Mental Age of between 8 and 12 years.

We offered Emma a program on the computer which required her to solve simple four-letter anagrams. This program does not use the keyboard letters to type in the correct solution, but instead it supplies a letter grid (see Figure 15.3) from which the letters for the correct solution has to be chosen. The user has access using only the letters Z and X on the keyboard. The letter Z could be used to select the required vertical column and the letter X has then to be used to select the required letter within that column; when the cursor lies over the required letter the user has to press the Z key to 'place' that letter on the solution line below the anagram. If an incorrect letter is selected nothing happens when the Z key is depressed. This is a complicated routine both to describe and to use; there are no on-screen instructions.

Emma was evidently able to recognise the nature of the main task and to solve the anagrams with ease, but she found the executive routine difficult and confusing. Initially she attempted to use the keyboard to type in the correct solution; the correct procedure was explained to her by a mixture of demonstration and written information. The task had two very different aspects: the solution of the anagram and then the use of the letter grid to place the solution upon the screen. Emma solved all of the four-letter anagrams correctly, but she managed the visuospatial scanning task of selecting the appropriate letter from the supplied grid with less ease until she had learnt to give up attempting to use the keyboard letters to produce the 'correct' word. Her speed of reaction to the actual task (measured by the interval between the presentation of the task and her search for the first letter of the resolved

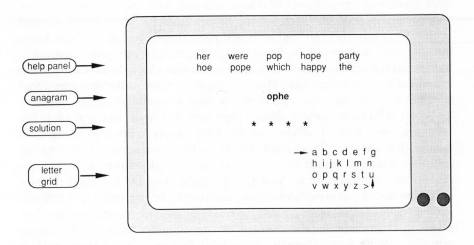

FIGURE 15.3 A schematic diagram of the screen showing the anagram and the grid which the subject had to use to find the letter to print the solution on the line below the anagram.

anagram) was much faster than the response time involved in extracting letters from the grid.

The client's ability to handle letters/words with facility was demonstrated by this session, as was her capacity for effective visuospatial scanning. She was able to concentrate on this abstract task for an hour and appeared calm, attentive and well motivated. New learning (the use of the grid) followed a normal pattern, being partly directed trial and error, partly copying a model and partly insight learning. On a day-to-day basis the client's difficulties appear to arise from an inability to communicate; she does not use her capacity to write spontaneously. It is as if she was unable to translate her demonstrable skill with words into effective communication with another person. Her ability to use the computer suggests that her main cognitive functions are relatively unimpaired and that her difficulties and apparent mental handicap arise in the social rather than the cognitive sphere. In other sessions playing computer games, the client was able to take turns with others and interact with them far more successfully than in ordinary face-to-face encounters. No doubt her success at the games contributed something to her ability to socialise success-fully in this manner, but it is an important gain for a normally isolated person to find any medium in which successful interaction can be achieved.

Relaxation therapy

Another and completely different use of our microprocessor system has been using it to teach relaxation through a simple bio-feedback technique. There are a number of our residents who have difficulty with impulse control. When they become excited they lack self-regulating strategies by which they might be able to reduce their arousal level and calm themselves. It has been found that for these and for other clients who are generally very tense, relaxation therapy which teaches the technique of relaxation through bio-feedback has considerable therapeutic value. There is little if anything in the literature about teaching self-induced relaxation to people with a mental handicap, although for people within the normal ability range such therapy is widely used. It has been suggested that of all the indices of relaxation heart rate is the most reliable (see, for example, Gatchel, 1979), so that after some attempts to use GSR as a measure, which were not successful, we decided to use the heart rate method with our clients. No doubt we might have had success with other measures and are currently exploring the possibility of using an electromyograph with clients whose main problem is muscle tension rather than excitement. However, for the moment we are using a system based on heart rate. The clients with whom we have tried this technique have a mild or moderate degree of handicap.

The method we chose was one which displayed the client's heart rate as a coloured bar on the TV monitor, which rose and fell with the client's averaged heart rate; it also displayed (as a horizontal bar) the target rate which the client was asked to achieve. The target rate was set about 10–20 beats below the starting rate, depending upon the degree of initial heart rate elevation above an assumed norm of 72 beats per minute. This system allowed the client to get visual feedback about his/her level of excitation/relaxation. Figure 15.4 shows the set-up with a client using it.

With some subjects, ambient music was used to help induce a more relaxed mood: other clients were encouraged to develop mental images of themselves in pleasant, relaxed situations.

The object of the exercise was to help the clients differentiate between an excited and a relaxed mood, as well as how to pass from state of tension and excitation to one which was calmer and more relaxed. The clients were seated in a comfortable chair from which they could see the screen easily and given verbal encouragement and reinforcement when the heart rate began to fall. In addition to bio-feedback they were also given social feedback until they had learnt to rely on the screen image to measure their own success.

At the end of each session the stored data for that session was printed out (through the network printer system) as a graph showing averaged heart rate against time. Figure 15.5 shows the print-out from a typical session.

With this system it has proved possible to teach relaxation to many clients with behavioural difficulties, who seem to have benefited from the training and to have found the experience pleasant and rewarding.

With several of the clients the therapy sessions have been conducted, and the print-out obtained, by a resident with a mild degree of handicap working

FIGURE 15.4   The bio-feedback system: showing the VDU and a client testing out the system before a relaxation training session.

with one of his peers. It was possible for the resident who ran the session to help us in this way because of the extent to which the system automated the process.

The extension of relaxation therapy to this handicapped group has been greatly facilitated by the use of the computer, which took care of many possibly confusing aspects of the learning task while leaving the locus of control with the client—where it belonged.

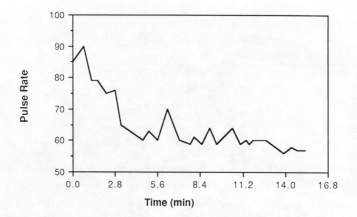

FIGURE 15.5 The print-out from a relaxation training session showing averaged heart rate over time.

Cost and management of the network

1   *Capital cost.* The original network was put in at a cost of £40 000 and was paid for out of the Royal Earlswood Trust Fund. There has been some small additional outlay involved in joining more wards to the network as the demand has arisen. The portable terminals (each comprising a BBC Master computer, VDU and trolley) have mostly been paid for by the hospital: a few residents have purchased their own personal terminals.

2   *Consumable costs.* There is an annual budget of £3000 for purchasing programs, discs, input devices, paper, etc. There is a library of input devices (some of which were listed above) which may be borrowed by any of the users and this was also maintained out of the consumable budget.

3   *Maintenance costs.* The network is updated and new material installed on the disc by a computer expert employed by the District Health Authority who spends one day a week in the hospital for this purpose. He also does some staff training. The only additional help comes from a Youth Training Scheme trainee who is at present working in the Psychology Department and from volunteers who join us from time to time. Members of the Psychology Department monitor the system and provide some help to other departments on an ad hoc basis. The maintenance cost is therefore negligible in terms of the Unit budget.

4   *Network management.* The disc storage has been set up in such a manner that each department head has an 'account' of disc space, some of which is allocated to individual clients and the rest is available for storing information about use. Individual users have access only to information about their own accounts. Each department head has access to information

about all their own 'users' and the system controller has access to all account information. The Personal Activity Record (PAR data) allows the department head or system controller to monitor the use made of the system by each user and from each terminal. Thus it is possible to know at any time what use has been and is being made of the system so that the 'accounts' can be adjusted to make optimal use of the hard disc space.

5   *Staff training.* Many staff in the hospital were initially rather nervous about using the network; they were not used to computers and felt they must be very complicated. It was therefore essential to have some system for making the staff familiar with the network so that they could in turn encourage the residents to make use of it. Some staff were given instruction in the use of the network by the district computer expert; the Psychology Department staff also did some informal training, but the main source of help came from making the network 'user-friendly', with immediate access to the news bulletin (updated weekly) and the help programs. In this way most of the staff who were interested rapidly became familiar with the network.

6   *Collection of data.* There is no general plan for collecting data about the patient's use of the network, or of monitoring progress, other than the routine collection of PARdata (see above). Different therapy and training departments make very different use of the network and each has its own way of keeping records or monitoring progress.

In the Psychology Department we keep extensive records where a research project is involved and more informal records of progress when doing clinical work and individual or group skills training. The cost of keeping complete records of the details of each session for every client is prohibitive. The mere accumulation of numerical data is worthless unless there is a hypothesis under test, so that we use detailed records for research and clinical notes for other purposes. The use of the network for relaxation training will serve as an example; it was initiated as a small carefully documented research project. We now use the technique as a clinical tool and keep fewer records; the graph is printed at the end of each session, examined and then given to the client. At present we have a research project on literacy skills and another exploring the relation between duration of presentation of a stimulus and the speed and accuracy of the response. Further research is planned as funding permits, but this is only a minor aspect of our present work.

Discussion

While the main use of our network is for the training and treatment of our clients, we also see it as a powerful tool for exploring some of the classical issues in cognitive psychology. The system has the great advantage of allowing us to gather data about response times, discrimination skills, problem-solving strategies and cognitive style in a natural setting. Our clients do not have to go to a laboratory; they can be studied in their own home doing something they are familiar with and will enjoy. Much psychological research can be and has been criticised because the environment in which it has been carried out is highly artificial and said to be remote from the realities of an everyday situation. Field-work in psychology, on the other hand, is often dismissed because it is impressionistic and imprecise.

Unlike some types of field-work, the work we are doing on the network is such that the stimulus parameters and response patterns can be as fully controlled and recorded as they could be in the laboratory. We anticipate that in addition to the immediate therapeutic advantage to our clients the network system will afford an opportunity to carry out research on cognitive functioning in people with learning difficulties. Such insights will in their turn benefit our clients by allowing us to offer them material which corresponds closely to their needs because it takes into account their particular cognitive deficits and areas of greatest competence.

We have tried to give sufficient information in this chapter to allow other people to see both the costs and the benefits of a microprocessor network for the use of a number of people with a mental handicap who live together or in close proximity to one another, in case they wish to set up a similar system. As a caveat we should add that in our experience it would be difficult, if not impossible, to set up and maintain such a system without expert technical advice.

In a multidisciplinary setting such as a hospital, it is not always easy to secure as much interdisciplinary coordination in helping the residents as one would wish. Staff from different disciplines work in different areas and at different tasks: they do not always have the time or resources to coordinate their work in the way that they know will be most effective. The network system can help here. It allows for some such additional coordination and cooperation without making additional demands on staff time and resources.

Computer-based or -aided learning cannot be expected to meet all the training needs of our clients. It can only supplement other more usual therapeutic input. Such a system can be a powerful source of extra enrichment for clients whose life experience and opportunities have been limited both by their own handicap and the restriction of their environment. This consideration applies as much to clients who live at home as to those who live in institutions. In an ideal world we would like to see a library of suitable computer programs obtainable through the telephone system, on a national or regional base, available to all people with a mental handicap, wherever they live.

Acknowledgements

We wish to acknowledge our great debt to Mr Nicholas Creasy of the East Surrey Health Authority Computer Service because he designed and set up the Royal Earlswood network and continues to maintain and enhance it.

We would like to thank Mr David Swann of the Psychology Department technical staff, Royal Holloway and Bedford New College, for giving us the computer program which we have used for relaxation treatment.

References

Aitken, S. (1988). Computer-aided instruction with the multiply impaired, *Journal of Mental Deficiency Research* **32**, 257–263.

Gatchel, R. J. (1979). Biofeedback and the treatment of fear and anxiety. In R. J. Gatchel and K. P. Price (eds), *Clinical Applications of Biofeedback: Appraisal and Status*. New York: Pergamon Press.

Lancioni, G. G. and Oliva, D. (1988a). A computer-aided program for promoting unsupervised activities for multiple handicapped adolescents, *Journal of Mental Deficiency Research*, **32**, 125–136.

Lancioni, G. G. and Oliva, D. (1988b). A computer-aided program for low functioning persons: a reply to Odar and Aitken, *Journal of Mental Deficiency Reseearch*, **32**, 265–269.

CHAPTER 16

Information technology in the treatment of aphasic disorders

Esme Burton and Andrew Burton

Introduction

Speech therapy is a clinical speciality concerned with communication problems. Disorders of speech and language may be developmental in origin, or acquired—when they are known as *aphasias*—following some kind of damage to the brain such as cerebrovascular accident or severe head injury. Problems encountered include those of comprehension, expression, voice production and non-verbal communication skills. There may also be accompanying emotional and behavioural problems consequent on the primary language disorder.

The therapist's task is to help the client to learn/relearn language use and/ or to provide alternative means of communication such as sign language or artificial aids. To do so, a series of decisions must be made (Howard and Hatfield, 1987). First, the therapist must decide what exactly the client's problems are, what is going wrong and how and which processes are impaired. Performance abilities are assessed, hypotheses as to the underlying deficits are drawn up, and performance areas selected for treatment together with achievement levels. Second, decisions must be made as to how to implement the treatment: what steps to use to get from present performance to target performance, the strategy and approach to be taken, the methods and materials to be used, and the organisation of these into a hierarchy with criteria for progression through it. Third, the client's progress must be constantly monitored to determine the rate at which he or she moves through the hierarchy of treatment, to adjust treatment as necessary and to decide when to end it.

Although these logical steps apply to all speech therapy, the details of treatment will obviously vary with factors such as the age of the client and the nature of his or her problems. This chapter is concerned mainly with

Microcomputers, Psychology and Medicine
Edited by R. West, M. Christie and J. Weinman
© 1990 by John Wiley & Sons Ltd

computer applications to the problems of language experienced by adults with acquired aphasia. In the majority of cases, the language disturbances are the result of a cerebrovascular accident ('stroke'). Many patients are relatively elderly and may also have some degree of motor disability. Generally speaking, there appears to have been very little empirical research into what information technology can offer the speech therapy practitioner and patient, although the potential advantages have been well aired in theory. This phenomenon is not unique to this area. As Mayntz (1984) says, speaking of information technology in general, 'the decision to introduce an information system is very often not triggered by a specific problem and a systematic search for solutions, but by the perception of an opportunity . . . computers are a kind of ready-made solution looking for possible applications.' The present authors have more than once encountered therapists who have acquired a microcomputer for their department but are unsure how best, or even how at all, to use it. Many understandably lack the expertise to make such decisions, and the time to decide how to integrate the computer into their clinical practice. As outlined above, the potential applications are numerous and include providing assistance with assessment, drawing up and delivering the treatment programme, monitoring and adjustment, and, in most cases, with the considerable administrative load of report writing, liaison with other professionals, appointment handling, etc. A mixture, therefore, of administrative and clinical processes is involved and application of information technology might be more appropriate for some (or all) of these. The main emphasis of the chapter will be on using computers to deliver treatment to the patient. The overlap between educational and speech therapy services is partly responsible for the increased interest in this possibility. Speech therapists working in special schools have been exposed to and have had the opportunity to use the new technology. In addition, various forms of microprocessor technology have been in use for some time in special applications such as the phonemic analysis of speech and to provide aphasic patients with alternative means of communication such as electronic wordboards. Computers have also been used with some success in training in second language learning by, for example, the armed forces. It seems natural therefore for professionals concerned with the problems of aphasic patients to have considered the possibility of using computer-based forms of language rehabilitation.

Potential benefits of computer-based language therapy

To what extent is it justifiable to claim that the introduction of computer technology into aphasia therapy would lead to an improvement in the service that could be offered to patients? Several potential benefits are easily indentified. First, computers offer the opportunity to extend therapy time. The case-load of speech therapists appears to be such that only one or two sessions of therapy per week can be offered to clients, often with long waiting lists. While one patient is being seen, therefore, others could be gaining extended practice on selected computer-based activities. Such an increase in potential therapy time might be particularly useful in the case of particular groups of patients, such as those with mild aphasia who, it has been argued (Marshall, 1987), may be less likely to receive therapy because of the minimal nature of their deficits but who are nevertheless capable of making significant functional gains. It also seems probable that such patients are likely to be the most capable of working at a computer keyboard with minimum supervision. A second useful gain would be in the increase in the range of information which could be collected about a patient's performance, such as the speed of completion of a particular item or set of items. This could be of value in helping to identify areas of language difficulty that might not be revealed by errors alone. Such feedback can also be provided instantly in a clearly presented form, stored permanently and retrieved quickly if required at some later time. Third, therapists would be able to spend proportionately less time on non-therapeutic activities such as routine record keeping and preparing materials for use in therapy sessions. In fact, modern storage technology would place a vast range of stimulus materials at the disposal of the therapist. Even a small microcomputer is capable of offering an alternative means of creating the many expensive and space-consuming sets of cards, sheets, lists and pictures which form an essential part of the equipment of the therapist. In principle, the technology is available which would allow the creation of a large national database of therapeutic material, both written and pictorial, for therapists to search and to select from using a variety of criteria.

There may, however, be an additional benefit, which is that the use of a computer would not only make possible an *extension* of therapy time but would also introduce some qualitative differences into the therapy that could be offered. The computer's capacity for carrying out repetitive, monotonous and time-consuming tasks with unerring accuracy makes it eminently suitable for use in routine drill-and-practice activities. Though this feature is important—in extended practice, for example—computer presentation of a task may bring additional benefits. As Self (1985) has pointed out in relation to computer-assisted learning in education, computers can be powerful motivators of learning. Children enjoy working at them and the opportunity to do so can be used as a powerful reward. The games format, with its obvious allure amounting in some cases to an addiction, can be valuable in improving skills such as reading which can occur as a result of playing an adventure game. It is not known whether the motivating power of computers is different for adults, for whom learning may be more acceptable as an end in itself. We have found very few aphasic patients who did not appear to enjoy working with computers, providing that the content and difficulty of the tasks were appropriate to their problems (Burton *et al.*, 1988). Therapists' reports attested to the interest and application of their patients—'wouldn't come and have his coffee—had to have another go', 'would have sat for hours'; etc. For elderly patients especially, initial apprehension soon gave way to pride at their ability to handle a high-status piece of equipment. In addition, it would seem that even if the computer is merely mimicking an activity that could be presented equally well by a teacher or therapist, the provision of an alternative, parallel form of presentation introduces variety and may help to sustain motivation and provide an additional context for the rehearsal of skills.

A further potential advantage discussed by Self (1985) is the power of the computer in activating responses from the user. Considerable emphasis has been placed on this in the educational field because of the widely accepted view that learning is enhanced through the active involvement of the learner. Bruner (1973), for example, has argued that new concepts and skills are more likely to be retained if learners are active, either in the sense of learning through active discovery and hypothesis testing rather than passive listening, or by exercising control and responsibility for the learning process, for example, by determining the timing of operations such as repetition and rehearsal. According to Adams (1988) computers can stimulate active participation in different ways. In their traditional role as tutors, computers present appropriate tasks and materials to the user. At the same time they are also tutees in the sense that the user needs to instruct and control them correctly in order to elicit information.

The role of tutee is of course one that has been further developed in various other ways, notably in applications such as LOGO, a high-level programming language which enables users to create procedures to 'teach' the machine to carry out tasks. Louie et al. (1985) found that children who had spent some time using LOGO had scores on a children's version of the *Internal v. External Locus of Control Scale* (Rotter et al., 1972) which were suggestive of greater internal locus of control. Greater internal locus of control is generally taken to indicate a stronger belief by the individual that life's events and experiences are within his or her control rather than simply at the mercy of social forces over which he or she has no influence. It would obviously be unwise to suppose that this result could necessarily be generalised to the aphasic population. Interestingly, however, Burton et al. (1988) found that many therapists judged that working with computers had increased both the concentration and confidence of their patients and that learning the simple sequence of responses needed to operate the programs had helped with general motor sequencing and control. This unexpected but welcome byproduct clearly needs more systematic investigation but serves as a useful demonstration that computers can play a number of different roles in the therapeutic context. Computer-based activities not only provide opportunities for extended practice on specific language activities but might also be used to foster the development of other more general cognitive skills involved in the planning, organisation and coordination of behaviour which are essential for successful language functioning. A final possible advantage which should certainly be considered is the increased social interaction which has been observed amongst groups of people working at computer-presented tasks (e.g. Underwood and Underwood, 1987). A related phenomenon is the increased spontaneous verbalisation by patients which has also been found to occur in aphasics and other language-impaired individuals during computer use (Burton *et al.*, 1988; Weir and Emanuel, 1976). This is particularly encouraging in the light of general fears that computers might have a socially isolating effect on patients and reduce them to automatons in thrall to their robot therapists!

There would appear, therefore, to be some strong arguments in favour of making use of computer-presented language activities in therapy for aphasic patients. The range and variety of tasks employed as well as the amount of therapy available to patients could be increased and the type and quality of information recorded about the performance of patients could be improved. Therapists themselves would also spend less time engaged in routine non-therapeutic activities. Research also suggests that many aphasic patients are capable of coping with computer-presented activities, enjoy and appear to benefit from them. The use of information technology in this area of speech therapy should not be seen, therefore, merely as an attempt to replace people by machines. As Greenfield (1987) has argued, each of the available media has its own distinctive contribution to make to learning and development. Each calls upon and develops a particular set of cognitive skills. Increasing the range of opportunities for aphasic patients to exercise their language competence can be seen as an important way of strengthening the skills which have been disrupted.

Hardware and software

It has been observed (Corder, 1985) that the process of successful technological innovation tends to go through three phases. During the first, the technology is experimental, the equipment unreliable and the work promoted and sustained mainly through the efforts of small bands of enthusiasts and dedicated researchers. The second phase begins as the technology becomes more reliable and the implications and commercial possibilities become more apparent. Money is invested in developing the technology and the product is manufactured and sold to the public. The technology is still relatively expensive and users need to rely on 'experts' to install it and regulate its expansion. In the final phase the advantages of the technology are widely acknowledged, most of the early teething problems have been ironed out, a mass market has developed, costs have considerably reduced and the product becomes accessible to, and easily usable by, the non-expert. The introduction of computer technology into speech therapy appears to be hovering on the margins of the second stage.

Many speech therapy departments have acquired at least one microcomputer, some software (programs) has appeared, specially written or adapted, for aphasic patients and there have been some preliminary attempts to evaluate its use and potential. At present there are several major obstacles to progress. Financial restrictions place the larger and more sophisticated machines beyond the budget which even a large department could realistically expect to receive. Much can of course be achieved using small microcomputers but such machines are inevitably limited in their storage and graphics capabilities and, more significantly, in their potential for synthetic and other forms of speech production which are obviously so desirable for use with aphasic patients. It is also our impression that many therapists, already stretched by busy case-loads, simply do not have sufficient time to draw up plans for their future information technology requirements or to decide how best to introduce computer technology into their clinicial work.

Even more important, however, is the present lack of software. Unfortunately, for various reasons, programs intended for educational use with children are generally unsuitable for adults with acquired language disorders. Such material is based essentially on a developmental model of language and learning. Although early approaches to the treatment of adult aphasia were aimed at the re-education of language using methods which were thought useful with children, modern approaches, although very diverse, suggest that it would be misguided to model therapy on the processes of first language learning (see Howard and Hatfield, 1987, for a review of therapies for aphasia). Educational software for children also present a number of practical difficulties. The vocabulary used and the style of presentation are designed for children. Many of the activities are presented as games. While this has been found to be a valuable source of motivation for children, our own observations suggest that patients can find this format irritating and feel that it devalues both their language difficulties and therapy. Educational software also often requires two-handed or other complex keyboard operations of a type which would be too difficult for hemiplegic patients. Program instructions can be quite complex and are usually presented in written form. Finally, the speed which the computer responds is often too fast, especially for elderly patients. Screen displays can change so rapidly following a key press that patients do not realise a change has occurred, or why. We have also observed patients turning round to their therapist on successful completion of a task, only to find that the program has moved on to the next stage and the response of which they are so proud is no longer to be seen.

Software for adult aphasic patients therefore needs to be written so that it meets the needs of the users. A proper understanding of these requires both a careful analysis of the particular problems such patients have and a knowledge of how they interact with and learn from computers (e.g. Katz, 1986). Burton *et al.* (1988) concluded that software for aphasic patients should:

1   Allow for a range of tasks, varying in level of both content and difficulty, since patients present with a wide range of deficits varying in severity.
2   Be written so that patients always feel in control of, rather than controlled by, the technology. Programs should be as 'transparent' as possible in their operation so that very little training is required. To this end, only a small number of responses of a very simple nature should be required of the user. The speed of operation of the programs should also be determined by the patient.
3   Should present stimulus material as simply and attractively as possible, using uncluttered screen layouts and double-height or other large-scale letters where appropriate.
4   Should never allow users to remain 'trapped' in the program through persistent error or inability to respond but should provide prompts and/or correct answers after a reasonable period.
5   Should provide *suitable* incentives and feedback on performance in a form that is immediately comprehensible and usable by both patients and therapists.

Burton *et al* (1988) also report the results of a preliminary study of how a large sample of aphasic patients responded to a set of computer-presented language activities meeting these criteria. A suite of programs for the BBC 'B' microcomputer was devised and written that allowed a variety of tasks, ranging from pre-reading activities to higher-level semantic tasks, to be presented in an identical format. In this format a single stimulus item appeared in magenta on the left of the screen and a number of response items (from three to nine according to level of difficulty) appeared in green on the right below a downward-pointing arrow (see Figure 16.1). All words, letters and numbers were printed as double-height characters, generally in lower case. One of the response items was related to the stimulus item, so that the two formed a pair (see Table 16.1). The task was to select the appropriate response item. The user could move up and down the right-hand list by pressing keys with up or down arrows (located on both the left and right of the keyboard to allow for operation by either hand). The current position in the list was indicated by that item changing colour from green to magenta. When a choice was made, the user indicated this by pressing a third key (the space bar). The left-hand item and the selected response item were than shown alone on the screen, in blue if correctly paired, in red if not. At the same time either a cheerful of mournful tune sounded. The next set of stimulus and response items was not displayed until the space bar was pressed again. Errors resulted in repetition of the previous set. If more than three consecutive errors occurred, the correct response was indicated but the user still had to select it in the usual manner. When all right-hand items had been correctly paired a results screen was

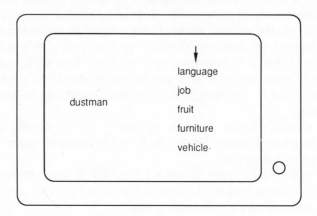

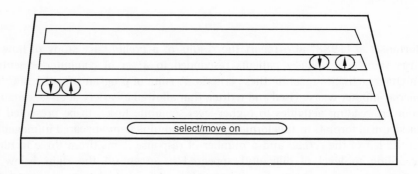

FIGURE 16.1   Schematic diagram showing parts of a microcomputer system and how they interact (see text for details).

displayed, listing for each pair of items the number of errors made and the time taken to make the correct response.

The programs thus met the criteria for software listed above. They were used by speech therapists for a three-month period and were found to be usable and enjoyable by nearly all patients, including the elderly. Generally speaking, however, not nearly enough is known about the population of aphasic patients to allow the sort of further detailed planning which is desirable for developing suitable integrated packages and to lay the foundations for future developments. A further general problem is the present lack of standardisation in hardware, making it difficult to coordinate and capitalise fully upon individual software projects. This not only leads to a wasteful duplication of

Table 16.1   Description of computer tasks, with examples

1	Shapes	Coloured geometric shapes are matched for both colour and shape
2	Blocks	A random block design is matched to an identical partner
3	Letter sequences	A meaningless letter string (increasing in length from 2 to 4) is matched to an identical string 'mtkp—mtkp'
4	Digit strings	As above, for sets of four digits '4123—4123'
5	Cross-case	Pairs of upper- and lower-case letters 'H—h'
6	Pairs	Pairs of verbal associates are matched 'brush—and comb'
7	Colours	An object is matched to a colour 'grass—green'
8	Instance groupings	An object is matched to two others from the same category 'rabbit—dog, cat'
9	Categories	A category and an instance of that category are matched 'chair—furniture'
10	Materials	An object is matched to a material 'shoe—leather'
11	Quantities	A product is matched to a quantity 'pint—of beer'
12	Verb–noun	A verb and its object are paired 'ride—the bicycle'
13	Synonyms	Two synonyms are matched 'wedding—marriage'
14	Compound words	Two words are paired to form a third word 'tight—rope'

research efforts but also contributes still more to an already fragmented program of software development. It is to be hoped that the Working Party on Computers and Speech Therapy recently set up by the College of Speech Therapists (the professional body representing speech therapists in the UK) will be effective in tackling these sorts of problems.

Implications and conclusions

Any significant expansion in the use of information technology in the treatment of patients with aphasic disorders would require an injection of resources at all appropriate levels. Funds would be required not only to meet the capital investment costs needed to purchase the necessary hardware and software but also for the provision of in-service training which would be so essential for effective use of the increasingly sophisticated capabilities the improved technology would bring. Since the provision of more computer facilities would entail a considerable initial financial outlay, it is inevitable that some demonstration would be required that such an investment would, in the long term, lead to an improvement in the cost-effectiveness of the service provided to patients. Considerations relevant to this include the increased therapy time available for each patient, the fact that more patients could receive some form of treatment and, more difficult to demonstrate, the improvement in the quality of the therapy which patients would receive as a result of the expanded facilities.

Ultimately, agreement is needed among those who deliver speech therapy services to patients on the role that they would like the computer to play in treatment. Our impression is that there is a general acceptance in principle that information technology has a part to play but much less consensus on exactly *how* it should be used. This is understandable. As many have argued (e.g. Fitter, 1987), the introduction of any new form of technology is not merely a technical process since it also has implications for the status, autonomy and professional roles of its users. Certainly, it is our impression that the relationship between therapist and patient is changed when both are working 'together' at the computer during a therapy session. Patients seem less reluctant to risk making mistakes and less upset and embarrassed when they cannot respond, or respond incorrectly. This may be partly because the patient perceives the tasks to have been set by the computer rather than by the therapist, who is freed from the traditional role as the patient's assessor and is able to concentrate more fully on providing support and encouragement. More research is clearly needed on such effects which suggest that the availability of computerised facilities could lead to a redefinition of the therapist's traditional role. Another issue concerns the use of auxiliary staff or volunteers. Since computer-based activities would be controlled, some tasks could be delegated to such suitably trained personnel, including the patient's relatives. Again, this suggests that therapists may come to be seen perhaps more as facilitators of language rehabilitation and as managers of therapeutic resources and less as primary therapy providers.

There are other reasons for the apparent lack of agreement on plans for future developments. Therapists might readily agree that they would like to improve the service they can offer. Since direct therapy with individual patients is at present probably the most enjoyable and satisfying aspect of the therapist's job, however, vague promises of extended practice opportunities and alternative learning contexts are not likely to be sufficient to justify an investment of time, effort and resources unless the promise of long-term benefits appears to have reasonably solid foundations. Therapists might argue, for example, with some justification, that the range of disorders experienced by aphasic patients is so complex and diverse it is hard to see how any computer program could be capable of providing language activities matched sufficiently closely to the particular needs of individual patients. Future developments in software engineering, of course, are likely to increase the power and availability of utilities such as authoring systems which would allow therapists to assemble a set of procedures capable of providing therapeutic exercises tailor-made to individual requirements. In the meanwhile, however, in order to make the optimum use of limited resources, it would be useful to identify the types of language disorder for which computer-based forms of therapy might be the most straightforward to administer, those which are the most effective and those patients who are most likely to respond positively to them. There is a lack of hard evidence on these and other important questions which therapists might legitimately ask. It is not known, for example, to what extent any improvements which might occur in a patient's performance on a computer-presented task are likely to generalise to other settings, nor whether the gains are genuinely the result of the use of computer presentation or merely the product of increased attention or change in therapy routine.

It is fortunate that many of the above questions and others which need to be addressed are amenable to empirical investigation since, in the absence of relevant information, it is unlikely that there will be enough agreement on the purpose of computer-based therapy and what it can be expected to achieve. Without some form of consensus, however, it will be difficult to make the sort of decisions necessary for initiating and sustaining a coherent program of software development which, arguably, provides the key to the future success of the whole enterprise. The benefits of further research are therefore considerable. Not only would it facilitate agreement about expectations and goals but it would also be of value in strengthening the arguments for continued support and increased resources being provided in the future.

The task of drawing up in advance a comprehensive set of procedures for all the possible forms of aphasia therapy for which computer presentation might be considered suitable is one before which even the most determined of speech therapists would understandably quail. A more realistic interim strategy might be to select specific 'target' aphasic problems and decide on detailed software programs for tackling them. In the short term this would produce a set of relatively isolated treatment 'modules' probably containing many points of treatment overlap. Through a process of constant review and evaluation, however, such areas of overlap between modules could be identified and the content of the modules adjusted accordingly. Such a strategy would therefore be capable of producing some tangible results fairly quickly, while enabling a more substantial integrated software package to emerge gradually through a process of refinement and evolution.

In conclusion, there are sound arguments for believing that information technology has an important role to play in helping with the language problems experienced by aphasic patients. More research is needed, however, for its precise uses to be defined sufficiently clearly for the all-important process of software development to be properly managed. With adequate provision of resources there would seem to be no reason why the availability of computer-based aids should not enhance the status and potential of speech therapy and increase the expertise and job satisfaction of its practitioners.

References

Adams, T. (1988). Computers in Learning: a coat of many colours, *Computers and Education*, **12**, 1–6.

Bruner, J. (1973). In J. Anglin (ed.), *Beyond the Information Given: Studies in the Psychology of Knowing*. New York: Norton.

Burton, E., Burton, A. and Lucas, D. (1988). The use of microcomputers with aphasic patients, *Aphasiology*, **2**, 479–491.

Corder, C. (1985). *Ending the Computer Conspiracy*. New York: McGraw-Hill.

Fitter, M. (1987). The development and use of information technology in health care. In F. Blackler and D. Oborne (eds), *Information Technology and People*. Leicester: British Psychological Society.

Greenfield, P. (1987). Electronic technologies, education, and cognitive development. In D. Berger, K. Pezdak and W. Banks (eds), *Applications of Cognitive Psychology*. Hillsdale, NJ: Erlbaum.

Howard, D. and Hatfield, F. (1987). *Aphasia Therapy: Historical and Contemporary Issues*. Hillsdale, NJ: Erlbaum.

Katz, R. (1986). *Aphasia Treatment and Microcomputers*. London: Taylor & Francis.

Louie, S., Luick, A. and Louie, J. (1985). Locus of control among computer using school children: a report of a pilot study, *Journal of Education Technology Systems*, **14**, 101–118.

Marshall, R. (1987). Reapportioning time for aphasia rehabilitation: a point of view. *Aphasiology*, **1**, 59–73.

Mayntz, R. (1984). Information systems and organisational effectiveness. In Th. Bemelmans (ed.), *Beyond Productivity*. Amsterdam: North-Holland.

Rotter, J., Chance, J. and Phares, E. (eds) (1972). *Applications of a Social Learning Theory of Personality*. New York: Holt, Rinehart & Winston.

Self, J. (1985). *Microcomputers in Education*. Brighton: Harvester Press.

Underwood, G. and Underwood, J. (1987). The computer in the classroom; a force for change? In F. Blackler and D. Oborne (eds), *Information Technology and People*. Leicester: British Psychological Society.

Weir, S. and Emanuel R. (1976). Using Logo to catalyse communication in an autistic child. *DAI Research Report No. 15*, Department of Artificial Intelligence, University of Edinburgh.

Conclusion: new micros—new applications

ROBERT WEST, JOHN WEINMAN AND MARGARET CHRISTIE

To many people, pychologists and medical doctors included, micros are mysterious and inaccessible. To others they offer an opportunity to practise a skill which is of no conceivable use in other walks of life—but to practise it with a profound dedication matched only by the irrelevance of the results. The contributions in this book have been aimed at that middle ground of people who believe that micros can be of use, and are not put off by the challenge of becoming familiar with their application.

Many will already be using micros, others may be teetering on the threshold. Hopefully, such readers will have been excited about the potential of modern micros to satisfy their requirements—the contributions may even have inspired new ideas about goals which might be achieved. However, micro users are well aware of the limitations of these tools and the frustrations involved in their use. This concluding chapter discusses the future of micros and the role of psychological and health practitioners in shaping the kinds of facilities which new generations of micros offer.

Future hardware

It sounds very impressive when one hears that a microcomputer can perform 2 million instructions per second, or has 4 million bytes of memory. One is tempted to say in the light of such achievements that there is little point in making faster microcomputers with even more memory. The fact is, however, that micros are nothing like fast enough yet and have nothing like enough memory. How can this be?

There are two major areas of stimulus presentation which are largely beyond the bounds of present-day micros because of their speed and memory limitations: sights and sounds! By 'sights and sounds' we do not mean the brief, highly stylised, static stimuli which are used in most present-day experiments;

Microcomputers, Psychology and Medicine
Edited by R. West, M. Christie and J. Weinman
© 1990 by John Wiley & Sons Ltd

we mean naturalistic, dynamic stimuli which contain the richness of detail and movement of the real world.

Let us consider this for a moment. To look realistic, a single frame of a graphic display should have a resolution of around 100 pixels per inch—in a mixture of colours. Representing one such image on a VDU can take more than one million bytes. Now consider that to create a moving image one needs around 50 frames per second. This means that one second's worth of animated display would require 50 million bytes! Even supercomputers such as the legendary Cray have difficulty creating high-resolution, realistic animated graphics. Most computer graphics (even that produced by expensive minicomputers) are highly stylised and lacking in richness of detail. It is not just the memory limitations which prevent realistic animated graphics—the speed of the processor is also critical. If a processor has to update an image made up from one million bytes, pixel by pixel, it is clearly going to have difficulty keeping up with the 50 frames per second needed to produce smooth animation. If the computer has to construct the image as it goes along (as would need to be the case in any but the simplest experimental implementation), the demands on the processor are clearly even greater.

Now we can consider the problem with regard to sounds. Sounds can be represented by using a number to represent the sound pressure level at particular moments in time. Thus a sound can be 'digitised' by sampling the sound pressure level at a particular frequency. The human ear can hear frequencies up to around 20 000 cycles per second (20 kHz). In order to faithfully represent sounds within the limit of human hearing, one needs to sample the sound pressure levels at 40 kHz. Each sound pressure level sample needs two bytes, thus one second of sound requires 80 000 bytes. This is nothing like as much of a problem as that posed by visual images, but it is still a major problem for current micros. It is relatively easy to use the micros to present discrete sounds lasting a few seconds, but storing and manipulating sounds lasting longer than this requires faster processors and more memory than are presently available.

However, realistic stimulus generation requires more. In the real world we see things in three-dimensions. Holographic images have given us one way of viewing objects in three dimensions; the use of special mirror arrangements and stereoscopes provide others. Whatever method one chooses, it clearly adds further processing and memory requirements. Similarly with sounds; these are usually heard located in space. The use of stereo speakers or headphones provides a crude approximation to naturalistic sound localisation. Creation of more realistic sound localisation involves accurate computing of timing and intensity difference from the sound sources which, as ever, impose an additional burden on the beleaguered microprocessor.

As Pat Rabbitt has pointed out earlier in the book, and as is apparent from the chapter by Margo George and Harvey Skinner, advances in technology can spark off new ideas for measurement which can in turn lead to the formulation of new theories. However, the converse is also true. Limitations in technology can restrict the way researchers think about their subject matter and the kinds of stimuli they consider appropriate. There can be no doubt that further advances in technology will enable more realistic stimulus generation and that this in turn will lead to more sophisticated theories about human behaviour.

We turn from stimulus generation to response recording. By far the most common response which experimental subjects use is the button press. The chapters by Wilson and by Parmar and Lawlor show that is possible to use other specialised devices, including voice-activated switches, 'concept keyboards', etc. But the basic idea is the same—respondents select from a fixed range of options. The option they choose is recorded, as is the time taken to make the response. In behaviour monitoring (see chapters by Hendrie and Rogers and by Blundell and Alikham) a wider range of responses can be recorded either by using an observer or some quantitative measurement device.

It is apparent that these simple response formats can hardly do justice to the richness and variety of behaviour. Perhaps the greatest need is for some kind of speech input. The fact that most respondents cannot type means that we cannot use computers to record open-ended responses to questionnaires, or monitor an interactive 'conversation' between computer and respondent. The processing of speech information requires a great deal of processing power and a memory capacity sufficient to store the speech sounds in raw form prior to processing. There are computer-based speech recognition systems. There are even add-ons to standard micros such as IBM PCs which will understand a range of spoken commands. However, these work with isolated words, not connected speech; they have to be specifically trained for the person whom they are supposed to understand; and they have a limited vocabulary.

Besides speech, there is movement. There are already systems which monitor human movement for the purposes of recreating it, for example, in factory automation. However, this typically involves wearing cumbersome suits with sensors at each of the joints to record the joint position 50 or so times a second. For psychological applications we need sensors which are less obtrusive. This may come about through miniaturisation or by a sophisticated 'remote sensing' device which uses a visual, magnetic or infrared sensor to record the position of parts of the body.

Finally, there is physiological measurement. Christine Temple mentions towards the end of her chapter the use of sophisticated micro-based systems for monitoring EEGs and ERPs from multiple electrode sites. These are beginning to be used for clinical and research applications. Fundamentally, they are no more than multichannel polygraph apparatus, but, by linking the data acquisition devices to a microcomputer there is the opportunity to produce graphical representations or 'mappings' of electrode activity over the surface of the scalp. Thus changes in location and amplitude of alpha can be readily observed. In current systems, limitations on the memory capacity and speed of the machines means that rates of sampling electrical activity over a large number of sites are restricted, as is the capacity to store the raw waveforms on disc for later analysis. One still needs devices such as FM tape recorders for this purpose. Also, rejection of artifactual data (e.g. arising from the electrical activity generated by movement) is crude. More sophisticated pattern-matching techniques are needed to determine what is artifact and what is the signal of interest. Even more importantly, pattern-matching techniques are needed to pick out characteristic instrusions into the EEG arising from clinical conditions such as epilepsy. However, these techniques require both processing power and speed.

Despite their being called 'microcomputers', portability of micros is still a major limitation. The standard micro takes up about half of a desk, and with a seperate keyboard, main-box and VDU requires quite a lot of 'lugging'. The emergence of portable computers has helped to some extent, but these are of limited use in stimulus presentation because they use monochrome screens which lack the contrast and clarity of standard VDUs. Also, they are only portable in the sense that a portable typewriter is portable. They cannot be kept on the person for use in the way that a pocket calculator might. There are, however, a small number of 'hand-held' computers, of which the most notable is the Psion Organiser. This is the size of a large pocket calculator but is in many respects like a standard microcomputer. Its screen is limited, being able to display only a few lines of text, but it offers considerable scope for human behaviour monitoring. An experimental subject can carry it around with him or her and be prompted by a 'beep' to record what he or she is doing at particular times or fill in a short questionnaire. At the end of a week, the computer can be returned and the data stored on it 'uploaded' to a standard microcomputer for analysis. Psion Organisers are already being used in this way by Saul Shiffman at the University of Pittsburgh. The opportunity that such devices have for providing a window into the lives of individuals (with their consent, of course) is very exciting. However, a decrease in size, the addition of speech recognition or just better screens and more memory would enhance the usability of such devices considerably.

Computer software

Advances in hardware must be accompanied by similar advances in software. In some cases, progress in software development can substitute for improvements in hardware. For example, more efficient 'algorithms' (procedures for performing some task) can make the same processor seem faster, and new ways of encoding data can make better use of available memory. Advances are already being made in computer high-level languages (see Introduction) which makes the programs written in them run faster. Give that BASIC is the most widely used language in psychological applications, it is important that newer versions of the language use compilers rather then interpreters, the former being considerably faster by and large. Also, the machine code produced by these BASICs is optimised for efficient running. There is no reason why this process should not continue, although the law of diminishing returns may be expected to apply at some stage. Efficient data encoding is an area of computer science which is receiving a great deal of attention, not merely to save computer memory but also to enable more information to be transmitted with existing telecommunication systems.

Probably the greatest need for psychologists in terms of software development is the creation of systems which minimise the expertise and time required to develop applications. Facility with computer languages requires an aptitude. There are, and will continue to be, psychologists and clinicians who do not have the necessary aptitude for programming, or who have no wish to devote time to developing programming skill. It may be that they will continue to use specialist programmers to assist them. However, there are drawbacks to this. Many readers will be only too aware of the difficulty in communicating to programmers exactly what is required. Moreover, if and when the programmer moves to another job, one is left with a system whose operation is mysterious and which cannot easily be improved or modified (or in some cases even be made to work!). It would be better if there were programming development tools which were flexible enough to meet the varied needs of clinicians and researchers but which could be used by non-specialists with little programming aptitude and experience. It should be possible for these packages to be used as word-processing programs are currently used: most users know little about computing, do not take advantage of their advanced facilities and seek help when things go wrong, whereas some users get to know them in detail and act as a kind of resource for a department.

Shaping future technology

By and large, the computer revolution has been 'supplier driven'. Manufacturers have put out a new machine with improved performance characteristics and users have (more or less) eagerly scrapped their old machines and upgraded to the new ones. In many cases, the upgrading exercise has been based on nothing more than a need to have the latest technology. As a result, there are thousands of micros sitting on people's desks which are performing tasks which could have been performed equally effectively by older machines at half the price. This is not to say that users do not know what they want. One only has to read the pages of computer magazines to know that the deficiencies of current micros and their associated software are well recognised. However, knowing what one wants and getting it are two different things.

This is particularly true for psychological applications because as a market we are minute compared with the commercial and business sector: the ubiquitous IBM clone, for example, has no built-in system for accurate timing (say to 100th of a second); there is no need for such a timer in business use—a clock counting once a second will do perfectly well.

The question then is whether psychological applications need remain a Cinderella of the computing market. One way of avoiding this is to form a kind of alliance with what is a potentially influential sector of the business community—market research organisations. For example, it is the needs of market research organisations much more than academic or clinical institutions which has led to the enormously beneficial enhancements to the statistics package SPSS. There is reason to hope that market research organisations will see the need for more sophisticated psychometric instruments and questionnaire packages and that clinicians and researchers will reap the benefits. Another possible alliance is with the artificial intelligence (AI) community. AI is big business. Billions of pounds and dollars are being spent by government and businesses to solve problems such as speech recognition. Vision research and robotics can also provide valuable spin-offs for psychology. For example, vision research has indicated ways in which the massive amount of memory required to present visual images may be reduced by computing the visual equivalent of a sound spectrogram. Instead of representing an image pixel by pixel, one can represent it in terms of the amplitude and phase of the spatial frequencies within it.

Finally, there are enough psychologists and clinicians to form a user base of sufficient size to sustain modest (by comparison with the business sector) research and development effort. Indeed, many of us spend significant proportions of our days programming. Many technical departments contain knowledgeable and creative engineers who are also capable of building sophisticated equipment. At present there is little coordination of this effort. It may be that in the future we will get fed up with continually reinventing the wheel and will establish structures designed to promulgate the fruits of our efforts.

Index